THE LIFE OF LADY
JOHANNA ELEONORA PETERSEN,
WRITTEN BY HERSELF

THE
OTHER VOICE
IN
EARLY MODERN
EUROPE

A Series Edited by Margaret L. King and Albert Rabil Jr.

RECENT BOOKS IN THE SERIES

Johanna Eleonora Petersen

THE LIFE OF LADY JOHANNA
ELEONORA PETERSEN,
WRITTEN BY HERSELF

*Pietism and Women's Autobiography
in Seventeenth-Century Germany*

᠅

*Edited and Translated by
Barbara Becker-Cantarino*

THE UNIVERSITY OF CHICAGO PRESS
Chicago & London

Johanna Eleonora Petersen, 1644–1724

Barbara Becker-Cantarino is research professor in German at Ohio State University. She is the author, editor, or translator of twenty books, most recently, *The Eighteenth Century: Enlightenment and Sentimentality.*

The University of Chicago Press, Chicago 60637
The University of Chicago Press, Ltd., London
© 2005 by The University of Chicago
All rights reserved. Published 2005
Printed in the United States of America

14 13 12 11 10 09 08 07 06 05   1 2 3 4 5

ISBN: 0-226-66298-5 (cloth)
ISBN: 0-226-66299-3 (paper)

Library of Congress Cataloging-in-Publication Data
Petersen, Johanna Eleonora, 1644–1724.
[Leben Frauen Joh. Eleonora Petersen, Gebohrner von und zu Merlau. English]
The Life of Lady Johanna Eleonora Petersen / written by
herself : Pietism and women's autobiography / Johanna Eleonora
Petersen; edited and translated by Barbara Becker-Cantarino.
p. cm. — (The other voice in early modern Europe)
Includes bibliographical references and index.
ISBN 0-226-66298-5 (cloth : alk. paper) — ISBN 0-226-66299-3 (pbk. : alk. paper)
1. Petersen, Johanna Eleonora.   2. Pietism—Germany.
3. Pietists—Germany—biography.   I. Becker-Cantarino, Barbara.   II. Title.   III. Series.
BR1653.P47 A3 2005
273'.7 B 22   2004015884

CONTENTS

ACKNOWLEDGMENTS

Johanna Eleonora Petersen's autobiography has interested me for quite some time. When I was searching for original texts written by women for my study *Der lange Weg zur Mündigkeit: Frau und Literatur in Deutschland, 1500–1800* (The Long Road out of Tutelage: Women and Literature in Germany, 1500–1800; Stuttgart 1987), this Pietist autobiography caught my eye because it was one of the very few authentic texts from a woman's pen. Not only had the text even been published, but it was also a complete, stylized, structured life story written in German. I am very grateful to Albert Rabil, editor of the Other Voice series, for giving me the opportunity to include a translation and presentation of the autobiography in the series where it, indeed, has found an appropriate place in the company of other unusual, distinguished texts of early modern Europe. Working with him has been a great pleasure, and his prompt and professional advice and editorial suggestions have greatly improved the manuscript.

My thanks go to the Alexander von Humboldt Foundation for supporting my work with a generous research award (*Forschungspreis*), which has enabled me to use the seventeenth-century collections in the libraries of Göttingen, Berlin, and Halle and to attend several specialized conferences and workshops in Germany. I am also indebted to Prof. Dr. Helwig Schmidt-Glintzer and to Dr. Gillian Bepler of the Herzog August Bibliothek, Wolfenbüttel, where a director's invitation supported my work in the winter of 2003. The College of Humanities and the Department of Germanic Languages and Literatures at the Ohio State University have always encouraged and supported my research and this book with a publishing subsidy, for which I am very grateful.

Research on Pietism has greatly flourished in Germany during the past decade or so (after many years of disinterest in religious texts on the part of literary scholars) and the invitation to the fall of 2002 conference on Johann Wilhelm and Johanna Eleonora Petersen came just at the right time for me. The conference took place in the beautifully restored ensemble of Pietist buildings in Halle, the Franckesche Stiftungen. I am indebted to Udo Strätter, director of the Interdisziplinäre Zentrum für Pietismusforschung at the University of Halle, and to Markus Matthias, University of Halle, for giving me the opportunity to read a paper on the Petersens' connections with the English spiritualist Jane Lead and the Philadelphians, as well as their emigration to America, an area I am continuing to explore. I learned a lot from the papers and discussions of other scholars interested in the Pietist couple, especially church historians and theologians with their different approaches to religious texts. Markus Matthias, who has done the most meticulous research to date on Johanna Eleonora and Johann Wilhelm Petersen, pointed me to Johanna Eleonora's supplication to the Frankfurt city council (translated in appendix A), for which I am very grateful. My longtime friend Brigitte Janssen deciphered accurately the ornate German handwriting of Petersen's supplication, a much-appreciated help. I also thank the library of the Franckesche Stiftungen for providing a copy of the rare early portrait of Johanna Eleonora Petersen used in this volume. And as always, I am grateful to my husband Vicente Cantarino, a Spanish medievalist by profession, for his help in questions of religion and the Bible.

Barbara Becker-Cantarino

THE OTHER VOICE IN EARLY MODERN EUROPE: INTRODUCTION TO THE SERIES

Margaret L. King and Albert Rabil Jr.

THE OLD VOICE AND THE OTHER VOICE

In western Europe and the United States, women are nearing equality in the professions, in business, and in politics. Most enjoy access to education, reproductive rights, and autonomy in financial affairs. Issues vital to women are on the public agenda: equal pay, child care, domestic abuse, breast cancer research, and curricular revision with an eye to the inclusion of women.

These recent achievements have their origins in things women (and some male supporters) said for the first time about six hundred years ago. Theirs is the "other voice," in contradistinction to the "first voice," the voice of the educated men who created Western culture. Coincident with a general reshaping of European culture in the period 1300–1700 (called the Renaissance or early modern period), questions of female equality and opportunity were raised that still resound and are still unresolved.

The other voice emerged against the backdrop of a three-thousand-year history of the derogation of women rooted in the civilizations related to Western culture: Hebrew, Greek, Roman, and Christian. Negative attitudes toward women inherited from these traditions pervaded the intellectual, medical, legal, religious, and social systems that developed during the European Middle Ages.

The following pages describe the traditional, overwhelmingly male views of women's nature inherited by early modern Europeans and the new tradition that the "other voice" called into being to begin to challenge reigning assumptions. This review should serve as a framework for understanding the texts published in the series the Other Voice in Early Modern Europe. Introductions specific to each text and author follow this essay in all the volumes of the series.

TRADITIONAL VIEWS OF WOMEN, 500 B.C.E.–1500 C.E.

Embedded in the philosophical and medical theories of the ancient Greeks were perceptions of the female as inferior to the male in both mind and body. Similarly, the structure of civil legislation inherited from the ancient Romans was biased against women, and the views on women developed by Christian thinkers out of the Hebrew Bible and the Christian New Testament were negative and disabling. Literary works composed in the vernacular of ordinary people, and widely recited or read, conveyed these negative assumptions. The social networks within which most women lived—those of the family and the institutions of the Roman Catholic Church—were shaped by this negative tradition and sharply limited the areas in which women might act in and upon the world.

GREEK PHILOSOPHY AND FEMALE NATURE. Greek biology assumed that women were inferior to men and defined them as merely childbearers and housekeepers. This view was authoritatively expressed in the works of the philosopher Aristotle.

Aristotle thought in dualities. He considered action superior to inaction, form (the inner design or structure of any object) superior to matter, completion to incompletion, possession to deprivation. In each of these dualities, he associated the male principle with the superior quality and the female with the inferior. "The male principle in nature," he argued, "is associated with active, formative and perfected characteristics, while the female is passive, material and deprived, desiring the male in order to become complete."[1] Men are always identified with virile qualities, such as judgment, courage, and stamina, and women with their opposites—irrationality, cowardice, and weakness.

The masculine principle was considered superior even in the womb. The man's semen, Aristotle believed, created the form of a new human creature, while the female body contributed only matter. (The existence of the ovum, and with it the other facts of human embryology, was not established until the seventeenth century.) Although the later Greek physician Galen believed there was a female component in generation, contributed by "female semen," the followers of both Aristotle and Galen saw the male role in human generation as more active and more important.

In the Aristotelian view, the male principle sought always to reproduce

---

1. Aristotle, *Physics* 1.9.192a20–24, in *The Complete Works of Aristotle,* ed. Jonathan Barnes, rev. Oxford trans., 2 vols. (Princeton, 1984), 1:328.

itself. The creation of a female was always a mistake, therefore, resulting from an imperfect act of generation. Every female born was considered a "defective" or "mutilated" male (as Aristotle's terminology has variously been translated), a "monstrosity" of nature.[2]

For Greek theorists, the biology of males and females was the key to their psychology. The female was softer and more docile, more apt to be despondent, querulous, and deceitful. Being incomplete, moreover, she craved sexual fulfillment in intercourse with a male. The male was intellectual, active, and in control of his passions.

These psychological polarities derived from the theory that the universe consisted of four elements (earth, fire, air, and water), expressed in human bodies as four "humors" (black bile, yellow bile, blood, and phlegm) considered, respectively, dry, hot, damp, and cold and corresponding to mental states ("melancholic," "choleric," "sanguine," "phlegmatic"). In this scheme the male, sharing the principles of earth and fire, was dry and hot; the female, sharing the principles of air and water, was cold and damp.

Female psychology was further affected by her dominant organ, the uterus (womb), *hystera* in Greek. The passions generated by the womb made women lustful, deceitful, talkative, irrational, indeed—when these affects were in excess—"hysterical."

Aristotle's biology also had social and political consequences. If the male principle was superior and the female inferior, then in the household, as in the state, men should rule and women must be subordinate. That hierarchy did not rule out the companionship of husband and wife, whose cooperation was necessary for the welfare of children and the preservation of property. Such mutuality supported male preeminence.

Aristotle's teacher Plato suggested a different possibility: that men and women might possess the same virtues. The setting for this proposal is the imaginary and ideal Republic that Plato sketches in a dialogue of that name. Here, for a privileged elite capable of leading wisely, all distinctions of class and wealth dissolve, as, consequently, do those of gender. Without households or property, as Plato constructs his ideal society, there is no need for the subordination of women. Women may therefore be educated to the same level as men to assume leadership. Plato's Republic remained imaginary, however. In real societies, the subordination of women remained the norm and the prescription.

The views of women inherited from the Greek philosophical tradition became the basis for medieval thought. In the thirteenth century,

2. Aristotle, *Generation of Animals* 2.3.737a27–28, in *The Complete Works*, 1: 1144.

the supreme Scholastic philosopher Thomas Aquinas, among others, still echoed Aristotle's views of human reproduction, of male and female personalities, and of the preeminent male role in the social hierarchy.

ROMAN LAW AND THE FEMALE CONDITION. Roman law, like Greek philosophy, underlay medieval thought and shaped medieval society. The ancient belief that adult property-owning men should administer households and make decisions affecting the community at large is the very fulcrum of Roman law.

About 450 B.C.E., during Rome's republican era, the community's customary law was recorded (legendarily) on twelve tablets erected in the city's central forum. It was later elaborated by professional jurists whose activity increased in the imperial era, when much new legislation was passed, especially on issues affecting family and inheritance. This growing, changing body of laws was eventually codified in the *Corpus of Civil Law* under the direction of the emperor Justinian, generations after the empire ceased to be ruled from Rome. That *Corpus*, read and commented on by medieval scholars from the eleventh century on, inspired the legal systems of most of the cities and kingdoms of Europe.

Laws regarding dowries, divorce, and inheritance pertain primarily to women. Since those laws aimed to maintain and preserve property, the women concerned were those from the property-owning minority. Their subordination to male family members points to the even greater subordination of lower-class and slave women, about whom the laws speak little.

In the early republic, the *paterfamilias*, or "father of the family," possessed *patria potestas*, "paternal power." The term *pater*, "father," in both these cases does not necessarily mean biological father but denotes the head of a household. The father was the person who owned the household's property and, indeed, its human members. The *paterfamilias* had absolute power—including the power, rarely exercised, of life or death—over his wife, his children, and his slaves, as much as his cattle.

Male children could be "emancipated," an act that granted legal autonomy and the right to own property. Those over fourteen could be emancipated by a special grant from the father or automatically by their father's death. But females could never be emancipated; instead, they passed from the authority of their father to that of a husband or, if widowed or orphaned while still unmarried, to a guardian or tutor.

Marriage in its traditional form placed the woman under her husband's authority, or *manus*. He could divorce her on grounds of adultery, drinking wine, or stealing from the household, but she could not divorce him. She could neither possess property in her own right nor bequeath any to her children upon her death. When her husband died, the household property passed not to her but to his male heirs. And when her father died, she had no claim to any family inheritance, which was directed to her brothers or more remote male relatives. The effect of these laws was to exclude women from civil society, itself based on property ownership.

In the later republican and imperial periods, these rules were significantly modified. Women rarely married according to the traditional form. The practice of "free" marriage allowed a woman to remain under her father's authority, to possess property given her by her father (most frequently the "dowry," recoverable from the husband's household on his death), and to inherit from her father. She could also bequeath property to her own children and divorce her husband, just as he could divorce her.

Despite this greater freedom, women still suffered enormous disability under Roman law. Heirs could belong only to the father's side, never the mother's. Moreover, although she could bequeath her property to her children, she could not establish a line of succession in doing so. A woman was "the beginning and end of her own family," said the jurist Ulpian. Moreover, women could play no public role. They could not hold public office, represent anyone in a legal case, or even witness a will. Women had only a private existence and no public personality.

The dowry system, the guardian, women's limited ability to transmit wealth, and total political disability are all features of Roman law adopted by the medieval communities of western Europe, although modified according to local customary laws..

CHRISTIAN DOCTINE AND WOMEN'S PLACE. The Hebrew Bible and the Christian New Testament authorized later writers to limit women to the realm of the family and to burden them with the guilt of original sin. The passages most fruitful for this purpose were the creation narratives in Genesis and sentences from the Epistles defining women's role within the Christian family and community.

Each of the first two chapters of Genesis contains a creation narrative. In the first "God created man in his own image, in the image of God he created him; male and female he created them" (Gn 1:27). In the second, God created Eve from Adam's rib (2:21–23). Christian theologians relied principally on Genesis 2 for their understanding of the relation between man and woman, interpreting the creation of Eve from Adam as proof of her subordination to him.

The creation story in Genesis 2 leads to that of the temptations in Genesis 3: of Eve by the wily serpent and of Adam by Eve. As read by Christian theologians from Tertullian to Thomas Aquinas, the narrative made Eve responsible for the Fall and its consequences. She instigated the act; she deceived her husband; she suffered the greater punishment. Her disobedience made it necessary for Jesus to be incarnated and to die on the cross. From the pulpit, moralists and preachers for centuries conveyed to women the guilt that they bore for original sin.

The Epistles offered advice to early Christians on building communities of the faithful. Among the matters to be regulated was the place of women. Paul offered views favorable to women in Galatians 3:28: "There is neither Jew nor Greek, there is neither slave nor free, there is neither male nor female; for you are all one in Christ Jesus." Paul also referred to women as his coworkers and placed them on a par with himself and his male coworkers (Phlm 4:2–3; Rom 16:1–3; 1 Cor 16:19). Elsewhere, Paul limited women's possibilities: "But I want you to understand that the head of every man is Christ, the head of a woman is her husband, and the head of Christ is God" (1 Cor 11:3).

Biblical passages by later writers (although attributed to Paul) enjoined women to forgo jewels, expensive clothes, and elaborate coiffures; and they forbade women to "teach or have authority over men," telling them to "learn in silence with all submissiveness" as is proper for one responsible for sin, consoling them, however, with the thought that they will be saved through childbearing (1 Tm 2:9–15). Other texts among the later Epistles defined women as the weaker sex and emphasized their subordination to their husbands (1 Pt 3:7; Col 3:18; Eph 5:22–23).

These passages from the New Testament became the arsenal employed by theologians of the early church to transmit negative attitudes toward women to medieval Christian culture—above all, Tertullian (*On the Apparel of Women*), Jerome (*Against Jovinian*), and Augustine (*The Literal Meaning of Genesis*).

THE IMAGE OF WOMEN IN MEDIEVAL LITERATURE. The philosophical, legal, and religious traditions born in antiquity formed the basis of the medieval intellectual synthesis wrought by trained thinkers, mostly clerics, writing in Latin and based largely in universities. The vernacular literary tradition that developed alongside the learned tradition also spoke about female nature and women's roles. Medieval stories, poems, and epics also portrayed women negatively—as lustful and deceitful—while praising good housekeepers and loyal wives as replicas of the Virgin Mary or the female saints and martyrs.

There is an exception in the movement of "courtly love" that evolved in southern France from the twelfth century. Courtly love was the erotic love between a nobleman and noblewoman, the latter usually superior in social rank. It was always adulterous. From the conventions of courtly love derive modern Western notions of romantic love. The tradition has had an impact disproportionate to its size, for it affected only a tiny elite, and very few women. The exaltation of the female lover probably does not reflect a higher evaluation of women or a step toward their sexual liberation. More likely it gives expression to the social and sexual tensions besetting the knightly class at a specific historical juncture.

The literary fashion of courtly love was on the wane by the thirteenth century, when the widely read *Romance of the Rose* was composed in French by two authors of significantly different dispositions. Guillaume de Lorris composed the initial four thousand verses about 1235, and Jean de Meun added about seventeen thousand verses—more than four times the original—about 1265.

The fragment composed by Guillaume de Lorris stands squarely in the tradition of courtly love. Here the poet, in a dream, is admitted into a walled garden where he finds a magic fountain in which a rosebush is reflected. He longs to pick one rose, but the thorns prevent his doing so, even as he is wounded by arrows from the god of love, whose commands he agrees to obey. The rest of this part of the poem recounts the poet's unsuccessful efforts to pluck the rose.

The longer part of the *Romance* by Jean de Meun also describes a dream. But here allegorical characters give long didactic speeches, providing a social satire on a variety of themes, some pertaining to women. Love is an anxious and tormented state, the poem explains: women are greedy and manipulative, marriage is miserable, beautiful women are lustful, ugly ones cease to please, and a chaste woman is as rare as a black swan.

Shortly after Jean de Meun completed *The Romance of the Rose*, Mathéolus penned his *Lamentations*, a long Latin diatribe against marriage translated into French about a century later. The *Lamentations* sum up medieval attitudes toward women and provoked the important response by Christine de Pizan in her *Book of the City of Ladies*.

In 1355, Giovanni Boccaccio wrote *Il Corbaccio*, another antifeminist manifesto, although ironically by an author whose other works pioneered new directions in Renaissance thought. The former husband of his lover appears to Boccaccio, condemning his unmoderated lust and detailing the defects of women. Boccaccio concedes at the end "how much men naturally surpass women in nobility" and is cured of his desires.[3]

---

3. Giovanni Boccaccio, *The Corbaccio, or The Labyrinth of Love*, trans. and ed. Anthony K. Cassell, rev. ed. (Binghamton, N.Y., 1993), 71.

WOMEN'S ROLES: THE FAMILY. The negative perceptions of women expressed in the intellectual tradition are also implicit in the actual roles that women played in European society. Assigned to subordinate positions in the household and the church, they were barred from significant participation in public life.

Medieval European households, like those in antiquity and in non-Western civilizations, were headed by males. It was the male serf (or peasant), feudal lord, town merchant, or citizen who was polled or taxed or succeeded to an inheritance or had any acknowledged public role, although his wife or widow could stand as a temporary surrogate. From about 1100, the position of property-holding males was further enhanced: inheritance was confined to the male, or agnate, line—with depressing consequences for women.

A wife never fully belonged to her husband's family, nor was she a daughter to her father's family. She left her father's house young to marry whomever her parents chose. Her dowry was managed by her husband, and at her death it normally passed to her children by him.

A married woman's life was occupied nearly constantly with cycles of pregnancy, childbearing, and lactation. Women bore children through all the years of their fertility, and many died in childbirth. They were also responsible for raising young children up to six or seven. In the propertied classes that responsibility was shared, since it was common for a wet nurse to take over breast-feeding and for servants to perform other chores.

Women trained their daughters in the household duties appropriate to their status, nearly always tasks associated with textiles: spinning, weaving, sewing, embroidering. Their sons were sent out of the house as apprentices or students, or their training was assumed by fathers in later childhood and adolescence. On the death of her husband, a woman's children became the responsibility of his family. She generally did not take "his" children with her to a new marriage or back to her father's house, except sometimes in the artisan classes.

Women also worked. Rural peasants performed farm chores, merchant wives often practiced their husbands' trades, the unmarried daughters of the urban poor worked as servants or prostitutes. All wives produced or embellished textiles and did the housekeeping, while wealthy ones managed servants. These labors were unpaid or poorly paid but often contributed substantially to family wealth.

WOMEN'S ROLES: THE CHURCH. Membership in a household, whether a father's or a husband's, meant for women a lifelong subordination to others.

In western Europe, the Roman Catholic Church offered an alternative to the career of wife and mother. A woman could enter a convent, parallel in function to the monasteries for men that evolved in the early Christian centuries.

In the convent, a woman pledged herself to a celibate life, lived according to strict community rules, and worshiped daily. Often the convent offered training in Latin, allowing some women to become considerable scholars and authors as well as scribes, artists, and musicians. For women who chose the conventual life, the benefits could be enormous, but for numerous others placed in convents by paternal choice, the life could be restrictive and burdensome.

The conventual life declined as an alternative for women as the modern age approached. Reformed monastic institutions resisted responsibility for related female orders. The church increasingly restricted female institutional life by insisting on closer male supervision.

Women often sought other options. Some joined the communities of laywomen that sprang up spontaneously in the thirteenth century in the urban zones of western Europe, especially in Flanders and Italy. Some joined the heretical movements that flourished in late medieval Christendom, whose anticlerical and often antifamily positions particularly appealed to women. In these communities, some women were acclaimed as "holy women" or "saints," whereas others often were condemned as frauds or heretics.

In all, although the options offered to women by the church were sometimes less than satisfactory, they were sometimes richly rewarding. After 1520, the convent remained an option only in Roman Catholic territories. Protestantism engendered an ideal of marriage as a heroic endeavor and appeared to place husband and wife on a more equal footing. Sermons and treatises, however, still called for female subordination and obedience.

THE OTHER VOICE, 1300–1700

When the modern era opened, European culture was so firmly structured by a framework of negative attitudes toward women that to dismantle it was a monumental labor. The process began as part of a larger cultural movement that entailed the critical reexamination of ideas inherited from the ancient and medieval past. The humanists launched that critical reexamination.

THE HUMANIST FOUNDATION. Originating in Italy in the fourteenth century, humanism quickly became the dominant intellectual movement in

Europe. Spreading in the sixteenth century from Italy to the rest of Europe, it fueled the literary, scientific, and philosophical movements of the era and laid the basis for the eighteenth-century Enlightenment.

Humanists regarded the Scholastic philosophy of medieval universities as out of touch with the realities of urban life. They found in the rhetorical discourse of classical Rome a language adapted to civic life and public speech. They learned to read, speak, and write classical Latin and, eventually, classical Greek. They founded schools to teach others to do so, establishing the pattern for elementary and secondary education for the next three hundred years.

In the service of complex government bureaucracies, humanists employed their skills to write eloquent letters, deliver public orations, and formulate public policy. They developed new scripts for copying manuscripts and used the new printing press to disseminate texts, for which they created methods of critical editing.

Humanism was a movement led by males who accepted the evaluation of women in ancient texts and generally shared the misogynist perceptions of their culture. (Female humanists, as we will see, did not.) Yet humanism also opened the door to a reevaluation of the nature and capacity of women. By calling authors, texts, and ideas into question, it made possible the fundamental rereading of the whole intellectual tradition that was required in order to free women from cultural prejudice and social subordination.

A DIFFERENT CITY. The other voice first appeared when, after so many centuries, the accumulation of misogynist concepts evoked a response from a capable female defender: Christine de Pizan (1365–1431). Introducing her *Book of the City of Ladies* (1405), she described how she was affected by reading Mathéolus's *Lamentations:* "Just the sight of this book . . . made me wonder how it happened that so many different men . . . are so inclined to express both in speaking and in their treatises and writings so many wicked insults about women and their behavior."[4] These statements impelled her to detest herself "and the entire feminine sex, as though we were monstrosities in nature."[5]

The rest of *The Book of the City of Ladies* presents a justification of the female sex and a vision of an ideal community of women. A pioneer, she has

4. Christine de Pizan, *The Book of the City of Ladies,* trans. Earl Jeffrey Richards, foreword by Marina Warner (New York, 1982), 1.1.1, pp. 3–4.
5. Ibid., 1.1.1–2, p. 5.

received the message of female inferiority and rejected it. From the fourteenth to the seventeenth century, a huge body of literature accumulated that responded to the dominant tradition.

The result was a literary explosion consisting of works by both men and women, in Latin and in the vernaculars: works enumerating the achievements of notable women; works rebutting the main accusations made against women; works arguing for the equal education of men and women; works defining and redefining women's proper role in the family, at court, in public; works describing women's lives and experiences. Recent monographs and articles have begun to hint at the great range of this movement, involving probably several thousand titles. The protofeminism of these "other voices" constitutes a significant fraction of the literary product of the early modern era.

THE CATALOGS. About 1365, the same Boccaccio whose *Corbaccio* rehearses the usual charges against female nature wrote another work, *Concerning Famous Women*. A humanist treatise drawing on classical texts, it praised 106 notable women: ninety-eight of them from pagan Greek and Roman antiquity, one (Eve) from the Bible, and seven from the medieval religious and cultural tradition; his book helped make all readers aware of a sex normally condemned or forgotten. Boccaccio's outlook nevertheless was unfriendly to women, for it singled out for praise those women who possessed the traditional virtues of chastity, silence, and obedience. Women who were active in the public realm—for example, rulers and warriors—were depicted as usually being lascivious and as suffering terrible punishments for entering the masculine sphere. Women were his subject, but Boccaccio's standard remained male.

Christine de Pizan's *Book of the City of Ladies* contains a second catalog, one responding specifically to Boccaccio's. Whereas Boccaccio portrays female virtue as exceptional, she depicts it as universal. Many women in history were leaders, or remained chaste despite the lascivious approaches of men, or were visionaries and brave martyrs.

The work of Boccaccio inspired a series of catalogs of illustrious women of the biblical, classical, Christian, and local pasts, among them Filippo da Bergamo's *Of Illustrious Women*, Pierre de Brantôme's *Lives of Illustrious Women*, Pierre Le Moyne's *Gallerie of Heroic Women*, and Pietro Paolo de Ribera's *Immortal Triumphs and Heroic Enterprises of 845 Women*. Whatever their embedded prejudices, these works drove home to the public the possibility of female excellence.

THE DEBATE. At the same time, many questions remained: Could a woman be virtuous? Could she perform noteworthy deeds? Was she even, strictly speaking, of the same human species as men? These questions were debated over four centuries, in French, German, Italian, Spanish, and English, by authors male and female, among Catholics, Protestants, and Jews, in ponderous volumes and breezy pamphlets. The whole literary genre has been called the *querelle des femmes,* the "woman question."

The opening volley of this battle occurred in the first years of the fifteenth century, in a literary debate sparked by Christine de Pizan. She exchanged letters critical of Jean de Meun's contribution to *The Romance of the Rose* with two French royal secretaries, Jean de Montreuil and Gontier Col. When the matter became public, Jean Gerson, one of Europe's leading theologians, supported de Pizan's arguments against de Meun, for the moment silencing the opposition.

The debate resurfaced repeatedly over the next two hundred years. *The Triumph of Women* (1438) by Juan Rodríguez de la Camara (or Juan Rodríguez del Padron) struck a new note by presenting arguments for the superiority of women to men. *The Champion of Women* (1440–42) by Martin Le Franc addresses once again the negative views of women presented in *The Romance of the Rose* and offers counterevidence of female virtue and achievement.

A cameo of the debate on women is included in *The Courtier,* one of the most widely read books of the era, published by the Italian Baldassare Castiglione in 1528 and immediately translated into other European vernaculars. *The Courtier* depicts a series of evenings at the court of the duke of Urbino in which many men and some women of the highest social stratum amuse themselves by discussing a range of literary and social issues. The "woman question" is a pervasive theme throughout, and the third of its four books is devoted entirely to that issue.

In a verbal duel, Gasparo Pallavicino and Giuliano de' Medici present the main claims of the two traditions. Gasparo argues the innate inferiority of women and their inclination to vice. Only in bearing children do they profit the world. Giuliano counters that women share the same spiritual and mental capacities as men and may excel in wisdom and action. Men and women are of the same essence: just as no stone can be more perfectly a stone than another, so no human being can be more perfectly human than others, whether male or female. It was an astonishing assertion, boldly made to an audience as large as all Europe.

THE TREATISES. Humanism provided the materials for a positive counterconcept to the misogyny embedded in Scholastic philosophy and law and inherited from the Greek, Roman, and Christian pasts. A series of humanist treatises on marriage and family, on education and deportment, and on the nature of women helped construct these new perspectives.

The works by Francesco Barbaro and Leon Battista Alberti—*On Marriage* (1415) and *On the Family* (1434–37)—far from defending female equality, reasserted women's responsibility for rearing children and managing the housekeeping while being obedient, chaste, and silent. Nevertheless, they served the cause of reexamining the issue of women's nature by placing domestic issues at the center of scholarly concern and reopening the pertinent classical texts. In addition, Barbaro emphasized the companionate nature of marriage and the importance of a wife's spiritual and mental qualities for the well-being of the family.

These themes reappear in later humanist works on marriage and the education of women by Juan Luis Vives and Erasmus. Both were moderately sympathetic to the condition of women without reaching beyond the usual masculine prescriptions for female behavior.

An outlook more favorable to women characterizes the nearly unknown work *In Praise of Women* (ca. 1487) by the Italian humanist Bartolommeo Goggio. In addition to providing a catalog of illustrious women, Goggio argued that male and female are the same in essence, but that women (reworking the Adam and Eve narrative from quite a new angle) are actually superior. In the same vein, the Italian humanist Mario Equicola asserted the spiritual equality of men and women in *On Women* (1501). In 1525, Galeazzo Flavio Capra (or Capella) published his work *On the Excellence and Dignity of Women*. This humanist tradition of treatises defending the worthiness of women culminates in the work of Henricus Cornelius Agrippa *On the Nobility and Preeminence of the Female Sex*. No work by a male humanist more succinctly or explicitly presents the case for female dignity.

THE WITCH BOOKS. While humanists grappled with the issues pertaining to women and family, other learned men turned their attention to what they perceived as a very great problem: witches. Witch-hunting manuals, explorations of the witch phenomenon, and even defenses of witches are not at first glance pertinent to the tradition of the other voice. But they do relate in this way: most accused witches were women. The hostility aroused by supposed witch activity is comparable to the hostility aroused by women. The evil deeds the victims of the hunt were charged with were exaggerations of the vices to which, many believed, all women were prone.

The connection between the witch accusation and the hatred of women is explicit in the notorious witch-hunting manual *The Hammer of Witches* (1486) by two Dominican inquisitors, Heinrich Krämer and Jacob Sprenger. Here the inconstancy, deceitfulness, and lustfulness traditionally associated with women are depicted in exaggerated form as the core features of witch behavior. These traits inclined women to make a bargain with the devil—sealed by sexual intercourse—by which they acquired unholy powers. Such bizarre claims, far from being rejected by rational men, were broadcast by intellectuals. The German Ulrich Molitur, the Frenchman Nicolas Rémy, and the Italian Stefano Guazzo all coolly informed the public of sinister orgies and midnight pacts with the devil. The celebrated French jurist, historian, and political philosopher Jean Bodin argued that because women were especially prone to diabolism, regular legal procedures could properly be suspended in order to try those accused of this "exceptional crime."

A few experts such as the physician Johann Weyer, a student of Agrippa's, raised their voices in protest. In 1563, he explained the witch phenomenon thus, without discarding belief in diabolism: the devil deluded foolish old women afflicted by melancholia, causing them to believe they had magical powers. Weyer's rational skepticism, which had good credibility in the community of the learned, worked to revise the conventional views of women and witchcraft.

WOMEN'S WORKS. To the many categories of works produced on the question of women's worth must be added nearly all works written by women. A woman writing was in herself a statement of women's claim to dignity.

Only a few women wrote anything before the dawn of the modern era, for three reasons. First, they rarely received the education that would enable them to write. Second, they were not admitted to the public roles—as administrator, bureaucrat, lawyer or notary, or university professor—in which they might gain knowledge of the kinds of things the literate public thought worth writing about. Third, the culture imposed silence on women, considering speaking out a form of unchastity. Given these conditions, it is remarkable that any women wrote. Those who did before the fourteenth century were almost always nuns or religious women whose isolation made their pronouncements more acceptable.

From the fourteenth century on, the volume of women's writings rose. Women continued to write devotional literature, although not always as cloistered nuns. They also wrote diaries, often intended as keepsakes for their children; books of advice to their sons and daughters; letters to family members and friends; and family memoirs, in a few cases elaborate enough to be considered histories.

A few women wrote works directly concerning the "woman question," and some of these, such as the humanists Isotta Nogarola, Cassandra Fedele, Laura Cereta, and Olympia Morata, were highly trained. A few were professional writers, living by the income of their pens; the very first among them was Christine de Pizan, noteworthy in this context as in so many others. In addition to *The Book of the City of Ladies* and her critiques of *The Romance of the Rose*, she wrote *The Treasure of the City of Ladies* (a guide to social decorum for women), an advice book for her son, much courtly verse, and a full-scale history of the reign of King Charles V of France.

WOMEN PATRONS. Women who did not themselves write but encouraged others to do so boosted the development of an alternative tradition. Highly placed women patrons supported authors, artists, musicians, poets, and learned men. Such patrons, drawn mostly from the Italian elites and the courts of northern Europe, figure disproportionately as the dedicatees of the important works of early feminism.

For a start, it might be noted that the catalogs of Boccaccio and Alvaro de Luna were dedicated to the Florentine noblewoman Andrea Acciaiuoli and to Doña María, first wife of King Juan II of Castile, while the French translation of Boccaccio's work was commissioned by Anne of Brittany, wife of King Charles VIII of France. The humanist treatises of Goggio, Equicola, Vives, and Agrippa were dedicated, respectively, to Eleanora of Aragon, wife of Ercole I d'Este, duke of Ferrara; to Margherita Cantelma of Mantua; to Catherine of Aragon, wife of King Henry VIII of England; and to Margaret, Duchess of Austria and regent of the Netherlands. As late as 1696, Mary Astell's *Serious Proposal to the Ladies, for the Advancement of Their True and Greatest Interest* was dedicated to Princess Anne of Denmark.

These authors presumed that their efforts would be welcome to female patrons, or they may have written at the bidding of those patrons. Silent themselves, perhaps even unresponsive, these loftily placed women helped shape the tradition of the other voice.

THE ISSUES. The literary forms and patterns in which the tradition of the other voice presented itself have now been sketched. It remains to highlight the major issues around which this tradition crystallizes. In brief, there are four problems to which our authors return again and again, in plays and catalogs, in verse and letters, in treatises and dialogues, in every language: the problem of chastity, the problem of power, the problem of speech, and the problem of knowledge. Of these the greatest, preconditioning the others, is the problem of chastity.

THE PROBLEM OF CHASTITY. In traditional European culture, as in those of antiquity and others around the globe, chastity was perceived as woman's quintessential virtue—in contrast to courage, or generosity, or leadership, or rationality, seen as virtues characteristic of men. Opponents of women charged them with insatiable lust. Women themselves and their defenders—without disputing the validity of the standard—responded that women were capable of chastity.

The requirement of chastity kept women at home, silenced them, isolated them, left them in ignorance. It was the source of all other impediments. Why was it so important to the society of men, of whom chastity was not required, and who more often than not considered it their right to violate the chastity of any woman they encountered?

Female chastity ensured the continuity of the male-headed household. If a man's wife was not chaste, he could not be sure of the legitimacy of his offspring. If they were not his and they acquired his property, it was not his household, but some other man's, that had endured. If his daughter was not chaste, she could not be transferred to another man's household as his wife, and he was dishonored.

The whole system of the integrity of the household and the transmission of property was bound up in female chastity. Such a requirement pertained only to property-owning classes, of course. Poor women could not expect to maintain their chastity, least of all if they were in contact with high-status men to whom all women but those of their own household were prey.

In Catholic Europe, the requirement of chastity was further buttressed by moral and religious imperatives. Original sin was inextricably linked with the sexual act. Virginity was seen as heroic virtue, far more impressive than, say, the avoidance of idleness or greed. Monasticism, the cultural institution that dominated medieval Europe for centuries, was grounded in the renunciation of the flesh. The Catholic reform of the eleventh century imposed a similar standard on all the clergy and a heightened awareness of sexual requirements on all the laity. Although men were asked to be chaste, female unchastity was much worse: it led to the devil, as Eve had led mankind to sin.

To such requirements, women and their defenders protested their innocence. Furthermore, following the example of holy women who had escaped the requirements of family and sought the religious life, some women began to conceive of female communities as alternatives both to family and to the cloister. Christine de Pizan's city of ladies was such a community. Moderata Fonte and Mary Astell envisioned others. The luxurious salons of the French *précieuses* of the seventeenth century, or the comfortable English drawing rooms of the next, may have been born of the same impulse. Here women not only might escape, if briefly, the subordinate position that life in the family entailed but might also make claims to power, exercise their capacity for speech, and display their knowledge.

THE PROBLEM OF POWER. Women were excluded from power: the whole cultural tradition insisted on it. Only men were citizens, only men bore arms, only men could be chiefs or lords or kings. There were exceptions that did not disprove the rule, when wives or widows or mothers took the place of men, awaiting their return or the maturation of a male heir. A woman who attempted to rule in her own right was perceived as an anomaly, a monster, at once a deformed woman and an insufficient male, sexually confused and consequently unsafe.

The association of such images with women who held or sought power explains some otherwise odd features of early modern culture. Queen Elizabeth I of England, one of the few women to hold full regal authority in European history, played with such male/female images—positive ones, of course—in representing herself to her subjects. She was a prince, and manly, even though she was female. She was also (she claimed) virginal, a condition absolutely essential if she was to avoid the attacks of her opponents. Catherine de' Medici, who ruled France as widow and regent for her sons, also adopted such imagery in defining her position. She chose as one symbol the figure of Artemisia, an androgynous ancient warrior-heroine who combined a female persona with masculine powers.

Power in a woman, without such sexual imagery, seems to have been indigestible by the culture. A rare note was struck by the Englishman Sir Thomas Elyot in his *Defence of Good Women* (1540), justifying both women's participation in civic life and their prowess in arms. The old tune was sung by the Scots reformer John Knox in his *First Blast of the Trumpet against the Monstrous Regiment of Women* (1558); for him rule by women, defects in nature, was a hideous contradiction in terms.

The confused sexuality of the imagery of female potency was not reserved for rulers. Any woman who excelled was likely to be called an Amazon, recalling the self-mutilated warrior women of antiquity who repudiated all men, gave up their sons, and raised only their daughters. She was often said to have "exceeded her sex" or to have possessed "masculine virtue"—as the very fact of conspicuous excellence conferred masculinity even on the female subject. The catalogs of notable women often showed those female heroes dressed in armor, armed to the teeth, like men. Amazonian heroines romp through the epics of the age—Ariosto's *Orlando Furioso* (1532) and Spenser's *Faerie Queene* (1590–1609). Excellence in a woman was perceived as a claim for power, and power was reserved for the masculine realm. A woman who possessed either one was masculinized and lost title to her own female identity.

THE PROBLEM OF SPEECH. Just as power had a sexual dimension when it was claimed by women, so did speech. A good woman spoke little. Excessive speech was an indication of unchastity. By speech, women seduced men. Eve had lured Adam into sin by her speech. Accused witches were commonly accused of having spoken abusively, or irrationally, or simply too much. As enlightened a figure as Francesco Barbaro insisted on silence in a woman, which he linked to her perfect unanimity with her husband's will and her unblemished virtue (her chastity). Another Italian humanist, Leonardo Bruni, in advising a noblewoman on her studies, barred her not from speech but from public speaking. That was reserved for men.

Related to the problem of speech was that of costume—another, if silent, form of self-expression. Assigned the task of pleasing men as their primary occupation, elite women often tended toward elaborate costume, hairdressing, and the use of cosmetics. Clergy and secular moralists alike condemned these practices. The appropriate function of costume and adornment was to announce the status of a woman's husband or father. Any further indulgence in adornment was akin to unchastity.

THE PROBLEM OF KNOWLEDGE. When the Italian noblewoman Isotta Nogarola had begun to attain a reputation as a humanist, she was accused of incest—a telling instance of the association of learning in women with unchastity. That chilling association inclined any woman who was educated to deny that she was or to make exaggerated claims of heroic chastity.

If educated women were pursued with suspicions of sexual misconduct, women seeking an education faced an even more daunting obstacle: the assumption that women were by nature incapable of learning, that reasoning was a particularly masculine ability. Just as they proclaimed their chastity, women and their defenders insisted on their capacity for learning. The major work by a male writer on female education—that by Juan Luis Vives, *On the Education of a Christian Woman* (1523)—granted female capacity for intellection but still argued that a woman's whole education was to be shaped around the requirement of chastity and a future within the household. Female writers of the following generations—Marie de Gournay in France, Anna Maria van Schurman in Holland, and Mary Astell in England—began to envision other possibilities.

The pioneers of female education were the Italian women humanists who managed to attain a literacy in Latin and a knowledge of classical and Christian literature equivalent to that of prominent men. Their works implicitly and explicitly raise questions about women's social roles, defining problems that beset women attempting to break out of the cultural limits that had bound them. Like Christine de Pizan, who achieved an advanced education through her father's tutoring and her own devices, their bold questioning makes clear the importance of training. Only when women were educated to the same standard as male leaders would they be able to raise that other voice and insist on their dignity as human beings morally, intellectually, and legally equal to men.

THE OTHER VOICE. The other voice, a voice of protest, was mostly female, but it was also male. It spoke in the vernaculars and in Latin, in treatises and dialogues, in plays and poetry, in letters and diaries, and in pamphlets. It battered at the wall of prejudice that encircled women and raised a banner announcing its claims. The female was equal (or even superior) to the male in essential nature—moral, spiritual, and intellectual. Women were capable of higher education, of holding positions of power and influence in the public realm, and of speaking and writing persuasively. The last bastion of masculine supremacy, centered on the notions of a woman's primary domestic responsibility and the requirement of female chastity, was not as yet assaulted—although visions of productive female communities as alternatives to the family indicated an awareness of the problem.

During the period 1300–1700, the other voice remained only a voice, and one only dimly heard. It did not result—yet—in an alteration of social patterns. Indeed, to this day they have not entirely been altered. Yet the call for justice issued as long as six centuries ago by those writing in the tradition of the other voice must be recognized as the source and origin of the mature feminist tradition and of the realignment of social institutions accomplished in the modern age.

We thank the volume editors in this series, who responded with many suggestions to an earlier draft of this introduction, making it a collaborative enterprise. Many of their suggestions and criticisms have resulted in revisions of this introduction, although we remain responsible for the final product.

PROJECTED TITLES IN THE SERIES

Isabella Andreini, *Mirtilla*, edited and translated by Laura Stortoni

Tullia d'Aragona, *Complete Poems and Letters*, edited and translated by Julia Hairston

Tullia d'Aragona, *The Wretch, Otherwise Known as Guerrino*, edited and translated by Julia Hairston and John McLucas

Francesco Barbaro et al., *On Marriage and the Family*, edited and translated by Margaret L. King

Laura Battiferra, *Selected Poetry, Prose, and Letters*, edited and translated by Victoria Kirkham

Francesco Buoninsegni and Arcangela Tarabotti, *Menippean Satire: "Against Feminine Extravagance" and "Antisatire,"* edited and translated by Elissa Weaver

Rosalba Carriera, *Letters, Diaries, and Art*, edited and translated by Catherine M. Sama

Madame du Chatelet, *Selected Works*, edited by Judith Zinsser

Vittoria Colonna, Chiara Matraini, and Lucrezia Marinella, *Marian Writings*, edited and translated by Susan Haskins

Princess Elizabeth of Bohemia, *Correspondence with Descartes*, edited and translated by Lisa Shapiro

Isabella d'Este, *Selected Letters*, edited and translated by Deanna Shemek

Fairy-Tales by Seventeenth-Century French Women Writers, edited and translated by Lewis Seifert and Domna C. Stanton

Moderata Fonte, *Floridoro*, edited by Valeria Finucci and translated by Julia Kisacki

Moderata Fonte and Lucrezia Marinella, *Religious Narratives*, edited and translated by Virginia Cox

Catharina Regina von Greiffenberg, *Meditations on the Life of Christ*, edited and translated by Lynne Tatlock

In Praise of Women: Italian Fifteenth-Century Defenses of Women, edited and translated by Daniel Bornstein

Louise Labé, *Complete Works*, edited and translated by Annie Finch and Deborah Baker

Lucrezia Marinella, *L'Enrico, or Byzantium Conquered*, edited and translated by Virginia Cox

Lucrezia Marinella, *Happy Arcadia*, edited and translated by Susan Haskins and Letizia Panizza

Chiara Matraini, *Selected Poetry and Prose*, edited and translated by Elaine MacLachlan

Alessandro Piccolomini, *Rethinking Marriage in Sixteenth-Century Italy*, edited and translated by Letizia Panizza

Christine de Pizan, *Life of Charles V*, edited and translated by Nadia Margolis

Christine de Pizan, *The Long Road of Learning*, edited and translated by Andrea Tarnowski

Madeleine and Catherine des Roches, *Selected Letters, Dialogues, and Poems*, edited and translated by Anne Larsen

Oliva Sabuco, *The New Philosophy: True Medicine*, edited and translated by Gianna Pomata

Margherita Sarrocchi, *La Scanderbeide*, edited and translated by Rinaldina Russell

Justine Siegemund, *The Court Midwife of the Electorate of Brandenburg* (1690), edited and translated by Lynne Tatlock

Gabrielle Suchon, *"On Philosophy" and "On Morality,"* edited and translated by Domna Stanton with Rebecca Wilkin

Sara Copio Sullam, *Sara Copio Sullam: Jewish Poet and Intellectual in Early Seventeenth-Century Venice,* edited and translated by Don Harrán

Arcangela Tarabotti, *Convent Life as Inferno: A Report,* introduction and notes by Francesca Medioli, translated by Letizia Panizza

Laura Terracina, *Works,* edited and translated by Michael Sherberg

Katharina Schütz Zell, *Selected Writings,* edited and translated by Elsie McKee

Joh[ann] Stridbeck, Johanna Eleonora Petersen, copperplate, 122 × 80 mm. Courtesy of the Portrait Collection (C 4197), the Library, the Francke Foundation.

JOHANNA ELEONORA PETERSEN, NÉE VON MERLAU (1644–1724): FROM NOBLEWOMAN TO RADICAL PIETIST

THE OTHER VOICE

In an age in which most women in Germany remained silent, because most of them could neither read nor write and those who could were usually muted, Johanna Eleonora Petersen, née von Merlau (1644–1724), found her own voice. Growing up in a desolate and difficult time right after the end of the Thirty Years' War that had left large parts of Germany destitute, ravaged by marauding soldiers, impoverished, and starving, she became a writer of religious books and revelations, exhibiting her individual faith and visions. Hers was "another voice" in the chorus of almost exclusively male authors not only because of her gender but also because of her way of writing and her message: she insisted on her right as a believer, though a woman and thus a layperson, to publish her readings of the Book of Revelation and of theological questions. While the Pauline dictum that women should be silent in church was still strictly enforced in her lifetime, she found her own voice as a believer and as a woman as she published her experience with biblical readings. Her writings and her life were accompanied by controversy especially in orthodox Protestant circles, since she became a voice for the "radical pietists," those most at odds with orthodox Lutheran ministers and their teachings, and a voice for pious women. In order to defend her religious calling, her change from noblewoman to radical Pietist, she published her autobiography, the subject of this book. It is the first autobiography known to me by a woman written in the German language.

Already as a single young woman, Johanna Eleonora von und zu Merlau set an example as a leader in a devotional gathering of women in Frankfurt, the "Saalhof Pietists," named after the stately Frankfurt residence at which they met. Her supplication to the Frankfurt City Council, who considered expelling her from the city, already shows her independent spirit (see the translation of her letter, "A Supplication," in appendix A). Von Merlau's circle was visited by, among others, William Penn (in 1677), and helped in the preparation of the first group of German immigrants to settle in Pennsylvania. Von Merlau was inspired and supported by the noted Pietist theologian Johann Jakob Spener, then also living in Frankfurt. She kept her independence from Spener's conventicles, the "Collegia Pietatis," until she married—the circumstances to be discussed later in this introduction—at age thirty-six the Protestant minister (and commoner) Johann Wilhelm Petersen in 1680. She spent the rest of her life writing and preaching Pietist beliefs, moving, and traveling with her husband.

All her religious writings—some fourteen original works—and her autobiography appeared in print between 1689 and 1718, when she was married to Petersen (see the annotated bibliography of her works following this introduction). Her writings exhibit her visionary religiosity, her "heart's experience and true practice," as the English translator of one of her religious tracts stated in 1772 (see appendix B: "The Nature and Necessity of the New Creature in Christ"). They can be compared to, among others, the writings of the English visionary Jane Lead (1623–1704), who inspired and provided the theoretical basis for Philadelphianism and whom Johanna Eleonora Petersen read and corresponded with. While their theological explications are today only of interest to theologians, both women fervently believed in and preached "brotherly love," a reconciliation of all warring factions religious and otherwise, still a very valid cause in our time.

Of special interest is her autobiography, translated below: The Life of Lady Johanna Eleonora Petersen, née von und zu Merlau, Wife of Dr. Johann Wilhelm Petersen, Written by Herself and Given to the Public Because of Many Edifying Events, As a Sequel to Her Husband's Memoirs. Paid for by Worthy Friends. She published the first part in 1689 as an appendix to her first book, and an expanded version in 1718. Petersen's autobiography went beyond the presentation of and reflection on the religious life; her way of writing later became customary among Pietists, who usually composed their spiritual autobiographies when facing death. In her autobiography Petersen defended her "other path," her choice of becoming a Pietist, of a marriage outside of her class, and the publication of her religious thoughts against the accusations and lies of other people. She described in detail her secular life: her rather desolate childhood in the wake of the Thirty Years' War, her service at court, her life as a Pietist in Frankfurt, and her marriage. Her religious visions concluded the volume as a climax of her inner biography, her destiny since childhood. At the same time she defended herself against the attacks of (unidentified) enemies and others, of whose worldly lifestyle she disapproved. Petersen ended her autobiography with mystic images of a religious calling, reminiscent of Jacob Boehme and Jane Lead.

CHILDHOOD AND SERVICE AT COURT

The seventeenth century was an age of religious and civil conflicts escalating into wars in much of Europe. In Germany the Thirty Years' War (1618–48) began as an internal rebellion, a dispute about sovereignty and the election of the emperor, but it became a civil and international war, and ended with a weakened empire and an impoverished country fractured into a large number of mostly small principalities. The Peace of Westphalia (Münster and Osnabrück) in 1648 meant the end of hostilities between the big powers. But marauding soldiers, lingering local conflicts, and new regional wars—Louis XVI's occupation of Alsace, Lorraine, and of the Palatinate, Brandenburg-Prussia's war against Sweden, the Turkish invasion of Hungary and siege of Vienna—plagued the people for years to come. The peace in 1648 was essentially a religious peace; it officially marked the end of more than a century of bitter religious conflict and wars. With the peace agreement, the rights of the three major Christian denominations—Catholic, Lutheran, and Calvinist communities established before 1624—were guaranteed by imperial law. For the rest, religious freedom was granted from above by decree and was dependent on princes and magistrates. The provisions accounted largely for a marked decline in religious prosecutions after 1648, but the troubles were by no means over as hostile feelings between members of different denominations persisted, and acrimonious theological debate among scholars about religious questions was the order of the day.

Johanna Eleonora von und zu Merlau was born on April 25, 1644,[1] during the final phase of the Thirty Years' War, in Frankfurt, an Imperial Free City and heavily fortified, where her parents had moved for protection during the war. Her childhood (1644–56) coincided with the most difficult

---

1. Her life is relatively well documented for a woman in the seventeenth century. In addition to her autobiography is that of her husband Johann Wilhelm Petersen's autobiography, *Das Leben Jo. Wilhelmi Petersen* (1717); letters to other noted Pietists like Johann Jakob Spener, Jakob Schütz, the Duchess Sophie Elisabeth von Sachsen-Zeitz, and others; and documents relating to her family, her stay in Frankfurt (see appendix A), and her husband's employment and activities. (Seventeenth-century German women are usually best documented, if at all, through their prominent husbands or male relatives.) For the best summary of archival sources, see Markus Maththias, *Johann Wilhelm Petersen und Johanna Eleonora: Eine Biographie bis zur Amtsenthebung Petersens im Jahre 1692*, Arbeiten zur Geschichte des Pietismus, 30 (Göttingen: Vandenhoeck & Rupprecht, 1993), 341–46.

years of reconstruction, which was to extend well into the eighteenth century. Her entire life was overshadowed by the lingering memory of war, continuing difficulties of making a living, and religious conflicts. This was the seedbed for her religiosity, spiritual illuminations, and speculations about God's will and intent, about the role and fate of humanity, and about what the future had in store.

The Merlaus were an old Hessian noble family, with an estate at Merlau near Grünberg, south of Alsfeld; they belonged to the Knights of the Rhine and as such they were immediate to the emperor, thus not subject to any princely ruler. This relatively independent status was reflected in Johanna Eleonora's pride in and frequent references to her social standing—all her publications bore the "von und zu Merlau" on the title page. Her father, Georg Adolph von und zu Merlau (d. 1681), came from an impoverished sideline of the Merlaus; he was an educated man who struggled to make a living. Orphaned at an early age, he and his older brother were taken in by the widowed Anna von Solms in Laubach, a small residential town in Hesse, both serving as pages and being trained for service at court. While the older Merlau[2] made it to privy councillor at the important court of the Duke of Württemberg in Stuttgart, the younger brother, Johanna Eleonora's father, married several times,[3] and got entangled in a lengthy lawsuit over the war-damaged manor house at Philippseck near Heddernheim (today a suburb of Frankfurt)[4] claimed by relatives. After the Peace of Westphalia, he obtained a position as steward of the household[5] for the Landgrave of Hesse in the town of Homburg; later he served as steward of the Landgrave's divorced wife.

Johanna Eleonora's mother, Maria Sabina Ganß von Utzberg, moved with the children—Johanna Eleonora was the second of four daughters—after the war to Philippseck, but she died in 1653, when Johanna Eleonora

2. Johanna Eleonora mentions her uncle's authority in the family and his veto at one of the marriages proposed to her; see her autobiography, §§ 3 and 9. His position as older brother, as well as his political career and social standing, gave him authority in family affairs.

3. Three wives died in childbirth, a rather common death for women at the time; Johanna Eleonora's mother was the second wife.

4. The lawsuit over Philippseck was not decided until 1746 (!) by the imperial court at Wetzlar for a grandson of Johanna Eleonora's, an indication of the inefficacy and disorder of the imperial court that was responsible for, among other things, property disputes among those of closest kin to the emperor.

5. The position, *Hofmeister*, was in the seventeenth century an administrative job of managing the entourage of the prince, all ceremonies at court, and all of the prince's social engagements (it is not to be confused with the late-eighteenth-century *Hofmeister*, who was a tutor). It was not a political or policy-making position for the princely territories.

was nine years old. The mother seems to have been very pious; Johanna Eleonora remembered fondly her protection in connection with the threats of marauding soldiers, her prayers, and her tears over a friend's moral decline. She feared her father, a stern authority figure, who may well have been displeased with the lack of a male heir and the burden of four young daughters.[6] The father hired a succession of housekeepers, who cared little for the welfare of the children, even permitting robbers to clean out the already dilapidated estate. When Johanna Eleonora's older sister was sent to her uncle, the privy councillor at the court in Stuttgart—as was customary for the young ladies in search of a suitable husband—she took over the sister's job of supervising the household personnel.

At age twelve Johanna Eleonora was sent to live with the Countess Barbara Maria von Solms-Rödelheim at her estate in Rödelheim; this was arranged apparently with some haste, because another nobleman laying claim to Philippseck simply occupied it and the three remaining young Merlau daughters needed a place to live. Unfortunately, the countess was mentally unstable, and Johanna Eleonora's father soon took her out of this position and placed her as lady-in-waiting[7] with her godmother, the Duchess Anna Margaretha, a Landgravine of Hessen-Homburg by birth and the second wife of the Duke Philipp Ludwig of Schleswig-Holstein-Sonderburg. They resided at Wiesenburg Castle in Saxony near the city of Zwickau, some three hundred miles away from Frankfurt.

Johanna Eleonora's service at court (1657–74) was an important phase in her life; it laid the foundation for her later turn away from secular life and the affairs of her class. At first she enjoyed the experience and lifestyle, taking part with pleasure and satisfaction in elaborate marriage festivities in Linz[8] and as the personal assistant of the duchess in all social activities in which the lady was involved. It was also the time for finding a suitable husband. Her father and the duke first agreed to the marriage proposal of a Herr von

6. A stepbrother was born later; Johanna Eleonora's father remarried at least once and had several more children. For an epistle to her sisters, see Johanna Eleonora's "The Nature and Necessity of the New Creature in Christ" (appendix B).

7. At the more prestigious courts, the position of lady-in-waiting (*Hofjungfer*) was usually reserved for noblewomen, *Jungfer* denoting an unmarried noblewoman. The position entailed helping the women of the ducal family with dressing, assisting at all social events, and often also reading aloud to the lady. In seventeenth-century Germany, a duchess had only a small staff of women with her, attached to the much larger entourage of the duke.

8. The duke's daughter from his first marriage was being married to Count Sinzendorf, a president of the Imperial Chamber. However, because of the count's limited financial means, Johanna Eleonora could not continue as lady-in-waiting with the young countess; instead she returned and stayed with the Duchess Anna Margaretha.

Bretewitz, who was employed as cornet[9] and who was later to take over his father's charge as a chief lieutenant. After some years, however, he found a wealthier prospect and the engagement with Johanna Eleonora was called off. A few years later in 1674, the marriage proposal of a well-established, widowed clergyman was rejected by her family because of the difference in social class.

Traveling by boat on the Main River to the spa Bad Ems[10] in the summer of 1672, Johanna Eleonora met by chance the theologian Philipp Jakob Spener (1635–1705), the father of German Pietism,[11] who since 1666 had been the senior preacher at the Barfüßer Church in Frankfurt. Spener's religious views were in harmony with von Merlau's, and an exchange of letters concerning religious questions ensued.[12] One of Spener's letters in particular expounded upon the reasons for and against marriage, after von Merlau had received the marriage proposal from the clergyman in 1674. Spener pointed to the goal of a Christian life shared by her and the clergyman and how von Merlau could support the minister's work in the community, but he also realized "that the greatest obstacle to your marriage is having to give up the single life so much enjoyed until now." There would be much less time and leisure as well for the "enjoyable contemplations and devotions and their delight."[13] He counseled her to leave the decision entirely to her father, who rejected the proposal. Strengthened by Spener's advice, von Merlau turned to a religious life in Christian simplicity and humility, rejecting all worldly ambitions and withdrawing from the diversions and social activities at court. Her request to be dismissed from her position at court was denied by the

---

9. A cadet in the cavalry; the fact that Bretewitz joined the military suggests that he was not the family heir and impoverished like the Merlaus.

10. Von Merlau, of course, did not travel independently for pleasure but as a companion of the Princess Sophie Elisabeth, a daughter from the second marriage of Duke Philipp Ludwig von Holstein-Sonderburg, who was going to the spa Bad Ems to improve her health.

11. See the thorough study by Johannes Wallmann: *Philipp Jakob Spener und die Anfänge des Pietismus*, Beiträge zur historischen Theologie, 42, 2d enlarged ed. (Tübingen: Mohr, 1986); and K. James Stein, *Philipp Jakob Spener: Pietist Patriarch* (Chicago: University of Chicago Press, 1986).

12. In 1701 Spener published ten of his letters of the original correspondence of 1772–74 under the title "To a Noble Lady" as examples of his religious advice, views, and the nobility's interest in Pietism. Spener's letters are now being made available in *Philipp Jakob Spener: Briefe aus der Frankfurter Zeit, 1666–1686,* ed. Johannes Wallmann with Udo Sträter and Markus Matthias (Tübingen: Moht Siebeck, 1992), vol. 1. Volume 3 contains the only two surviving letters of Johanna Eleonora to Spener.

13. Spener's letter of June 1774 counseled von Merlau on marriage; see *Briefe*, vol. 1, 762–69, here 764. The clergyman was Johann Winckler (1642–1705). See also her version in her autobiography, § 18.

duchess and duke, who rebuked her and tried to change her mind but in the end allowed her to pursue her religious inclinations while she continued in court service. Her father called her away to care for a newly born stepsister after the stepmother died in childbirth. After the stepsister also died, von Merlau did not return to court service but moved to Frankfurt in the spring of 1775 in order to join Spener's congregation.

Johanna Eleonora von Merlau received permission from her father to board with the widowed Maria Juliana Baur von Eyseneck, née von Hynsberg (1641–84), in the ancient imperial Saalhof Castle,[14] where she lived until her marriage in September 1680. In his correspondence with von Merlau Spener had recommended the widow as a like-minded, pious soul and suitable companion, and von Merlau mentioned her in her autobiography with great affection. Von Merlau needed her father's permission for such a move, since unmarried women were under the tutelage of their fathers or their closest male relative or appointed male guardian. As a lady of rank she could not live alone but had to join another household of her class. This also was more economical as good living quarters in the city were relatively scarce and expensive. Von Merlau's income[15] from her court position enabled her to make the move to Frankfurt, a step into a state of some independence, rarely possible for an unmarried woman of her time in Germany. She used her new freedom to expand her correspondence with theologians and other women interested in religious questions, to learn Hebrew from a Frankfurt Jew, and to teach at a school Mrs. Baur had established for girls. She taught daily a group of eight to twelve girls ages six to ten, instructing them in household tasks and "female" skills for upper-middle-class women (singing, manners, embroidery, managing a household, servants, and finances). She also gave the girls Bible lessons and had them memorize biblical passages. Together she and Mrs. Baur wrote prayers for children and devotional texts, and von Merlau even taught Greek to a few of the older girls. She also took in a niece, her godchild. Von Merlau herself had never had formal instruction in a school, nor any tutors that we know of; she acquired her knowledge

---

14. The Saalhof was the former imperial palace of the Hohenstaufen dating back to the twelfth century; among the later owners was the Hynsberg family (old Hessian nobility) of which Juliana Baur von Eyseneck was a member. Today only one tower and the private chapel remain of what must have been very stately quarters. In the seventeenth century, parts of the building were used by wealthy merchants from the Lower Rhine and the Netherlands attending the Frankfurt trade fairs.

15. Von Merlau received payment for her services at court; she related how the duchess wanted her to come back and even promised to double her pay and give her a supervising position. See § 25 in the autobiography.

as an autodidact with her wide reading. She seems to have had a fabulous memory, as she mentioned in passing that she remembered sermons verbatim afterward and could repeat them even after a year's time.

EMERGING PIETISM IN FRANKFURT, WILLIAM PENN, AND INDEPENDENCE

During these years Pietism, a reform movement within the Protestant churches, especially in Germany throughout the late seventeenth and eighteenth centuries, began to evolve in Frankfurt. Pietists emphasized a religious life in accordance with Christian ethics for the individual and for the representatives of the church. They turned against the rigid orthodoxy of the Lutheran and Reformed Churches. "Pietist" was at first, and remained in some quarters, a derogative name used only from the early 1690s; in Germany Pietists preferred to call themselves *die Stillen im Lande* (the quiet ones in the land).

Spener[16] was the leading theologian of the early Pietist movement in Germany. In his widely read and best-known work *Pia Desideria, or Heartfelt Desire for a God-Pleasing Reform of the True Evangelical Church, Together with Several Simple Proposals Looking Toward This End* (1675–76), Spener pointed out the discrepancy between the religious teachings and the worldly lifestyle of individuals and Protestant Church officials. He set forth proposals for reforming the individual Christian and the church from within, while reaffirming the Lutheran tradition. He explained how conventicles should be used for teaching and learning about the Bible, for the education of the individual and for an inner reform of entire congregations. Spener called for a basic change in the soul, a "rebirth" introduced into Lutheran spirituality. Originally the *Pia Desideria* were published as a preface to a book of sermons by Johann Arndt (the *Postille*). Arndt's *Das wahre Christentum* (True Christianity; 1605–9) was the most popular devotional work in seventeenth-century Germany. Both Arndt and Spener were very influential in promoting piety and spirituality; Arndt was more mystical in orientation. A loose network of followers embraced Arndt's and Spener's piety; they looked to Spener as the leader of the reform movement.

Inspired by Spener, von Merlau became a leading personality in Frankfurt's religious community. Spener also introduced her to other prominent,

---

16. See the informative chapter "Spenerian Pietism" in Richard L. Gawthrop, *Pietism and the Making of Eighteenth-Century Prussia* (Cambridge: Cambridge University Press, 1993), 104–20; and Stein's excellent 1986 biography, *Philipp Jakob Spener: Pietist Patriarch* (see note 11).

like-minded citizens like the lawyer Johann Jakob Schütz (1640–90). She gathered a small circle of friends around her, the so-called Saalhof Pietists, who met in Mrs. Baur's apartment. They had split off from the larger, "pious" gatherings, the *Collegia Pietatis* or conventicles that Spener had held at his house since the summer of 1670, in addition to the regular church services and prayer hours. In the Saalhof a devout group of mostly laypeople, including students, met with the goal of gaining edification in Christian living. They read scripture and devotional literature, prayed and spoke about biblical passages; here even women could speak. That was not the case at Spener's meetings, where women had to sit in a side room unseen by the men[17] and could not participate in the discussion.

Von Merlau's gatherings attracted prominent visitors. In 1677 William Penn (1644–1718) was on his second trip through Germany together with George Fox, Robert Barclay, George Keith, and other leading Quaker personalities. On his visit to Frankfurt, he stayed at the house of the Dutch merchant Jacob van der Valle, where he was introduced to Johanna Eleonora von Merlau. He then visited the Saalhof on two days and was asked by von Merlau to preach. Five days later on his return through Frankfurt he visited there again and held another religious meeting in her residence. On August 21, 1677, Penn noted in his travel diary:

> Of these Persons there were two women, one a virgin, the other a widow, both of noble birth; who had a deep sense of that power and presence of god, that accompanyed our Testimony: & their hearts yearned strongly towards us. The virgin giving us a particular Invitation to her house the next morning: where we had the most blessed opportunity of the three.[18]

Penn also described the conversion of a young student of theology and of a "doctor" through his preaching and then quoted von Merlau: "Sayd the young Virgin, *Our quarters are free for you, let all come that will, & lift up your voices without fear: for (sayd she) it will never be well with us, till persecution come, & some of us be*

17. This was typical for northern Europe; the learned Anna Maria van Schurman, a benefactor and instrumental in the establishment of the University of Utrecht, could sit only in a side balcony covered by a curtain during the university's inaugural celebration in 1636, for which she had written dedicatory poetry in Latin and Dutch. She was not allowed to listen to any lectures or classes, not even while hidden from the men. And after the educated Luise Kulmus married the Leipzig professor of literature Gottsched in 1734, she could only listen to his lectures in a side chamber hidden by a curtain. Satirical poems circulated about such "unfeminine" women.

18. *The Papers of William Penn*, ed. Mary Maples Dunn and Richard S. Dunn (Philadelphia: University of Pennsylvania Press, 1981), vol. 1 (1644–79), 447–48.

lodg'd in the Stadthouse, that is, *the prison.*"[19] Penn's report underscores the leading role of von Merlau among the Saalhof Pietists and her expectation of some sort of persecution to come (von Merlau would in fact get into trouble with the city authorities). Penn, on the other hand, was more interested in making converts and in gathering settlers among the educated, religiously motivated, and well-to-do for his newly acquired territory, the later colony of Pennsylvania.[20] Johanna Eleonora gave Penn a letter of introduction to Charlotte Auguste Dhaun von Falkenstein und Broich in Mühlheim an der Ruhr and she most likely introduced him to many of her Pietist friends among the nobility in Hesse and the Rhineland. Von Merlau corresponded with Penn, who remained in contact with the Frankfurt Pietists. In November of 1782 a number of prosperous Frankfurt citizens had started an enterprise, the so-called Frankfurter Compagnie, and invested money in it with which they bought land shares in Pennsylvania and financed poor emigrants; by 1686 Johanna Eleonora von Merlau (then married to Petersen) had acquired shares in the company.[21]

In February of 1677, the Frankfurt city council apparently wanted to revoke von Merlau's residence permit in the city and requested that she leave. Agitating for this request was the head superintendent of churches for that region as well as court chaplain Balthasar Mentzer, whose fear of heretical activities prompted him to investigate the newly formed gatherings in Frankfurt.[22] Such suspicion and intrigue was emblematic of the general climate of envy and distrust, wherein authorities attempted to control

19. Ibid., 448.

20. Penn accepted as his inheritance from the king the colonial territory of what was to become Pennsylvania in lieu of the large sum his father had lent to the Crown and the services he had rendered as admiral of the fleet during the English-Dutch War. The actual deal was not concluded until 1681. Already in 1681 Penn had published in German a description and advertisement of the colony in order to attract settlers. The promotional pamphlet read: *Eine Nachricht wegen der Landschaft Pennsylvania in Amerika, welche jüngstens unter dem großen Siegel in England an Wm. Penn . . . übergeben worden* (Amsterdam 1681: News about the territory of Pennsylvania in America, recently deeded in England to Wm. Penn under the great seal).

21. This was most likely a business proposition; there is no indication that von Merlau wanted to emigrate. The *Frankfurter Compagnie* also supported the group of Krefeld families who emigrated in 1683 and founded Germantown in Pennsylvania, now a district in Philadelphia. It was the beginning of religious settlements by Germans—mostly Protestant dissidents—in North America in the late seventeenth and early eighteenth centuries.

22. In 1676–77 the Frankfurt magistrate investigated Spener and his friend, a Mrs. Kißner, who also held private religious meetings in her house. Spener was politically very astute and took several measures to avoid being censored, or worse, dismissed and expelled from the city; he had an ordained minister lead such gatherings, strictly limited conversations to biblical passages and religious questions, and insisted that gatherings be an open affair and take place in church buildings. Later he argued that these *collegia* were not at all regular meetings, but social gatherings

adherents of different religious tenets and practices, sects or groups, single women, and strangers. Von Merlau represented all those categories, and her spirited defense was her insistence on her noble birth and her impeccable lifestyle (see her *Supplication* to the Frankfurt city council in appendix A).

In her autobiography, von Merlau did not elaborate beyond her reference to Penn of "persecutions to come." She recounted only carefully selected events to document her social role and her fulfillment of obligations, as well as to defend or establish her good reputation with the public, especially her critical peers in the nobility and church circles. Her remarks were directed against a public that was hostile and slanderous toward her. Yet concrete details of the Pietist assemblies and circles during these important and eventful years in Frankfurt have but a weak resonance in Johanna Eleonora's autobiography. A reference to her personal religious conversion is made in the metaphorical anecdote about her being caught in a storm during a boat ride when her prayer and fearlessness of death greatly impressed the other passengers and saved her and the people aboard. The lack of more specific details and names of the Saalhof Pietists was perhaps due to the sectarian circle's elitist and hermetic stance. The group took on "more and more clearly the form of a closed circle"[23] under the leadership of Merlau and Schütz, modeled after the Netherlands Labadists led by Jean de Labadie and Anna Maria van Schurman,[24] with whom von Merlau and Schütz corresponded.

AN ACTIVIST MARRIAGE

In 1680 Johann Wilhelm Petersen (1649–1727) proposed to Johanna Eleonora von Merlau. He had studied theology at the orthodox Lutheran university in Giessen and had visited Spener's *collegia* in Frankfurt. Spener taught him the spiritual understanding of scripture and remained his lifelong friend. After a position as professor of poetry in Rostock (where he received his master's in theology), and then serving as minister for the major church in Hannover, he landed (with Spener's and a relative's help) the post of superintendent of churches and court chaplain to the duke of Holstein-Gottorp in 1678 in Eutin, close to his hometown Lübeck. Petersen had probably attended also a meeting at the Saalhof and briefly seen von Merlau there in 1675. Petersen involved Spener and his network of friends with the nobility

---

among friends who conversed about religious instead of worldly affairs. See Matthias, *Johann Wilhelm Petersen und Johanna Eleonora: Eine Biographie bis zur Amtsenthebung Petersens im Jahre 1692*, 90.

23. Wallmann, *Philipp Jakob Spener und die Anfänge des Pietismus*, 235.

24. See pp. 37–38.

and eventually won von Merlau's and her father's approval. Perhaps Spener himself had suggested the pious von Merlau as a suitable match to Petersen.

Von Merlau herself seems to have been at first still generally opposed to marriage; with her religious life she had embraced the commonly held ideal of virginity among independent Pietist women. In a 1680 letter to the Duchess Sophie Elisabeth von Sachsen-Zeitz, she reported her impending wedding and wrote: "God knows how strange the married state will be to me; I can well say that I am a bride and am none. Yet I would rather fulfill God's will than retain my own while staying single, though I did not intend to stay single just for myself, but I thought I could serve God better that way."[25] This explains only partly the account in her autobiography that she quietly waited for a divine sign and left the decision to her father. She elaborated on how and why objections from family members—because Petersen was only a commoner—should be disregarded. Her marriage is portrayed as a sign or missive from God.

Marriage was then an important family affair and a business; the dowry, the family fortune, social status, and future inheritance all were to be considered before a marriage contract was drawn up. For von Merlau, her marriage would also alleviate the problems she had with the Frankfurt city council, since she would leave town. Personally, marriage meant a certain degree of financial and social stability. Thus her defense of marriage outside of her class occupied quite a bit of space in her autobiography; it was of course a time in which strict borders between the social classes were still firmly entrenched in German society. But her discussion of class barriers also shows that values other than money and status were then being considered. Petersen was a religious person, and he was also looking for a wife of like belief, reputation of virtue, and social standing; the elite of Protestant clergymen sought wives among the lower (impoverished) nobility at the time. This foreshadowed changes in marriage patterns and greater porosity of class divisions to come only a century later.

On September 7, 1680, Spener married the couple; he based his wedding sermon[26] on this passage from the Epistle to the Ephesians: "Wives,

25. Letter of August, 19, 1680; Markus Matthias, "Mutua Consolatio Sororum: Die Briefe Johanna Eleonora von Merlaus an die Herzogin Sophie Elisabeth von Sachsen-Zeitz," *Pietismus und Neuzeit* 22 (1996): 90. Von Merlau is referring to 1 Cor. 7:34: "The unmarried woman careth for the things of the Lord, that she may be holy both in body and in spirit; but she that is married careth for the things of the world, how she may please *her* husband."

26. Spener published the sermon: *Bey Gelegenheit der Ehelichen Trauung . . . Herrn Johann Wilhelm Petersen . . . und . . . Johanna Eleonora von und zu Merlau . . . So geschehen zu Frankfurt am Mayn/ den 7. September 1680* (Frankfurt: David Zunner, 1680).

submit yourselves unto your own husbands, as unto the Lord. For the husband is the head of the wife, even as Christ is the head of the church, and gave himself for it" (5:22–24). Spener emphasized that human marriage has a special meaning since it symbolizes the original joining of Christ with the church and the individual soul. Thus marriage takes its significance and dignity from the notion that it is an image of God's earlier act of redemption. Christ is the mediator and all goodness in men comes from him—everything points to a "Christus in nobis" (Christ within ourselves). Reaching out to individuals, Spener saw and considered the individual souls as church, and a church that was not a distant, lifeless body or organization for him.

After their wedding, the Petersens traveled by boat from Frankfurt to Holland, where they visited theologians and purchased books in Leiden, Rotterdam, Utrecht, Amsterdam, Groningen, and Franeker. Johann Wilhelm fell ill in Emden, and in Bremen a doctor had to be consulted. By way of Hamburg, they reached Lübeck, where Johanna Eleonora's niece, whom they had taken along, fell ill, and eventually also Johanna Eleonora herself became gravely ill. Petersen did not fully recover for three months, at which time they moved to Eutin.

In Eutin Johanna Eleonora continued her pious life and intensified her biblical readings—she gave 1685 as the year in which she had a vision and began to understand the Book of Revelation. She began to write devotional literature and started a family. She gave birth to two sons and two daughters, a considerable achievement considering that she married at age thirty-six. Only one son, August Friedrich, lived to adulthood. Born on August 2, 1682,[27] he became a Prussian civil servant, not the theologian or noted Pietist the parents had hoped for. He had a worldly career, inherited his uncle's noble title, had a large family, and died in 1732, outliving his mother by only eight years. Perhaps because female children were generally considered less important, Johanna Eleonora did not mention the birth of two daughters (but they are acknowledged in Johann Wilhelm's autobiography).[28] Likewise, she did not comment in her autobiography on her children's welfare, nor on her son's career and family. She only expressed the commonly held opinion at the time that "being blessed with child" was a woman's God-given role—but she stopped right here. Motherhood was not a topic for her; in her religious

---

27. See § 28 of her autobiography, *Das Leben Jo. Wilhelmi Petersen,* for the special circumstances surrounding the birth of this child. Johann Wilhelm mentions their children more then Johanna Eleonora does; see his autobiography (note 1), 397. One daughter, Maria Johanna, also had children, but (typically for women) nothing is known about her but her name.

28. See note 1, p. 397.

notions all people were part of a community of Christians, without reference to family, class, or nation.

In 1688, Johann Wilhelm accepted the position of superintendent in Lüneburg, but he encountered unexpected difficulties with his predecessor Sandhagen, the ducal government, and the consistory in Celle. Grounds for the complaints against him were his theological views, especially his millenarianism,[29] which he openly expressed from 1690 in sermons and writings, and his public defense of allowing the visionary Juliane von Asseburg[30] into his house in 1691. In addition, Johanna Eleonora's religious publications under her own name, *A Heart's Conversations with God* (1689) and *Conversations about Faith* (1691),[31] were considered a provocation of the authorities; the latter was suppressed by them only a few weeks after its appearance. Both Petersens actively participated in and also were the victims of constant polemical battling over the nature of "pure doctrine" within the Lutheran community.

On February 3, 1692, Johann Wilhelm Petersen was summarily dismissed and ordered to leave the city of Lüneburg within four weeks. The Petersens mobilized their Pietist friends and network and, after a short stay in the principality of Braunschweig-Wolfenbüttel (where the women in the ruling ducal family were somewhat inclined toward Pietism), they received permission from the Elector Friedrich III of Brandenburg[32] to settle in his

---

29. Millenarianism (chiliasm) entailed speculations about the nearness of the millennium (mentioned in Rev. 20) and fulfillment of the Christian prophecy, the end of the world, the return of the savior for a truly Christian interregnum. Any such speculations had been explicitly condemned in the Augsburg Confession (1530), which was binding for Lutherans. See also pp. 19–28 below.

30. Rosamunde Juliane von Asseburg (1672–1712) came from an impoverished noble family in Magdeburg and had visions and revelations about the future of the church. The Petersens traveled to Magdeburg in the fall of 1689, were greatly impressed by Asseburg, and invited the visionary with her mother and sisters to live with them in their official residence in Lüneburg. Johann Wilhelm published a pamphlet in 1691 that considers whether her revelations are divine (translated into English in 1695 by Francis Lee: *A Letter to some Divines, Concerning the Question, Whether GOD since Christ's Ascension, doth any more Reveal himself to Mankind by means of Divine Apparitions? . . .*). Asseburg attracted many visitors, among them the Duchess Sophie von Braunschweig-Lüneburg (second wife of Duke Ernst August), Leibniz, and Spener (who supported her for a while). There were a number of visionary women (and some men) at the time, a topic of intense debate as to their veracity or divine mission; see the study by Barbara Hoffmann, *Radikalpietismus um 1700: Der Streit um das Recht auf eine neue Gesellschaft*, Geschichte und Geschlechter, 15 (Frankfurt: Campus Verlag, 1996).

31. See pp. 25–26 below.

32. The Elector, later King Friedrich I of Prussia, reigned until 1713, continued the policies of the Great Elector and promoted reconciliation and ecumenical relations. He pursued the goal of institutional unification of the Lutheran and Reformed Churches.

territory. Johann Wilhelm was also awarded an annual pension of 700 thalers. The Petersens moved into an abandoned farm, whose owners had perished during the Thirty Years' War, in Nieder-Dodeleben (a small town in the vicinity of Magdeburg).[33]

The Mark Brandenburg and in particular the area around Magdeburg had suffered greatly during the war; fifty years after its end about one-third of the farms and rural estates were still abandoned. Already Friedrich Wilhelm III (the Great Elector, reigned 1640–88) had invited religious dissidents from as far away as Scotland and Silesia, mostly well-educated or high-ranking individuals, to settle in his impoverished territories, with the promise of religious freedom, partial tax relief, and other economic privileges, if they would become productive subjects. After 1672, when the almost continuous warfare on the continent led to increased harassment of Protestants by Catholic governments, Brandenburg-Prussia received sizable numbers of refugees from France, the Palatinate, the Hapsburg territories, and the upper Rhine region. Later, Friedrich III took in large numbers of Huguenots and Calvinist immigrants. The university of Halle was founded in 1692 as a Lutheran university, and leaders of Lutheran Pietism were appointed to important positions there. In 1691 Jacob Spener moved to Berlin and became a respected figure in the city ministry. It was in this climate of governmental support for Pietists that the Petersens were able to purchase the estate with the assistance of noble patrons. They were freed from taxation and military contribution and received special privileges such as firewood and hunting. Reconstructing the farm was a major job, mostly carried out by Johanna Eleonora.

JANE LEAD, THE PHILADELPHIANS, AND THE PIETIST NETWORK

In the early 1690s Baron Dodo von Knyphausen, a privy councillor at the Berlin court who had sponsored the Petersens' move to Brandenburg-Prussia, solicited their opinion of a manuscript of *The Wonders of God's Creation Manifested in the Variety of Eight Worlds* by Jane Lead (London, 1695).[34] As the Petersens assert in their respective autobiographies, they both examined the

33. The former bishoprics of Magdeburg and Halberstadt became part of Brandenburg formally only in 1680, a compensation for the Elector's loss of western Pomerania in the Peace of Westphalia.

34. See the autobiography, § 36. Johann Wilhelm also reported about this in his autobiography (*Das Leben Jo. Wilhelmi Petersen* [1717]; see note 1), 299. He mentions that it was "still in manuscript form"; such writings customarily first circulated among friends before being printed, some not being published at all.

text independently and after initial doubts, they "became quiet, as if some-one cut into our speech and hampered our pen."[35] They agreed that Jane Lead's views were indeed based in scriptures, even if "not actually proven," Johanna Eleonora stated, and "based plainly in Revelation only."[36] The Petersens reported their positive view to Knyphausen, who supported the impoverished Mrs. Lead. He sent her money toward the rent of a house and a yearly pension.[37]

Jane Lead[38] was, of course, by that time becoming well known as a visionary and mystic, and a correspondence between her and the Petersens ensued. Since 1681 Lead had published a few visions and revelations beginning with *The Heavenly Cloud Now Breaking*, and the edition of John Pordage's *Theologia Mystica* (1683).[39] She had become the spiritual leader of the small group of Protestant mystics in London, the Philadelphian Society for the Advancement of Divine Philosophy, mostly followers of the German mystic Jacob Böhme (1575–1624). The Philadelphians held that divine wisdom was derived from mystical contemplation on scripture, and they wanted to gather all "awakened" Christians (according to Rev. 1:11 and 3:7–13) in a communion of "brotherly love" (the meaning of the Greek word *philadelphos*). In 1689 Nonconformists became officially tolerated in England, and in 1695 the Licensing Act lapsed, ending prepublication censorship. The newly available freedom and tool of print enabled the Philadelphians, like their contemporaries the Quakers and other Nonconformists, to publish their religious views and spread their message. Going blind but assisted by Francis Lee and

35. Johann Wilhelm's autobiography, *Das Leben Jo. Wilhelmi Petersen* (1717) (note 1), 299.

36. Johanna Eleonora's autobiography, § 36: "sondern sich nur plat auf die Offenbarung gründete."

37. After Lead's death in 1704, her successor and son-in-law Francis Lee ("Dr. Lee") wrote letters of thanks to her benefactors, among them to the widow of Knyphausen.

38. See Catherine Smith's informative "Jane Lead: The Feminist Mind and Art of a Seventeenth-Century Protestant Mystic," in *Women of Spirit: Female Leadership in the Jewish and Christian Tradition*, ed. Rosemary Ruether and Eleanor McLaughlin (New York: Simon and Schuster, 1979), 184–203. Smith considers Lead's mystic writings as "a significant form of women's protest and self-affirmation" (187). There is only one dissertation on Lead: Joanna Magnani Sperle, "God's Healing Angel: A Biography of Jane Lead" (Ph.D. diss., Kent State University, 1995).

39. John Pordage (1607–81) was a physician and an Anglican minister before he was expelled from the church in 1654. One of the earliest commentators on the German mystic Jacob Böhme, Portage's devotional works were widely read in England and Germany. English devotional literature was translated into German and found a huge market there in the second half of the seventeenth century, as has been shown for the popular works of Lewis Bayly, Matthew Hale, and others. See Udo Sträter, *Sonthom, Bayly, Dyke und Hall: Studien zur Rezeption der englischen Erbauungsliteratur in Deutschland im 17. Jahrhundert*, Beiträge zur historischen Theologie, 71 (Tübingen: Mohr, 1987); and Edgar C. McKenzie, "British Devotional Literature and the Rise of German Pietism" (Ph.D. diss., University of St. Andrews, 1984).

by Richard Roach—both fellows of St. John's College of Oxford—Mrs. Lead published her spiritual diary, *A Fountain of Gardens* (London, 1697–1701), a record of her mystical visions and spiritual experience over the period of 1670–86, and eleven more books. The society collectively authored a periodical, *Theosophical Transactions* (1697), in which Johanna Eleonora also published "Of the Heavenly New Jerusalem,"[40] a chapter from her important 1696 publication *Instructions for a Thorough Understanding of Christ's Holy Revelations*. The journal also contained the second part of the English feminist Mary Astell's proposal for women's education, *A Serious Proposal to the Ladies*,[41] and an advertisement for Lady Conwell's *Principles of the Most Ancient and Modern Philosophy* (1691). The presence of several women's texts may well have been more than a coincidence, signaling changing times and the importance of women's voices in Jane Lead's circle, a model for other women. After 1695, all of Jane Lead's numerous books and tracts were translated into German by the schoolteacher Loth Fischer, who had been expelled from Nuremberg and then lived in Amsterdam. He was paid for the translations by Knyphausen and the Philadelphians. Lead's writings were to gather friends and converts for the Philadelphian Society, especially among the Pietists in Germany.

This episode is characteristic of the Pietist network; they formed groups and friendships according to religious views and their writings, even if they could not personally meet. They approached persons of means and in high office who would, if like-minded, assist with favors and money. On the other hand, the Petersens (and many other Pietists) were hospitable to visitors from Germany and from abroad who shared their beliefs. The Petersens' part of the Pietist network reached from Protestant Germany into the Netherlands and England.

A WOMAN PREACHER?

Preaching their theological views, both Petersens continued to publish and to gain converts for their brand of millenarianism. It seems that Johanna Eleonora did not shy away from preaching and speaking at religious gatherings, perhaps even at church services in Pietist congregations, as is reported in observers' private letters (although not in her autobiography)

---

40. See *Theosophical Transactions of the Philadelphian Society* 3 (1997): 142–51; a rare copy is in the British Library. Only five issues of the periodical appeared.

41. Part 1 had appeared in 1694; part 2 in 1697. Astell's project was to establish a religious community and a school for "ladies of quality," funded by their dowries. *A Serious Proposal for the Ladies* was to become the most famous treatise on women's education in England. See Mary Astell, *A Serious Proposal to the Ladies: For the Advancement of Their True and Greatest Interest*, ed. with an intro. and notes by Patricia Springborg (London: Pickering & Chatto, 1997).

about her frequent visits to Laubach[42] and Berleburg, two small principalities with Pietist sovereigns. A woman preacher was still an absolute taboo in Germany—unlike England, where Quaker women, though criticized or satirized in many quarters, did claim the pulpit. Johanna Eleonora Petersen's outspokenness in religious matters, in print, in daily affairs, and in conversations, offended and angered many who otherwise sympathized with her views. For instance, the services (or simply private prayer meetings?) the Petersens conducted in their new barn in Niederdodeleben angered the clergy in that area, while local farmers envied the privileges connected with their estate (they tore down the fence the Petersens had built for their sheep around their land). The local minister published pamphlets accusing Johanna Eleonora of speaking about religious dogma forbidden to women and of meddling with theology and men's business. With their new publications on chiliasm and on the Book of Revelation during the 1690s, the Petersens made even more enemies among the clergy in Brandenburg, so that in 1708 they moved once more, to the estate Thymer near Zerbst in the province of Magdeburg-Halberstadt, a relatively new addition to Brandenburg-Prussia. The episode in Niederdodeleben illustrates the deep divide and distrust among members of the same faith who disagree about the understanding of certain religious tenets. It also shows the desolate conditions brought on by the religious wars.

From the 1690s onward, Johanna Eleonora accompanied her husband on most of his trips throughout Germany, to (among other places) Berlin, Erfurt, Gotha, Stuttgart, Tübingen, Frankfurt, and Leipzig. They seemed to have toured the German Protestant lands like missionaries for their religious views. They met with and often stayed at the homes of religious friends, noble patrons, scholars, and clergymen. More often than not they followed up on invitations or received contributions to cover their travel expenses; they were by no means wealthy but they were comfortable. In May of 1705 they traveled to Altdorf, seat of a famous Latin School and university close to Nuremberg, and visited with the local dignitaries and professors. Upon Johann Wilhelm's request, both Petersens were inducted into the Society of the Pegnitz Shepherds.[43] Johanna Eleonora, inducted only several months

---

42. The ruling count was the son of Benigna von Solms-Laubach, a friend of Johanna Eleonora's from her days at court and to whom she dedicated her first publication, *A Heart's Conversations with God* (on which see below).

43. A well-known literary society (*Sprachgesellschaft* or "language academy") in Nuremberg, still in existence today but without the importance it had for seventeenth-century letters. Johann Wilhelm Petersen was also an accomplished poet who wrote Latin poetry and hymns; some were set to music and entered the Evangelical songbook.

after her husband at the end of 1705, received the name "Phoebe—Filled by the Light of Life."[44] The dedicatory poem composed by the society's secretary was written in her voice: "My heart is by nature like the dark moon / who receives the full light from the sun / and here my Jesus gives my soul light and life." The sun-moon metaphor was of course a proverbial phrase at the time referring to the male and female: he is the sun, she is the moon. In her thank-you letter Johanna Eleonora ensured that the metaphor be applied not to her husband but to Christ and herself by writing, "May I always do honor to the name of Phoebe and follow my life's sun, and become like him."

Little is known about Johanna Eleonora's last years before her death in 1724, as her health seemed to have faded away and illness took over. Her autobiography in its second, enlarged version of 1718 was her last work and her last authentic sign of life. Her husband published not the customary funeral sermon but a Latin elegy on her death.

THE RADICAL PIETIST AND AUTHORSHIP

Johanna Eleonora Petersen is usually counted among the radical Pietists[45] or unorthodox Protestants, signaling her innovative readings of scripture, her spiritualist and mystic leanings, and her speculative thinking. "Radical" Pietist is not a historical term, nor does it denote a certain organized group; it was coined in nineteenth-century research on Pietism to designate those individuals who advanced speculative theological views, often for a new order trying to break away from the church. The Petersens, however, wanted not to form a new sect but to reform the Lutheran Church according to their religious tenets. Johanna Eleonora Petersen's belief in God's will and in human values became increasingly important in her autobiography. A carefully chosen sequence of events illustrated and justified her path to God, her inner change away from the superficialities of courtly life and toward a religious life, willed by God. Again and again she emphasized prayer in her writing. Every experience derived its true meaning through divine providence, even the intrigues at court that led to a revoked engagement but in the end brought her an inner freedom and peace of mind.

44. [Johann Herdegen], *Historische Nachricht von deß löblichen Hirten- und Blumen-Ordens . . . von Amarantes* (Nuremberg: Riegel, 1744), 595–98.

45. The term "radical Pietist" is ambiguous, as there was no clear historical distinction among (nor a binding, clear definition of) radical Pietism, separatism, spiritualism, and mysticism. For a good historical discussion, see Hoffmann, *Radikalpietismus*, 7–19.

She placed the decision into the hands of those who initiated the actions: the authorities of the patriarchal society—namely, God and her own father as the executor of God's will; she was "so quiet as if it did not concern"[46] her, she wrote on the occasion of Johann Wilhelm's marriage proposal. Was her quietist attitude merely indicative of using religion as an inner escape, a sanctimonious ostentation spoken by Petersen as a victim of war, repeated misfortune, and the inability to live a life expected of a woman of her class? Was her depiction a compensation for her lower social prestige or a conscious choice of different, religious values? Inwardness as compensation, or as an expression of a newly discovered religious set of values? A modern reading of quietism would imply that Johanna Eleonora "unconsciously" manipulated this lack of will or positioned herself into willing subjection and sacrifice; but this remains purely speculation and transfers twenty-first-century concepts of autonomy onto the religious experience of the seventeenth century.

Petersen saw herself as a spiritually awakened, visionary woman, as a "doer of the Word."[47] She concluded her autobiography by describing her visions and depicting her own role as that of a nightingale who raises her voice and with her singing opens doors. The nightingale was already in medieval literature a symbol for the soul's desire for heaven, for the god-loving soul, as it appeared for example in the well-known painting by Martin Schongauer, *Mary in the Rose Grove.* According to Petersen's self-portrayal, she followed the calling of her inner voice, which repressed everything external. It was neither her individual achievement nor her individual voice in the (modern) sense of an independent person, but rather a picture of religious awakening and a pious interpretation of life. In the section of the autobiography added in 1718, there is no place allotted for concrete social events; there are no more reflections about her marriage or about other pietists (for example, the disturbing story of the visionary Juliane von Asseburg), no mention of the expulsion from Lüneburg, of the country estate near Magdeburg, or of the travels. The experience of religious inwardness and spiritual piety and her visionary interpretation completely displaced the outer world. She built a Christian utopia within herself.

Johanna Eleonora stated in her autobiography that she had visions and dreams from the time she was eighteen years old, that secrets had been revealed to her in dreams before and after she was married. She neatly

46. See § 27 below of her *Life.*
47. "Täterin des Wortes." See § 28 of her autobiography and (§ 38 for the nightingale image).

structured these revelations into six major religious questions, three each before and after her marriage; this parallelism of the number three also highlighted the importance she placed in her marriage for her life in this world. These revelations or illuminations in understanding certain passages in scripture had (unintended) social ramifications beyond religious dogma. First, she came to the realization that the salvation from hell would be granted to everyone, even to sinners and those of another faith.[48] This touched a hotly debated topic in seventeenth-century theology, as most Christian denominations taught that eternal damnation and hell would await all sinners. Fear of hell and of Judgment Day was especially great in those sects where eschatological questions were held very important. Only the more optimistic eighteenth century did away with most popular imaginations of hellish tortures, shifting to the aspect of possible salvation. Goethe's Faust "is saved" in the very end. In this respect, Johanna Eleonora Petersen anticipated a more modern, conciliatory view for believers.

Such optimism was all the more apparent in her second revelation (in a 1664 dream), which predicted the future conversion of the Jews and the "heathens."[49] In Petersen's view, this would not be a crusade with fire and sword; her dream portrayed several suns merging into the one light of divine truth. Another tenet[50] concerned the significance of human works and efforts vis-à-vis God's grace when men are called before him. The Apostle Paul appeared to her in a dream and directed her to his epistles, which taught her God's love and grace for humanity. This brought her to love Luther's teachings—there was always the attempt to show compliance with the Lutheran tradition and not to appear as a sectarian. Again her image of God is that of a loving, caring deity.

In 1685 (in her "married state") she gained spiritual illumination—simultaneously with her husband—of the Book of Revelation, an understanding that she associated with the renewed persecution of the Huguenots in 1685 (the abolition of the Edict of Nantes).[51] This revelation was given to her—she used the first person "I," only referring to herself, not to "us," the couple—in connection with reading Jane Lead's writings; it signaled the

---

48. See § 32 of her *Life* and the discussion of her work *The Eternal Gospel of the Return of All Creatures* (1698), below.

49. See § 33 of her *Life*. In her later publications she developed these and the following notions in much more detail and with much more stringency. See the discussion of her oeuvre below.

50. See § 34.

51. See § 35.

beginning of her millenarianism, speculations about the impending end of the world.[52] In 1708 her visions became even more speculative; she received illumination about the nature of Christ—whom she called the "heavenly God-Man" and his "God-Humanity" in her autobiography.[53] By coining new words for her religious concepts—as Jacob Böhme and other spiritualists had done—she pointed to the extraordinariness and ineffability of her visions in received religious terminology. With this she presented herself as a visionary in the tradition of mystic spiritualism; on the other hand she always mentioned her own thinking, when not understanding an issue, and her searching for other biblical passages in order to gain spiritual illumination about those things formerly arcane or veiled to her.

Her last vision—the end and the highlight of her autobiography—was that of a Trinity with a female element in it. She saw "father, son, and mother in one room," and understood by the latter the "Holy Ghost who, according to the Hebrew language, is of female gender and expressed by a fruitful mother and a breeding dove."[54] She went back to the biblical language (Petersen had learned Hebrew in Frankfurt) to establish a female element in the Divine. Such an amalgamation of male and female elements in the Divine existed from the beginning, according to Petersen, and was then implied in the Book of Revelation, which made the Divine—the origin and the end of humanity—manifest to human beings. While other spiritualists like Jacob Böhme, Gottfried Arnold, and Jane Lead envisioned God's wisdom as a "Sophia," a female and a mother figure, Petersen imagined a merging of the male and female elements in an all-encompassing divine spirit.[55]

Seen from a modern perspective, Petersen was very conscious of her role as a woman who entered theological debate, that it was a contested field for her because of her sex. She insisted on her female voice and stylized herself as visionary throughout her autobiography, leading to the crowning image

---

52. See § 36. There were many speculations about the end of the millennium and the return of Christ that would establish God's realm in historical times; this was based mostly in interpreting Rev. 20. The radical chiliasts believed in a return of the Lord at the beginning of the interregnum in historical time, the moderates in a return and judgment at the end of time. Johanna Eleonora Petersen believed in the reconciliation and redemption of all "creatures," regardless of creed or deed, for which she developed an elaborate scheme and time frame.

53. See § 37. Petersen speaks of the "Gemeinschaft seiner himmlischen Gott-Menschheit" (union with his divine God-Humanity). Her concept is not identical to but reminiscent of Jacob Böhme's notion of an androgynous first man who is free of sin; it was the wish for the separation into the two sexes that was, according to Böhme, the origin of sin.

54. See § 38.

55. See also her *Instructions for a Thorough Understanding of Christ's Holy Revelation* (1696), discussed below.

of the nightingale, a "singer" illuminated by and striving for the divine. In her theology, she represented a holistic view in which gender itself merged within a Trinity or the Divine Spirit, but the female element was neither forgotten nor suppressed as it had been in the patriarchal church.

Feminist theology has pointed to the patriarchal, male-oriented, and male-defined mode in which much of Judeo-Christian dogma has been couched and to the completely male structure and control over the Christian church until very recent times.[56] Protestant theology had done away with the active female elements in Christian teaching, the female saints and the Virgin Mary cult, both of which had valued and showcased motherly, female qualities such as compassion, pity, and piety. During the Protestant Reformation these images had been removed from churches, ransacked by the iconoclasts. Many a *Marienkirche* (Saint Mary's Church) in Germany and the Low Countries had its altarpiece of a Madonna and Child or a Mater Dolorosa removed to be (often later) replaced by a crucifix, the favorite Lutheran representation from the Bible, which remains to this day. Such a replacement can be understood as a sign for the renewed shift during the Reformation to patriarchy and an effacement of the female in religion. And while Luther to a certain extent revolutionized the church by allowing— even requiring—the ministers to marry, he still had no room for women in the organization of the church and certainly not in the priesthood; even women's voices in theological and church matters were forbidden. This was enforced by constant reference to Paul's interdiction "let women be silent in Church." Moreover, women were seen as "daughters of Eve," as the culprits for man's expulsion from Paradise and for the curse of hereditary sin; they were generally believed inferior to men, because God created woman after Adam and then only from Adam's rib, not from his head. Misogynist lore abounded, certainly a factor in the notorious witch hunts and witch burnings that reached a peak in the early seventeenth century.

To counter such low esteem and distortion of women even in theological quarters, feminist theology has searched for positive representations in early modern texts, especially in the concept of Sophia, a female voice of divine wisdom as first conceptualized by Jacob Böhme (1575–1624). The "cobbler from Görlitz" and lay theologian had been ordered to stop writing; his works were banned and circulated privately in manuscript form. In *The Way to Christ* (published without his knowledge and consent in 1624), he presented a dialogue between the virgin Sophia and the soul in the form

---

56. For the first and still most incisive feminist criticism of Judeo-Christian theology, see Mary Daly, *Beyond God the Father: Toward a Philosophy of Women's Liberation* (Boston: Beacon Press, 1973).

of conversations or prayers; Sophia was cast as the soul's bride, as a mediator of divine wisdom who brought water from the eternal spring. Böhme believed in "three Principles of the godhead, manifested in the creation through seven 'fountain-springs' as reflected in the Virgin Sophia."[57] Gottfried Arnold (1666–1714) developed a more systematic concept of a female religious force in *The Secret of Divine Sophia or Wisdom* (Leipzig, 1700), a Sophia as an independent divine agent, a pure divinity emanating from God and at the same time residing within him; Sophia's attributes were couched in a gendered language connoting the female.

Johanna Eleonora Petersen read Böhme and Arnold and was familiar with the contemporary theological discussion of Sophia. In 1708 her husband published *The Secret of the Apocalyptic Woman Giving Birth in the Last Days of Time*, a treatise containing quite a few speculations about female prophets or divines. Johanna Eleonora Petersen's thinking about the divine led her to envision a merging of gendered signs in a whole, all-encompassing Trinity. She was not, of course, a feminist in the modern sense, but she was acutely aware of the status of women in the theology of her times and she worked to recover a female voice and to let it be heard.

In her autobiography she repeatedly emphasized the simultaneity of her own and her husband's God-given, spiritual illumination (interpretations of certain biblical passages).[58] Johanna Eleonora related how she showed her notes to her husband in 1685 and found that he himself had written the same basic ideas, concluding that God had revealed the same truths to each of them.[59] But she carefully avoided in her writings any signs of a competition between the two, while always focusing on their religious calling as a *couple;* this was also reflected in their missionary work and preaching for their religious beliefs. Perhaps she also contributed to Johann Wilhelm's texts,[60] as she certainly did through conversations about religious questions. Johann Wilhelm in turn mentioned her graciously and warmly (in his autobiogra-

---

57. B. J. Gibbons, *Gender in Mystical and Occult Thought: Behmenism and Its Development in England* (Cambridge: Cambridge University Press, 1996), 19.

58. See § 35.

59. Theology and church history are mostly concerned with the notions of the "polemic outsider" Petersen, yet while Johanna Eleonora Petersen seems to have been the spiritually more significant personality, her work is usually subsumed under his work. One new study assesses her theology: Ruth Albrecht, "Johanna Eleonora Petersen als theologische Schriftstellerin" (Habilitations-schrift, University of Hamburg, 2000).

60. Johann Wilhelm Petersen's publications are much more voluminous; his list of publications, which he appended to his autobiography, in 1719 (the second edition) comprised 67 printed and 101 unpublished manuscripts. By contrast, Johanna Eleonora does not mention her other publications at all in her autobiography.

phy) and apparently did not interfere with, supervise, or censor her writing in any way. This is the picture she gave about their respective roles, one of unison. It should be noted though that originality of thought and innovation were not valued in the seventeenth century as they are today, and that individual achievement was a man's prerogative and not a virtue for a woman, for whom obedience, humility, and fitting in were considered female virtues. A marriage in spiritual harmony was the Pietists' goal, with the woman definitely taking second place after her husband, serving him and his welfare.[61] Johanna Eleonora presented an attempt at spiritual equality in her marriage, though as a visionary she seemed to have had the stronger and more radical voice.

Since it was very unusual that a woman—and a noble lady at that—would publish her writings and then under her own name, and since women were not to speak in religious matters, Johanna Eleonora Petersen asked her husband's friend Christian Kortholt,[62] the prominent theologian and professor at the University of Kiel, to write a preface for her first publication. This would lend stature and authority to the book. In his address "To the Christian Reader," Kortholt put the question whether there were more pious persons among men or among women. He quoted the Dutch theologian Gisbert Voetius,[63] who had stated that in the Low Countries more women were attending church services and prayer meetings than men; he had adduced a number of biblical quotes to prove his point. Kortholt then offered a large number of exemplary women from the Bible and from history attesting to women's greater piety and religiosity, admonished the men to rival the women in piety, and concluded by praising Johanna Eleonora Petersen as a shining example. Such an introduction was to pave the way for women's writings and forestall the vocal critics of women's voices in church matters.

61. Spener repeatedly preached and wrote about a woman's vocation: marriage, childbearing, and responsibility for the family's piety. Spener emphasized conjugal love, assistance, and duties as much as the woman's subordination under the husband's "regiment"; marriage was true service to God. See Jakob Spener, *Kurtze Catechismuspredigten* (1689; reprint, Hildesheim: Olms, 1982), and *Lehrreiche Zuschrift an seine Frau Tochter von denen nöthigen Pflichten Einer jeden sonderlich aber einer Priester-Frau* (Leipzig, 1690), advice to his daughter about female duties, especially those of a minister's wife.

62. Kortholt (1633–94) had corresponded with Johann Wilhlem Petersen since 1776.

63. The Utrecht professor Gisbertus Voetius (1589–1676) was a leading defender of Dutch Reformed theology and a revered authority in ecclesiastical matters of the Reformed Church. In his *Politica Ecclesiastica* (The State of the Church; 1663–66) he had a section concerning women; see his "The Spiritual and Ecclesiastical Status of Women," in *Anna Maria van Schurman: Whether a Christian Woman Should Be Educated and Other Writings from Her Intellectual Circle*, ed. and trans. by Joyce Irwin, Other Voice in Early Modern Europe (Chicago: University of Chicago Press, 1998), 130–39.

More interesting, however, are Petersen's own prefaces, one of which she seems to have written in defense of her first publication. In her "Address to My Heartily-Beloved Husband" of 1691, she articulated her illumination and calling from God as the basis for her writing: "I can assure you, dear reader, in the presence of God that you will receive the true explication of Holy Revelation as it has been illuminated by God to his humble servant and to others, each to his measure."[64] Against any criticism she insisted on her right to speak out in religious matters:

> Moreover, I am well aware that even more criticism will be issued against this work than was given to my previous work. I can tolerate this criticism well, since I did not seek my honor with it. Whoever does not want to believe that in this writing there is a gift I received from the Lord may do so. It is enough that I know what the Lord has given me and that it is evidence of truth not to be shattered and that I will with God's grace render an account about anything contained in this book to anyone orally or in writing. . . .

She considered her writing a gift from God and she insisted on using her spiritual gifts. She is a prophet, not a teacher. Based on biblical passages, she silenced her critics:

> Some will reproach me with Paul's words (1 Cor. 14:34 and 1 Tim. 2:12) that a woman should not teach in God's community. But they should know that these words do not pertain to me. I respect what the Holy Ghost has said through Paul and with reference to a woman's dutiful submission and I do not claim to teach in God's community. But this I know very well: that just as for Christ's grace and spirit there is no difference between man and woman (Gal. 3:28), God's grace cannot be dampened nor be suppressed in a woman, according to Paul's admonishment (1 Thess. 5:19). Rather, all spiritual gifts whether they appear in a man or in a woman are worthy to be presented and applied to the common good (1 Cor. 12:7). Therefore the Holy Ghost has given witness (through Joel 2:28[65] and Acts 2:17–18) that not only

64. This dedication ("Meinem Hertz-geliebten Mann D. Johann Petersen/ Wohl-verordneten Superintendenten in Lüneburg") appeared for the first time in her second publication, *Conversations on Faith* (1691), here p. a4r; it was dated July 11, 1691, used Johann Wilhelm's title, and thus was written before he was dismissed from office. This dedication was later reprinted with the 1715 edition of her first work, *A Heart's Conversations with God*, and similar prefaces were added to several works.
65. "And it shall come to pass afterward, that I will pour out my Spirit upon all flesh; and your sons and your daughters shall prophesy . . ."

the sons but also the daughters of Israel may prophesy and that the Lord will pour out his Spirit not only over his male but also over his female servants. And Paul himself who has forbidden women to teach in the community attributes the gift of prophecy to both, men and women, in that very Epistle (1 Cor. 2:4–5). Since the Lord in his grace has given me the gift of such illumination from his spirit, I do know my humble place in the community, but I do also know that I have received the Lord's gift not in order to hide it but in order to make the most of it, to apply it for his honor and to the benefit of my neighbor. And I know that no one who with God's blessing holds a just opinion will accuse me of teaching. This I leave to the judgment of God's community for examination.

As to publishing under her own name, she could praise her husband's generosity and support of her voice:

Some will say: it would have been more proper if my dear husband had issued this work under his name. To these I answer: I would have agreed, had my dear husband issued this book under his name; but since he is not of such a proud mind that, because of his authority as a male, he would not have allowed that divine truth be told by a weak and low instrument, he willingly and readily allowed that in praise of God the name of a weak and low instrument can introduce what the Lord had accomplished through the weak, low, and scorned one.

Petersen also had to assure the public that she would not neglect her duties as a wife and mother and to appear as a humble, unselfish author, a servant to God:

Some will say that I have neglected my duties as a wife and house-mother and presumed something that was not proper for me. This opinion likewise does not concern me, since before God and all his children who know me, I can attest that I always strive to be faithful to my husband and to my wifely duties. That I use the remaining time allowed to me by God in order to bear witness to him, that is not a sin.

And if, finally, one wants to accuse me of arrogance and greed for honor, I have to endure even this judgment. However, I do find a different witness in my God and I know that I have been awakened through the good impetus of his Spirit in order to communicate this gift, in humility and with pure love for his glory alone and for the benefit of my neighbor, with the hope that it will be beneficial for many souls today and in future generations. With this, dear reader, with Christian wishes your humble servant in Christ, Johanna Eleonora Petersen, née von und zu Merlau, takes leave from you.[66]

Petersen takes up and then answers point for point, with passages from the Bible, all the reasons brought up to subdue female authorship in religious visions and writing. She had to answer contemporary critics who verbally named and attacked her, like the Danzig preacher Friedrich Christian Bücher in his pamphlet *A Loyal Warning against the Revolutionary Quaker-Spirit* [67] and Johann Heinrich Feustking's notorious *School for Fanatical Women Heretics, Or History and Description of False Female Prophets, Quakers, Enthusiasts, and Other Such Sectarian Woman-Kind.*[68] Feustking attacked Johanna Eleonora Petersen in a lengthy chapter devoted to her and scolded her for ineptitude, womanish weakness, stubbornness, and—worst of all—evil influence on her husband.

Petersen did not answer in kind (an aggressive tract by a woman would have been totally improper and only given more credence to the male critic). Her inner drive, her missionary zeal, and her visionary voice were stronger than contemporary slander. She went public with polite and well-reasoned addresses to the reader repeatedly printed in most of her works; they were her answer. Her insistence on her authorship is a reflection of her self-consciousness; her missionary zeal is based in her strong belief in divine illumination *and* her understanding of scripture, in her belief in love as a divine power, in human beings' divine origin and eventual return to the divine, beliefs that were nurtured by millenarian visions of a better future.

JOHANNA ELEONORA PETERSEN'S OEUVRE

Petersen's religious concepts evolved and were presented more clearly in a series of devotional and theological works, altogether fourteen religious books (besides her autobiography) that she published during almost three decades, 1689–1714. Most of her writings were issued under her own name. Her three most important works will be discussed briefly below; her auto-biography and an epistle to her sisters, "The Nature and Necessity of the

---

66. Petersen's preface ("To My Dear Husband . . .") to her *Conversations on Faith* (1691), b4v–c1v.

67. *Treuhertzige Warnung für den Auffrührerischen Quacker-Geist* (Danzig: Simon Reiniger, 1700).

68. *Gynaeceum Haeretico Fanaticum, Oder Historie und Beschreibung der falschen Prophetinnen, Quäckerinnen, Schwäremerinnen, und andern sectirerischen und begeisterten Weibes-Personen* (Frankfurt and Leipzig, 1704). This contemporary account of seventeenth-century visionary women was written from an orthodox Lutheran position; the author's hostility toward women makes this a characteristic example of misogyny in theological literature at the time.

New Creature in Christ," can be found in this volume in translation, and a short descriptive list of all her works is contained in the annotated bibliography following this introduction. As to Johanna Eleonora Petersen's religious publications in comparison to Johann Wilhelm's and other (male) Pietist theologians, we must take into consideration that she lacked any formal theological training and that she was not allowed to write about questions of dogma openly. Thus she clothed much of her writing in spiritual, sometimes mystic, sometimes visionary imagery and language, vigorously defending her visionary publications in the prefaces of several of her works, as we saw above.

In 1689, nine years after her marriage to Johann Wilhelm, she published under her own name her first work, *A Heart's Conversations with God*,[69] a handsomely produced volume of devotional readings in which the soul—or "I"—seeks comfort and illumination in direct conversations with Jesus. Attached to the end of the volume is the first part of her autobiography (see below). It is a collection of meditations on biblical passages, mostly from the Psalms and the Song of Solomon (Song of Songs), that are placed at the head of prayerlike elaborations of no more than two to four pages each. The second part contains "conversations" following the pattern of a then immensely popular book of devotion, the Jesuit Herman Hugo's *Pia Desideria* (Pious Desires, 1624),[70] with its emblematic pictures from the tradition of Jesus and the soul portrayed in the form of a heart. Each of the fifty sections begins with an illustration, starting with "Jesus' Heart Given to the Lover" and each naming a particular activity or lesson like "Jesus Protects the Heart," "Jesus Knocks at the Heart's Door," "Jesus Scrutinizes the Heart," "Jesus Cleans the Heart," and so on. Like an emblem in the then immensely popular emblem books, each picture is followed by a short statement (a biblical verse) and a

---

69. *Hertzengespräche mit Gott* (1689); see the annotated bibliography of Petersen's works. The volume's first part is dedicated to the Duchess Christine von Schleswig-Holstein, née von Sachsen-Weißenfels, wife of the Petersens' sovereign; part 2 was dedicated to the Countess Benigna von Solms-Laubach, a prominent Pietist, the grandmother of Count Zinzendorf, the founder of Pietist Herrnhut. Johanna Eleonora had met Benigna von Solms-Laubach during her service at court in Wiesenburg, when Benigna lived at Wildenfels, only a few miles away from Wiesenburg, before she moved to Laubach.

70. The Jesuit Hugo turned the fashion of worldly love emblem books to religious service in his *Pia Desideria* (1624) by transferring the heart and love stories to the relationship between Christ and the human soul (as the mystics had done before him). Hugo's religious emblem book was printed in more than fifty editions in Latin until the mid-eighteenth century and sixteen different German translations (some with several editions). Johanna Eleonora Petersen probably owned and used as a model the German version by the early Pietist Christian Hohburg, *Emblemata Sacra, Das ist Göttliche Andachten . . .* (Frankfurt, 1661).

longer prose explication. Such a three-tier structure allowed for a threefold consideration of the "moral" or "problem" at hand, a guide for contemplation and learning. Petersen's prose is emotional, involves the senses, is comforting and enlightening, gives easy access to the biblical passages, and serves as a guidance for a Christian life. Such were the characteristics of the vastly popular and rich production of devotional literature in all European vernaculars (replacing Latin in the Catholic books of meditation exercises) in the seventeenth century.

Petersen may well have already written such devotional prose during the 1670s in Frankfurt; perhaps she even practiced writing such devotional exercises then, certainly using devotional models. Novelty, individuality, revolutionary ideas, or formalistic perfection—valued so highly for literary texts in our age—were unimportant and ephemeral for the devotional literature. What counted was the arousal of spirituality, the practice of prayer, and the motivation for a Christian life. Petersen structured her *Conversations* accordingly; most important was "the word"—that is, the spiritual meaning, not the structural shell.

For the first edition in 1689, the plates—an expensive item—for the text were not yet ready and the printing (without illustrations) proceeded; only the second edition of 1694 and the third of 1715 contained the illustrations that were still surprisingly similar to Hugo's originals, in spite of the many editions and translations that work had gone through. It seems that the engraver had a copy of Hugo's *Pia Desideria* before him and followed his pictorial designs. In a letter of 1686 Petersen stated:

> About two years ago I was asked by a good friend to write some Heart's conversations on the copperplates of the well-known Hermann Hugo. I refused for quite some time, but when I finally sat down last fall, considering that with all my housework there might be some time for devotion to God in this, I neither could nor do anything but write. I noted down what I have experienced in my life and how these biblical passages have been understood by me.[71]

While unnamed "good friends" are a standard excuse for writing and publication, Petersen's reliance on "experience" (*Erfahrung*) is noteworthy. It is her personal involvement and psychological insight into the plights of a Christian soul that make her *Conversations* so lively and immediate. At the same time

---

71. In Petersen's March 2, 1689, letter addressed to the Kiel theologian Kortholt, asking for a preface for her work; see Markus Matthias, "Enthusiastische Hermeneutik des Pietismus, dargestellt an Johanna Eleonora Petersens 'Gespräche des Herzens mit Gott' (1689)," *Pietismus und Neuzeit* 17 (1991): 41.

her book exhibits a well-balanced, formal construction that invites reading and contemplation.

Petersen's second book followed two years later: *Conversations with God on Faith in Three Parts; Part 1 on the Workings of Faith in Power; Part 2 on the Testimony, Power and Cordiality of Faith; Part 3 on the Goal of Faith Meaning the Souls' Bliss* (1691).[72] It was less a purely devotional book than a call for renewed faith in view of what Petersen believed to be the coming of an age of "so many people falling away from faith"[73] —the early signs of the Enlightenment and the coming secularization in the eighteenth century were already noticeable. Petersen dedicated this work not to any nobility but to her husband who had fought for his belief and who might have to suffer with her on account of her publishing these *Conversations*. She openly defended in public for the first time their newfound interest in millenarianism, in "the blessed thousand-year kingdom in which the kingdom of Israel will be established upon this earth" that she wished "to announce to the entire world with a trumpet."

More important and original was her next work in which her millenarianism is fully developed. Its lengthy, still very baroque title also tells of the program: *Instructions for a Thorough Understanding of Christ's Holy Revelation, Which He Sent and Explained to His Servant and Apostle John through His Angel. Observed in Its Final and Prophetic Meaning and in the Larger Parts of Its Complete Fulfillment During the Latter Days Whom We Are Near. Arranged in Its Proper Order in a Table in Which Holy Revelation Is Presented in Harmony with Things and Time. With a Preface Serving as Preparation and a Three-fold Appendix. Told and Edited According to a Measure of Grace by Johanna Eleonora Petersen, née von und zu Merlau* (1696).[74] This monumental work comprising almost five hundred pages in the large quarto format was published by the well-known Johann Daniel Müller in Germany's two centers of the book trade, Frankfurt and Leipzig, a sign of its importance for the religious market. Its handsome appearance, illustrations, tables, and title pointing to the nearness of the millennium—1700 was only four years away and the object of much chiliastic speculation—helped find many readers, especially among the aristocracy, including Duchess Sophie Elisabeth of Braunschweig-Lüneburg, who studied the *Instructions for a Thorough Understanding of Christ's Holy Revelation* carefully.[75] The work was dedicated to two Danish princesses whom Petersen had met while Johann Wilhelm was court

---

72. *Glaubens-Gespräche mit GOTT* (1691; see the annotated bibliography of Petersen's works).

73. Ibid., preface, 2r.

74. *Anleitung zu gründlicher Verständniß der Heiligen Offenbahrung Jesu Christi* (1696; see the annotated bibliography of Petersen's works).

75. The copy in the Herzog August Bibliothek, Wolfenbüttel, contains Sophie Elisabeth's signature as owner, some annotations from her hand, and underlining throughout.

chaplain in Eutin and who were interested in Pietism. More important, both had since then assumed important positions through marriage, Anna Sophia as the wife of the Elector of Saxony and Wilhelmine Ernestine as the wife of the Elector of the Palatinate.

In her foreword, "In the Name of Jesus: A Preface to the Christian Reader," Petersen assured the aristocratic readership that they had nothing to fear from the kingdom to come:

> Kings, princes, and magistrates need not fear the Quiet in the Land [Pietists]. For the empire that the children of this kingdom proclaim will not bring unrest but peace, salvation, and blessing: it does not announce the overthrow of the very sovereigns themselves, but it gives testimony of a time to come when the kings of this earth can bring their honor to this empire (Is. 60 and Rev. 21:24) and God will be with the people on earth, when the princes, kings, and people will be united in one people of the God of Abraham.[76]

Petersen's preface was to assure her readers—the professional middle class and aristocracy—that she was not a subversive radical preaching revolution; hers was a utopian vision of future communion and unity in a spiritual realm. Even if such a vision was purely speculative and considered to border on heresy by orthodox Lutherans, it stimulated her contemporary audience's thinking about their religious belief and ultimately also about their secular station and that of their community.

The elaborate frontispiece to Petersen's *Instructions for a Thorough Understanding of Christ's Holy Revelation* visualized the thrust of her illumination. Her detailed "Explanation of the Frontispiece, Of the Sun-Clad Woman Giving Birth" described the image and taught the reader its meaning. The picture is divided into three parts: in the upper part is the Trinity, signifying Zion. In the center is the miraculous Mother, a woman clothed in the sun, and in the star of David with the seven tribes of Israel signifying the stages of tribulations of humanity and our world. Below is the seven-headed dragon spitting fire and flame, and other creatures out to destroy humanity, allegorized by the whore of Babylon riding a dragon. Of special interest is the woman in the center: she is decked out in the iconographical signs of the female in the Judeo-Christian tradition: a wreath of flowers, full-length wavy hair encompassing her body, standing on the moon's sickle. In her round, seemingly very pregnant belly lies the seventh tribe of Israel, the new Jerusalem or Philadelphia, with the inscription: "Let yourself be

---

76. *Anleitung zu gründlicher Verständniß* . . . , a3v.

purified." This new Philadelphia is at the very center of the picture with all kinds of evil forces at work on the side margins to hinder its birth or coming. This figure appeared again in a large section of Petersen's text; she was the redeemer's mother, the spirit of Israel, Zion, and the true church: "Let yourself be comforted, you blessed mother of the child, who through your painful delivery will yourself be delivered, and so esteemed by God that you will give birth to the son of the Highest who will occupy the royal throne in heaven and on earth, in God's and David's realm, as the rightful heir."[77] Woman has a dual role, that of mother and church; the feminine is present in her vision.[78] In Petersen's visionary style, temporal sequence may defy our logic while images often do not really match and are (intentionally) conflated or merge several concepts. But her strong insistence on the female and her role in the divine and in the process of the life cycle of birth and rebirth emerges again and again like an anchor for her own positioning in her theological system of beliefs, which centers in this work on the coming of Christ's realm based on a reading of the Book of Revelation.

In 1698, inspired by Jane Lead's visions, Johanna Eleonora Petersen published the treatise *The Eternal Gospel of the Return of All Creatures*, explaining the restoration of all things.[79] This dogma of *Apokatastasis panton* (the salvation of all) became the centerpiece of the theology of both Petersens: all people were eventually to be redeemed and saved, regardless of their sins; this theological position adopted and elaborated the ancient doctrine of universal salvation and the restoration of all things.[80] Johanna Eleonora Petersen breathed new life into this dogma, which was, according to her, "based in Scriptures, prefigured in nature and deeply ingrained in our souls."[81] She developed an elaborate timetable and system for this redemption of all, rejecting the standard Protestant theological opinion according to which God may redeem an individual to eternal life or may condemn him or her to eternal damnation. Rather, Petersen envisioned a benevolent God who at the

77. Ibid., 121.

78. See the earlier discussion of the role of the female in her visions .

79. *Das ewige Evangelium Der Allgemeinen Wiederbringung Aller Creaturen* (see the annotated bibliography of Petersen's works, p. 47 below).

80. The German terms used in Petersen's texts are *Wiederbringung aller Creaturen* and *Allversöhnung*. See Stefan Luft, *Leben und Schreiben für den Pietismus: Der Kampf des pietistischen Ehepaares Johanna und Eleonora und Johann Wilhelm Petersen gegen die lutherische Orthodoxie* (Herzberg: Bautz, 1994), 239–71, for a detailed theological explication of the positions of both Petersens and the accepted Lutheran tradition. For an overview of the changing concept of hell, see D. P. Walker, *The Decline of Hell: Seventeenth-Century Discussions of Eternal Torment* (Chicago: University of Chicago Press, 1964).

81. *Das ewige Evangelium* . . . , 5.

end of his dealings with mankind would receive all "creatures" into a state of eternal, universal salvation. These "creatures" included all nonbelievers, even the fallen angels and the devil.[82] Petersen saw a sort of cosmic movement in which everything created—all "creatures"—would return to their creator, God: "His fire will not burn out until the last enemy, the death of time and of eternity, will have been absorbed, and God will be all in all."[83] Johanna Eleonora Petersen was convinced that "there will be a final, all-encompassing salvation, in which all of God's creation (not together but each according to its rank one after another) will be saved from their destruction and completely restored or placed into a state of bliss in which they were and have seen themselves at their creation or in their beginning."[84] The right time had come to spread this message. Petersen believed that God's final judgment was near and distinguished three categories or steps with a time frame for the impending salvation, which included even the "fallen Lucifer" and the false prophets.

Johanna Eleonora Petersen connected the doctrine of eternal salvation with chiliasm; for her it was the everlasting gospel, latent in scripture, though only a few Christians had seen and understood it until now, with the beginning of the Philadelphian Church. For her, both Testaments revealed God's infinite love and mercy. In her day this was a renewal of the image of a merciful God, a God who was connected to human beings and the human concept of time. It went against the contemporary fear of hell and damnation and suggested, albeit in religious terms, an almost utopian belief in a future of reconciliation. Johanna Eleonora fought against the "slavish fear"[85] that immobilized so many individuals who were giving in to imaginations of hellish punishments. To those who might think that a pious life was no longer necessary, she was quick to point out that only *eternal* damnation was impossible, but that some time of punishment would follow a sinful life. She emphasized a following of Christ and a life of "good works." Her theology had a fresh and optimistic outlook on God, human life, and this world that

---

82. The seventeenth century upheld elaborate constructions of the incarnation of evil, wherein fallen angels (or demons) and devils instead of praising God had opposed or fallen away from him. More important, these creatures were out to steal human souls away from God.

83. *Anleitung zur gründlichen Verständniß* . . . , 102.

84. Ibid., 94. Johanna Eleonora based her concept in reading in the "everlasting gospel" in Rev. 14:6–7: "And I saw another angel fly in the midst of heaven, having the everlasting gospel to preach unto them that dwell on earth, and to every nation, and kindred, and tongue, and people, Saying with a loud voice: 'Fear God and give glory to him; for the hour of his judgment is come . . .'"

85. *Anleitung zur gründlichen Verständniß* . . . , 68.

energized her readers (or listeners). She would not rest until she gained "understanding" (spiritual, rational, and emotional) of scripture through "experience" (reading and living it). In her spiritual optimism and missionary zeal she was a precursor of eighteenth-century Enlightenment with its zeal for happiness in this life, individual betterment, and education.

AUTOBIOGRAPHY AND PIETISM

Of Johanna Eleonora Petersen's later works only her autobiography is of interest here: *The Life of Lady Johanna Eleonora Petersen, née von und zu Merlau, Wife of Dr. Johann Petersen, Written by Herself and Given to the Public Because of Many Edifying Events[, As a Sequel to Her Husband's. Payed for by Worthy Friends].*[86] In the enlarged version of 1718 Petersen reviews, surveys, and justifies a long, productive life and spiritual awakening. Unlike modern authors of autobiography who usually aim at creating a literary work of what Goethe aptly called "poetry or fiction and truth,"[87] Petersen wrote in the tradition of religious autobiography. She was guided by a search for religious truth, not by a novel, fanciful or creative self-presentation. She did not write in the literary paradigm of modern aesthetics but she operated in a religious paradigm well capable of understanding and giving meaning to her own life.[88]

No scribe or mediator intervened with Petersen's text, as was to a certain extent the case with *The Life of Saint Teresa of Avila*, the Spanish nun's *Vida* (1588), which the Inquisition had regarded with suspicion and had tried to influence through her confessor. Having been given Saint Augustine's *Confessions* to read by her confessor, Teresa of Avila was stirred by some of the ecstatic passages in his narration and struck by the definitiveness of Augustine's conversion. She set out on her own quest for sanctity, disheartened by episodes of backsliding. Written as an address to her sisters, Saint Teresa's spiritual autobiography not only made it into print already during

---

86. See the annotated bibliography of Petersen's works; for publishing details see the introduction to the translation in this volume.

87. The title Goethe gave his 1812 autobiography, *Dichtung und Wahrheit*, is of course ambiguous, as *dichtung* can mean both poetry or fiction and invention.

88. Older scholarship dismissed first-person accounts of spiritual itineraries, especially women's, when a scribe or confessor was a possible mediator; see, for example, Roy Pascal, *Design and Truth in Autobiography* (London: Routledge, 1960), 24–25, 31–34. Present scholarship on the other hand speaks of autobiographics, ego documents, personal histories, autobiographical discourses and so on, often blurring or expressing disinterest in genre distinctions or historical variations; see Leigh Gilmore, *Autobiographics: A Feminist Theory of Women's Self-Representation* (Ithaca: Cornell University Press, 1994); and Gabriele Rippl, *Lebenstexte: Literarische Selbststilisierungen englischer Frauen in der frühen Neuzeit* (Munich: Fink, 1998).

her lifetime, but women and men religious interpreted it as authorization for the writing self. It became the model for a style of writing based on personal experience and direct expression, a paradigm for subsequent religious autobiography in the Catholic and especially the Spanish world.

Petersen probably did not read the Catholic Teresa of Avila, but she did know and mention repeatedly Saint Augustine's *Confessions* and Ana Maria van Schurman's autobiography of the 1670s. Like Saint Augustine's, Petersen's autobiography is a conversion narrative proceeding in a chronological, linear way. A series of inner and outer conflicts leads to the construction of the Christian individual, an illuminated self in accordance with God's will without a mediating priest or ecclesiastical institution. God is truth and the measure of human life; in order to find and understand the self, a person must seek its origin in God. In the concluding section of her autobiography,[89] Petersen mentioned the legend told of Saint Augustine's search of the divine, for the secret of the Trinity. Walking on the beach in deep thought, Saint Augustine saw a little boy digging a hole. When asked what he was doing, the boy responded that he wanted to catch the entire ocean in his hole. When Augustine pointed out to him that he would never be able to do that, the boy answered: "Just like you will never be able to understand the secret of the divine." This legend was a reminder for Petersen to subject herself to God and give up her reasoning. Subjecting herself to God meant for Petersen the study of scripture in order to gain illumination, and through this revelation some measure of understanding. The legend of Saint Augustine and the child underscored not the futility of the quest but the continuous effort necessary for what is *not* possible, a human's conscious, rational and full grasp of God. Like Augustine's description of his religious life after his conversion (in book 10) and his search for an understanding of God's word (books 11–13), Petersen described in the later segment of her autobiography her pious life in Frankfurt, her marriage in service to God (§§ 24–27), and her continuing search for illumination (§§ 28–38). Like Augustine, she used biblical language and ample quotes throughout her narrative, and both autobiographies are told with certainty and confidence in an ultimate spiritual outcome. In addition to these structural similarities, characteristic of the religious conversion narrative, Petersen charted her individual course and path to God. For unlike Augustine's dramatic conversion moment— the urging coming from a child's voice to read a biblical passage[90] —which

89. See § 38.

90. In book 8, Augustine reads Rom. 13:13–14: "Let us walk honestly, as in the day; not in rioting and drunkenness, not in chambering and wantonness, not in strife and envying. But put

was a highlight and turning point, Petersen outlined a step-by-step course toward God in a number of life-altering decisions she made in withdrawing from worldly affairs and a three-year trial period while still at court. It was not a sudden breakthrough or conversion, but a lifelong desire for God. Saint Augustine's *Confessions* were certainly an inspiration—of all the church fathers he was the one most revered and read by Luther and the Protestants, and his *Confessions* served as model for most Pietist autobiographies.

If there was also a contemporary inspiration for Petersen's autobiography, it was the religious account of the famous Dutch learned woman Anna Maria van Schurman (1607–78), who had written in Latin and Greek, been instrumental in the establishment of the University of Utrecht, and remained unmarried. After having become, already in her sixties, a vocal and the most distinguished follower of the charismatic French preacher and sectarian Jean de Labadie (1610–74) and suffering persecution with his followers, the "star of Utrecht"—as Schurman was known in scholarly circles—wrote a defense of her religious turn, her beliefs, and the Labadists' tribulation. In 1670 the followers of Labadie and Schurman were expelled from Amsterdam; they moved first to Herford, where Schurman's friend, the Abbess Elisabeth,[91] gave them a temporary refuge, then to the more liberal city of Altona (now a suburb of Hamburg). Finally in 1675 they were able to establish the separatist community in Wieuwerd (Friesland), where Schurman died in 1678. Schurman published the first part of her autobiography in 1673 in Altona shortly after Labadie's death, while the second part appeared posthumously in 1685. This autobiography, titled *Eukleria, or the Election of the Better Part,*[92]

---

ye on the Lord Jesus Christ." Petersen, unlike Saint Augustine, did not recount any extraordinary sins but presented a modest, humble life since childhood—very much in keeping with the contemporary image of women.

91. The unmarried Abbess Elisabeth was the daughter of Elisabeth Stuart and Frederic V of Bohemia, Count Palatine (the "Winter King" whose defeat triggered the Thirty Years' War); she had been installed in 1667 after spending time in the United Provinces where she had become acquainted with Descartes and with Van Schurman. Her sister was Sophie of Hannover, mother of the later King George I of England and correspondent of Leibniz. They represented the Protestant elite, many of whose members were intensely involved in religious questions. The convent at Herford housed fourteen aristocratic nuns and their large entourage of cooks, servants, four ministers, several deacons, etc.; it was a wealthy but tiny principality with Elisabeth claiming independence as princess of the empire. But the people of Herford and the clergy in northern Germany protested against their heretical teachings and immoral lifestyle.

92. *Eukleria* is Greek for "the right choice." A Dutch translation appeared in Amsterdam in 1684. The Labadists traveled with a printer and a printing press and produced their own books. A partial English translation of Schurman's autobiography can be found in Mirjam De Baar et al., eds., *Choosing the Better Part: Anna Maria van Schurman (1607–1678)*, Archives Internationales d'Histoire des Idées, 146 (Dordrecht: Kluwer Academic Publishers, 1996); and in Anna Maria

was written in Latin to defend her religious life to an audience of scholars and theologians. Schurman called her autobiography a public testimony to her newfound faith and a rejection of her former learned interests: "I recant in this place and by the light of the sun (after the example of Augustine, the most righteous of all church fathers) all my publications that carry the detestable, worldly odor of the vanity of my spirit: I no longer recognize them. Likewise I reject all the publications by others, and especially the panegyrics marked by a vain pride and a lack of piety."[93] Much of Schurman's argumentation was scholarly and rational, with missionary intent. She balanced her critique of her contemporary society, church, and individuals by detailing her new life, her newfound faith, the inner light, and the teachings of Labadie. Schurman stressed the new community in which she could play a useful part, where she had found "deep peace and great stillness"[94] in the turmoil of this world. Schurman's autobiography is more erudite, dogmatic, and descriptive than it is spiritual or emotional. Yet she objected to a merely intellectual appropriation of religious dogma; according to Schurman, these truths could be known truly only through divine illumination, which is given together with a new awakening in faith. Schurman's turn away from the world of learning and the Reformed Church toward a religious life in Labadie's community, her rejection of her former life and prominence, and her articulation of her faith and the "right choice" must have impressed— perhaps even influenced—Johanna Eleonora greatly.

Already in 1674, the Frankfurt lawyer and Pietist Schütz, who had visited Labadie and was interested in his teachings, had initiated an exchange of letters with Anna Maria van Schurman, who then also corresponded with Johanna Eleonora (then still) von Merlau. Schurman was, like the Frankfurt Pietist circle, also increasingly disappointed by the lack of reform in her own church. Petersen referred in her autobiography to Schurman by stating that she had been "commanded to choose the best part."[95] At court Petersen defended her choice to the ministers sent to change her mind, and she fought a hostile world of gossip, misunderstandings, and misinformation,

---

van Schurman, *Whether a Christian Woman Should Be Educated, and Other Writings from Her Intellectual Circle*, ed. and trans. by Joyce Irwin, Other Voice in Early Modern Europe (Chicago: University of Chicago Press, 1998), chaps. 1–2 (73–94).

93. *Eukleria* (Altona, 1673), 11 (my translation).

94. Ibid., 284.

95. "Mir ist befohlen das beste zu erwehlen," in § 21 of her autobiography. Johann Wilhelm Petersen mentioned Schurman and their admiration for her in his autobiography. His is full of references to persons and places where Johanna Eleonora only gives hints and rarely mentions persons by name.

just as Schurman had come out publicly to defend her new life, a daring and provocative step.

In the seventeenth century and before, very few women published their autobiographies. Those who did were mostly upper-class women in England like Lady Margaret Cavendish, Duchess of Newcastle, who first appended *A True Relation of My Birth, Breeding, and Life* to her collection of fictions, *Nature's Pictures* (1656) and later published it as an appendix to her husband's biography (composed by her, too). Petersen followed this publication pattern, apparently a sign of the decorum for women at the time rather than a conscious acknowledgment of Cavendish's practice. From the 1640s a few more women began to record their own life stories, but they were usually meant not for publication but for family members and friends, and came to light only in subsequent centuries, like the autobiographical notes and diary sections by Mary Rich, Countess of Warwick (1618–78), published only in the nineteenth century.[96]

Quakers, Puritans, and Pietists initiated a tradition of a religious introspection. With the burgeoning growth of Quakerism, which preached and practiced the equality of women—albeit in the limited sphere as "children of God"—Quaker women preached, traveled extensively, and wrote (toward the end of the seventeenth century) of their lives touched by God as examples for others.[97] The Quakers also believed in the power of the published word as a means of disseminating the truth and of furthering the aims of the society; here devotional, missionary, and experiential parts were mixed with accounts of travel, people, and events. Margaret Fell, for example, married the eminent Quaker John Fox at age fifty-five, and wrote about her life in *A Brief Collection of Remarkable Passages and Occurrences Relating to the Birth, Education, Life, Conversion, Travels, Services and Deep Sufferings of That Ancient, Eminent and Faithful Servant of the Lord, Margaret Fell, but by Her Second Marriage, Margaret Fox* published in 1710. Autobiography as a form or literary genre was less important than the autobiographical impulse for writing here.

Puritans began to require a spiritual autobiography for women who were seeking admission into the Church of Visible Saints in eighteenth-century

---

96. See *Autobiography of Mary Countess of Warwick*, ed. T. Crofton Crooker (London: Percy Society, 1848). Excerpts from her diaries were edited in 1817 as "memoirs," and her manuscript "Diary of Mary Rich, Countess of Warwick" remains unedited in its entirety in the British Library.

97. For American Quakers, see the fine essay by Carol Edkins in *Women's Autobiography: Essays in Criticism*, ed. Estelle C. Jelinek (Bloomington: Indiana University Press, 1980), 39–59; for mostly British Quaker women, see Luella Wright, *The Literary Life of the Early Friends* (New York: Columbia University Press, 1932).

New England. Likewise, Pietist autobiographies became a tradition in Germany in the eighteenth century. Called *Lebenslauf* (literally, life's course), they were writings asked of all believers in organized groups such as the Moravian Brethren in Herrnhut—the Pietist community established by Count Zinzendorf in Saxony and still active today—were required to record their own lives and conversion. This was read, or integrated into, the funeral sermon (*Leichenpredigt*) held at their burial. This practice evolved, however, quite late; only in the 1740s was an individual, personal component generally added to the memorial service; after 1757 autobiographical life stories written in the first-person narrative became a standard feature at the funeral.[98]

The tradition had developed slowly since Jakob Spener's and Johanna Eleonora Petersen's autobiographies. Already in 1683, Jakob Spener had composed what he called his *Lebenslauf.*[99] Not published during his lifetime, it circulated in manuscript as a model for others and was read at his funeral. Spener's autobiography is a rather short, condensed report with reflective comments on the most important events in his life; he represents himself as being guided by God to an exemplary life from birth to rebirth and beyond. He showed himself a child exposed to dangerous influences but rescued through the parents' loving education, strict teachers, and influential godparents. He claims he learned early in life to prepare himself for the prospect of a rebirth in God. Spener also mentioned his devotional readings of then popular works by Johann Arndt, Sonthom, and Bailey. His text became something of a model for Pietist lives and life stories in Germany, together with Gottfried Arnold's collection of exemplary, spiritual lives of religious dissidents in his *Unbiased History of the Church and Heretics* (1699–1700), which included well-known and obscure biographies up to 1688.[100]

---

98. The Unitäts-Archiv in Herrnhut contains thousands of handwritten autobiographies, *Lebensläufe,* written by members of the Herrnhut community since the second half of the eighteenth century. See Irina Modrow, "Religiöse Erweckung und Selbstreflexion: Überlegungen zu den Lebensläufen Herrnhuter Schwestern als einem Beispiel pietistischer Selbstdarstellung," in *Ego-Dokumente: Annäherungen an den Menschen in der Geschichte,* ed. Siegfried Schulze, Selbstzeugnisse der Neuzeit, 2 (Berlin: Akademie Verlag, 1996), 121–29.

99. Spener's autobiography appeared first in print as an appendix to the funeral sermon held for him in Conrad Gottfried Blanckenberg, *Das Leben der Gläubigen* (Frankfurt, 1705), 27–48; as an appendix to the funeral sermon for Spener under the title "Personalia" with the note that Spener had written his *Lebenslauf* and requested that it be used for the (much more elaborate) funeral sermon.

100. Gottfried Arnold's *Unpartheiische Kirchen- und Ketzerhistorie,* which appeared in four parts (two volumes) in Frankfurt between 1698 and 1700, was reprinted and enlarged several times until 1742 and read widely; together with the equally prolific Johann Henrich Reitz, *Historie der Wiedergebohrnen* [History of the Reborn] (1698–1701, with numerous enlarged editions

When Johanna Eleonora Petersen wrote her autobiography, the first part presumably during the late 1680s and the second part in the 1710s, she may well have known Spener's text, given the close spiritual relationship they had in Frankfurt and kept up through visits and correspondence. Yet while she also outlined her path to God under his guidance, her autobiography is quite independent from Spener's in her descriptive detail of postwar hardships and lack of parental protection, her life at court among unfeeling, worldly noblemen, her arranged but failed engagements, and her marriage. Unlike Spener's theological career, Petersen reflects a woman's socialization. And hers is a spiritual awakening, not a (sudden) breakthrough: from the small child's prayer to the meeting of her spiritual counselor and conscious decision "for the better part" as a young adult. Her spirituality became the center of her inner, religious autobiography. Unlike Spener's, Petersen's was offered to a broader audience through publication, as the individual experience of a woman with divine inspiration. Self-depiction and self-justification, predominant in the childhood phase, were no longer important in the latter part of the autobiography; instead the "edifying events" (the title page of 1718), made her story print-worthy. In place of scholarly dogmatism, rational theology, and arguments with professional colleagues that stand out in Johann Wilhelm Petersen's autobiography *Das Leben Jo. Wilhelmi Petersen* (1717), Johanna Eleonora Petersen interprets life in terms of biblical pictures with a personal, edifying piety, a piety fueled by an inner light, by faith in love as an ordering force, and by faith in the secret of the divine "God-Man" (*Gott-Mensch*), as well as by the chiliastic images of better times.

From a nonreligious perspective, Johanna Eleonora's autobiographical "I" appears reflective, searching, yet strong and individualistic. The early loss of her mother left a void that the father was unable and unwilling to fill; a loveless time is described without any mention of her faith in God or in the power of prayer to aid in desperate times, the low point of her childhood—and of her life. The pathetic episode of the fall from the tower only to wake up resting in her father's empty bed[101] seems to initiate her recognition of, and reliance on, her father (both her physical father and God) and to introduce her subsequent integration into the father's world; the initiation into the religious community follows. Her socialization as a

---

until 1748), which must have influenced the pious and their perception and of self. See Hans Jürgen Schrader's edited volume of *Historie der Wiedergebohrnen*, Deutsche Neudrucke Barock, 29 (Tübingen: Niemeyer, 1982).

101. See § 7 of her autobiography.

woman took place by her growing domestic responsibilities, which marked the end of her childhood development, as she succeeded her mother and sister in taking over the household. Her only learning consisted in her introduction into the patriarchal world of Christianity through her religious instruction (the only indication of formal lessons, as no home tutors are mentioned and schools were not open to girls). She placed the decision about her future—marriage—in the hands of those who initiated it, the authorities of the patriarchal society—namely, God and her own father as the executor of God's will. This quietist behavior can be read as her consciously manipulating an inescapable system to her best advantage; escaping into the freedom of faith and a religious life, she could and did live fully, asserting marriage to be the union of like-minded people with similar belief systems and goals.

Johanna Eleonora Petersen's was the first autobiography by a woman written in German to appear in print. Arguably it was also the first one written in Germany as a coherent, reflective experience in the literary form of autobiography. Before her there were a few chronicles, at best partial diaries or autobiographical sections written by women, such as the Abbess Caritas Pirckheimer's account of the closing of her convent in Reformation Nuremberg 1524–28,[102] Katharina Schütz's autobiographical section in her tract in defense of her husband,[103] or a one-page autobiographical preface that Maria Cunitz published in her work on astronomy, *Urania Propitia* (1650). Even with their more recent interest in personal histories—"ego documents"—scholars have unearthed very few such authentic texts written by women about themselves; during the seventeenth century only one Dutch autobiography by an upper-middle-class woman was published in 1695. But full-fledged personal accounts even from eighteenth- century women are scarce and rarely preserved. Also, very few women published in the seventeenth century in Germany, and for the most part these were women of the nobility who wrote religious poetry, devotional books, funerary memorials, or occasional poetry, but not plays, novels, or secular poetry. There are only two known exceptions: Anna Owena Hoyers (1584–1658) in her *Geistliche und Weltliche Poemata* (1550) included some contemporary poetry; and Sibylle Schwarz (1621–38), who died at age seventeen, wrote a number of Italianate sonnets for her posthumously published *Deutsche Poetische Gedichte* (1650). The eminent poet Katharina Regina von Greiffenberg (1633–94) confined herself to religious

102. For literary women in early modern Germany, see my study *Der lange Weg zur Mündigkeit: Frau und Literatur in Deutschland, 1500–1800* (Stuttgart: Metzler, 1987).

103. See the thorough study (in English with some translations) by Elsie Ann McKee, *Katharina Schütz*, 2 vols. (Leiden: Brill, 1999).

topics. Johanna Eleonora Petersen's oeuvre of religious texts extended this canon; her autobiographical reflections pointed to the eighteenth century.

Petersen served as an example for Susanna von Klettenberg and numerous other eighteenth-century women, many of whom were inclined toward Pietism but remained in their church and did not move to one of the few, separate Pietist communities like Herrnhut (in Saxony), Herrnhag, Laubach, or Berleburg (all in Hesse). The Frankfurt Pietist Klettenberg (1723–74), whose autobiography served Goethe in writing "Confessions of a Beautiful Soul," a central book in his novel *Wilhelm Meister's Apprenticeship* of 1796, did not publish her autobiography that is known to have existed (but has not been preserved). The "beautiful soul," an ethical and spiritual inwardness, became the predominant model for eighteenth-century women in Germany. At the turn of the century, however, Goethe offered an ironic and slightly critical twist: his "beautiful Soul" refuses to become a wife and mother for the sake of her piety, thus missing her "natural" calling, and is in the end marginalized in the newly blossoming, totally patriarchal society created by and mostly for men—a reflection of the increasingly fixed gender roles and gender dichotomy in patriarchal Germany around 1800.

Johanna Eleonora Petersen gave a voice to Pietist women; she was not a feminist but helped prepare the way for women's individual and collective expressions in the religious community and beyond. Her mystical-spiritual immersion in God's word and writings, calling herself "Doer of the Word" on various occasions, was a significant act for women who surrounded the Pietist clergymen as listeners, patronesses, and activists. While on the one hand she helped pave the way in her writings and her activist marriage, on the other hand she fostered development of "inwardness," which originated from the "Word" of the Bible and which found its expression in the literary form of devotional literature and the edifying autobiography. This was an important step for women in finding their own voice, in finding "a room of their own," a place and goal for their lives. Johanna Eleonora Petersen articulated her spiritual experience, while most remained silent, and created a body of devotional and religious texts as an exegesis of *the* book, the Bible. And while the theological debates are of interest only to specialists today, Petersen's life story contains a new understanding of spirituality and self-worth. It helped to change perceptions about women. These changed perceptions were potentially empowering for women in encouraging them to find their own voices.

VOLUME EDITOR'S
BIBLIOGRAPHY

ANNOTATED BIBLIOGRAPHY OF
JOHANNA ELEONORA PETERSEN'S WORKS

1689

A Heart's Conversations with God, Written by Johannna Eleonora Petersen, née von und zu Merlau. Ploen. Published by Siegfried Ripenau. Printed by Tobias Schmidt. 1689.
Gespräche des Hertzens mit GOTT/ Erster Theil. Auffgesetzet Von JOHANNA ELEONORA PETERSEN, Gebohrne von und zu Merlau. PLOEN/ verlegts Siegfried Ripenau. Gedruckt durch Tobias Schmidt/ 1689.

Two parts in one; each with an engraved frontispiece; new editions (with illustrations) in 1694 and 1715. Part 1 is dedicated to Duchess Christine von Schleswig Holstein, née von Sachsen-Weißenfels (Christine von Schleswig Holstein was the wife of the sovereign in Eutin, Johann Wilhelm Petersen's employer), part 2 to the Countess Benigna von Solms-Laubach (Benigna von Solms-Laubach was a well-known Pietist and friend of Jakob Spener's, whom Petersen had met during her court service in Wiesenburg.); a preface is written by the Kiel theologian Christian Kortholt. A devotional book; in the "conversations" the soul seeks a direct relationship with Jesus. Prayers and meditations about biblical passages are mostly from the Psalms and the Song of Solomon, illustrated by a picture (in the second and third edition; the engravings were not yet ready for the printing of the first) and followed prose passages. The first part contains fifty "conversations" and follows, in the pictures and biblical texts, Hermann Hugo's popular emblem book *Pia Desideria* (1624). The second part comprises twenty-four "conversations" from the tradition of "Cor Jesu Amanti Sacrum" of Antoon Wierix. Petersen chose the fitting biblical passages and wrote the prayerlike meditations. Added to part 2 (pp. 235–95) is the first printing of Petersen's autobiography: "A Short Narration How God's Guiding Hand Has Guided Me Hitherto,"

1691

Conversations with God about Faith. Written in Three Parts, So That Part I Represents the Work of Faith in Its Power, Part II the Testimony, the Power, and the Splendor of Faith, and Part III the End of Faith Which Is the Blessedness of Souls. In These Times without Faith to the Encouragement and Awakening of Faith. Written by Johanna Eleonora Petersen, née von und zu Merlau. Frankfurt and Leipzig. At Michael Brodthagen's. In the Year of Christ 1691.
Glaubens-Gespräche mit GOTT/ In Drey unterschiedene Theile abgefasset Also daß Der I. Theil/ Das Werck des Glaubens in der Krafft/ Der II. Theil/ Das Zeugniß/

die Macht und Herrlichkeit des Glaubens/ Der III. Theil/ Das Ende des Glaubens/ welches ist der Seelen Seligkeit/ vorstellet/ In dieser letzten Glaublosen Zeit zur Auffmunterung und Erweckung des Glaubens auffgesetzt von JOHANNA ELEONORA Petersen/ Gebohrne von und zu Merlau. Franckf. und Leipzig/ Bey Michael Brodthagen/ im Jahr Christi 1691.

Three parts, with an engraved frontispiece and seven illustrations, including a picture of the author (in the engraving, possibly done after an oil portrait, Petersen is pictured as a matron with an open book; this served as model for her picture in the 1718 edition). (See the frontispiece of our edition.)

The book is dedicated to Petersen's husband (dated Lüneburg, July 11, 1691); the preface ("to the Christian reader") answers her critics that God has given his spirit also to women and wants them to profess. Each of the three parts contains fifty devotional exercises based on biblical quotes containing the word "faith."

1696

Instructions for a Thorough Understanding of the Holy Revelation of Jesus Christ Which He Sent and Interpreted through His Servant and Apostle John with an Angel, Insofar As It Is Being Viewed in Its Very Last Prophetic Meaning and in Its Full Completion in the End of Time That We Are Approaching with the Largest Part Still Ahead. Organized in an Appropriate Table in Which Holy Revelation in Harmony with Things and Time Has Been Condensed. With a Preface Suitable for Preparation and a Threefold Appendix, In Well-Meaning Love and According the Measure of Grace Conveyed and Edited by Johanna Eleonora Petersen, née von und zu Merlau. Frankfurt and Leipzig: to be found at Johann Daniel Müller; 1696.

Anleitung zu gründlicher Verständniß der Heiligen Offenbahrung Jesu Christi welche er seinem Knecht und Apostel Johanni Durch seinen Engel gesandt und gedeutet hat/ sofern Sie in ihrem eigentlichsten letzten prophetischen Sinn und Zweck betrachtet wird/ Und in ihrer völligen Erfüllung in den allerletzten Zeiten/ denen wir nahe kommen sind/ grössten Theils noch bevorstehet/ Nach Ordnung einer dazu gehörigen TABELLE, Darinnen die heilige Offenbarung in der Harmonie der Dinge und Zeiten kürtzlich entworffen ist/ Mit einer zur Vorbereitung dienlichen Vor-Rede und Dreyfachem Anhange/ in wohlmeynender Liebe nach dem Maaß der Gnade mitgetheilet und herausgegeben von Johanna Eleonora Petersen/ gebohrnen von und zu Merlau. Franckfurt und Leipzig: zu finden bey Johann Daniel Müllern; 1696.

Quarto format; engraved, emblematic frontispiece; elaborate table with detailed explanation. The book is dedicated to Anna Sophie of Denmark (1647–1717), wife of the Elector Johann Georg III of Saxony, and to her sister Wilhelmine Ernestine of Denmark (1650–1706), wife of the Elector Karl II of the Palatinate. The monumental, elegant volume was addressed to readers of the nobility. In her preface ("To the Reader") Petersen explains her right and calling to publish. The volume contains a detailed presentation of Petersen's chiliasm, the coming of the thousand-year realm where the "tyrannical and godless government" will be destroyed and the entire creation rescued by Jesus Christ. A condensed version of the section "Of the Heavenly New Jerusalem" was published in London in *Theosophical Transactions of the Philadelphian Society* 3 (1697), pp. 142–51.

1698

The Eternal Gospel of the Universal Return of All Creatures. How This Is Deeply Rooted in the Right Understanding of the Middle Sphere of the Souls after Death and How This Will Occur after the Completion of God's Judgment. Presented in Praise of the Ever-Loving God and for the Awakening of a Holy Love in Return by a Member of the Philadelphian Society. At the End Has Been Added a Short Appendix with Harmonizing Passages from Scripture and Several Remarkable Testimonies by Luther. Printed in the Year of Christ 1698.

Das Ewige Evangelium Der Allgemeinen Wiederbringung Aller Creaturen./ Wie solche unter andern In rechter Erkäntnüß Des Mitlern Zustandes der Seelen nach dem Tode tieff gegründet ist/ Und nach Außführung der endlichen Gerichte GOttes dermaleins völlig erfolgen wird. Vorgestellet/ Und zum Preiß des ewig-liebreichen Gottes/ auch zur Erweckung einer heiligen Gegen-Liebe verkündiget/ Von einem Mitgliede der D. Ph. G. Zu Ende ist beygefüget ein kurtzer AHANG Von einigen harmonischen Schrifft-Stellen/ und verschiedenen sonderbahren Zeugnüssen LUTHERI. Gedruckt im Jahr Christi 1698.

A spirited defense of the dogma of universal return with speculations about the soul's fate after death. Philipp Jakob Spener had warned Petersen in a 1695 letter against publishing such views, which went against the accepted dogma of the Lutheran and the Reformed Churches. This may explain the anonymous publication without a place and publisher. The volume was reprinted in 1700 and attached to Johann Wilhelm Petersen's more learned but equally dogmatic and anonymous *Mysterion Apokatastaseos: That Is, The Secret of Universal Return . . .* 1700, printed again in 1705 and 1710.

1698

The Spiritual Fight of the Summoned, Select and Faithful Conquerors, In Which They Must Fight at the Beginning, Advancement, and End for the Crown of the Firstborn. Shown in the Image of the Seven Tribes to John in Revelation. Clearly and Lucidly Presented and Delivered into Print a Few Years Ago by Johanna Eleonora Petersen, née von und zu Merlau. Now for Everyone's Edification and Strong Arousal of Piety, Christian Patience, and Joy in Suffering Brought into This Convenient Form. Halle. Printer Chr. Henckel. 1698.

Der geistliche Kampff Der beruffenen/ auserwehlten und gläubigen Uberwinder/ Durch Welchen Sie beym Anfange/ Fortgange und Ausgange ihres Christen-thums die Krone der Erst-gebuhrt erstreiten müßen/ Unter dem Bilde der Sieben Gemeinen dem Johanni in der Offenbahrung gezeiget/ Klar und deutlich vor-gestellet/ Und vor einigen Jahren in Druck gegeben von Johanna Eleonora Pe-tersen gebohrnen von und zu Merlau/ Nunmehr aber zu mehrerer Erbauung und kräfftiger Erweckung wahrer Gottseeligkeit/ Christl. Gedult und Freudigkeit im Leiden/ in diese beqveme Form gebracht. Halle/ Druckts Chr. Henckel/ 1698.

Frontispiece shows "the woman clothed in suns," explained as the New Jeru-salem, whose birth is described in seven chapters. This short treaty of some sixty pages was published in the newly established center of Pietism, Halle. A second edition was published in 1719.

1699

Die Nothwendigkeit der Neuen Creatur in CHRISTO In einem Send-Schreiben Gezeiget Von Johanna Eleonora Petersen/ Gebohrnen von and zu Merlaw. Ge-druckt im Jahr Christi 1699.

See appendix 2 for the English translation of 1772:

The Nature and Necessity of the New Creature in Christ, Stated and Described According to Heart's Experience and True Practice. By Joanna Eleonora De Merlau. Translated from the German by Francis Okely, A. B. Formerly of St. John's College in Cambridge. Second Edition. London: Printed for the Editor; 1772.

1701

Proof of the Eternal Gospel. Presented to Dr. Johann Winckler, Senior and Official Preacher in Hamburg for Love of Truth by a Member of the Philadelphian Society. Printed in 1701.

Bewährung Des Ewigen Evangelii/ Dem Herrn D. Johann Wincklern/ SENIORI et PASTORI des MINISTERII zu Hamburg/ Auß Liebe der Wahrheit vorgestellet durch ein Mitglied der Philadelphischen Gemeine. Gedruckt im Jahr 1701.

A theological epistle addressed to a distinguished clergyman and friend of Spener's in Hamburg. (In 1678 Winckler had proposed to Johanna Eleonora but was rejected.)

Reprinted in 1703 in Johann Wilhelm Petersen's *Mysterion Apokatastaseos*.

1706

Jesus Christ's Revelation Explained According to Its Context and Meaning of the Spirit Shown Clearly by Johanna Eleonora Petersen, née von und zu Merlau. Printed in the Year of Christ 1706.

Die verklärte Offenbahrung JEsu Christi/ Nach dem Zusammenhang/ und Nach dem Sinn des Geistes/ deutlich gezeiget von Johanna Eleonora Petersen/ Gebohrnen von und zu Merlau. Gedruckt im Jahr Christi 1706.

Engraved frontispiece, a smaller copy (in octavo) of the frontispiece of her *Instructions* (1696, above). This readable treatise of 180 pages explains Petersen's ideas about chiliasm for the layperson. Petersen states in the preface that she had difficulty complying with a request to issue a short version of her voluminous *Instructions* because her writing "flows from her heart." A second printing (or issue with a slightly enlarged title page?) appeared in the same year, a new edition in 1717.

1711

The Secret of the Firstborn Who Is from the Beginning and Who Is God the Word, the God-Man Jesus Christ, Yesterday and Today the Same in Eternity. Through His Blessed Knowledge the Quarreling Parties in the Different Religions Could Come to an Agreement among Each Other. With a Summary Explanation of the Epistle to the Romans and Chapter 17 of John and about Some Other Passages Dealing with the Above Secret. Presented by Johanna Eleonora Petersen, née von und zu Merlau. Frankfurt. At Samuel Heyl and Gottfried Liebezeit, Booksellers. 1711.

Das Geheimniß Des Erst=Gebornen Der von Anfang ist/ und der da ist GOTT das Wort Der GOTT=Mensch JESUS Christus Gestern und Heute und Derselbe in Ewigkeit: Durch dessen seeliges Erkäntniß/ Die strittige Partheyen in den unterschiedlichen Reli= gionen unter sich könten vereiniget werden/ Sammt einer Summarischen Erklärung Über die Epistel an die Römer wie auch über das 17. Cap. Johanniß/ und über einige Schrifft= Oerter so von dem obigen Geheimniß handeln vorgetragen/ Von JOHANNA ELEONORA Petersen/ Gebohrne von und zu Merlau. [Vignette] Franckfurt/ bey Samuel Heyl und Gottfried Liebezeit Buchhändler 1711.

The work is dedicated to Sophie Luise, Queen of Brandenburg-Prussia, whom

Petersen knew from her years at court in Wiesenburg. (The Petersens were now living in the kingdom of Brandenburg-Prussia). Petersen encourages the king's efforts to unite Lutherans and Reformed. In the preface ("Dear Reader") she expresses her hope that "the God of love and peace is with us and gather together what is still divided in hatred." She tells the story of a 1708 meeting with a Lutheran and a Reformed in bitter dispute (see the autobiography, § 37), which gave her the idea for this book. The treatise is appended to Johann Wilhelm Petersen's work on the same topic, Christology, a theological explication of the nature and essence of Christ with an attempt to bridge the differences in interpretation between the Protestant denominations. Three sections deal with disunity, answers to often asked questions, and an interpretation of Paul's Letter to the Romans. The work contains several strong pleas for peace.

1714

Several Epistles Concerning the Necessity of Various Teachings Distrusted by Most Scholars Especially in Recent Times When the Preparation of the Lamb's Wedding Is to Take Place with Greater Zeal and Industry. Assembled upon the Wishes of Some Friends by Johanna Eleonora Petersen, née von und zu Merlau. Printed in the Year of Christ 1714.

Einige Send-Schreiben/ Betreffende die Nothwendigkeit Verschiedener bißher von den meisten Gelehrten in Verdacht gezogener Lehren/ Sonderlich in diesen letzten Zeiten/ da die Zubereitung zur Hochzeit des Lammes/ mit so größerem Eyfer und Fleiß geschehen soll/ Auff einiger Freunde Begehren verfertiget. von Johanna Eleonora Petersen Gebohrnen von und zu Merlaw. [Zierleiste] Gedruckt im Jahr Christi 1714.

In addition to a dedication to God, a preface to the reader, and preliminaries, in which Petersen tells of her illuminations in 1685 and 1708, the couple's trip to Silesia, and some of her dreams (later integrated in the last sections of her autobiography), this book contains three treatises: "Epistle On the Necessity of the New Creature," "Epistle On the Necessity of Teachings," and "Can We Hope in Truth for Better Times." Printed again in 1717 (?).

1715

Short Observations about the Sayings by the Most Holy Jesus Christ Known in the Spirit of Faith, with Which the Four Evangelists Have Dealt Partly According to His Sovereignty and Partly According to his Humility, and Partly to Both. In the Testimony and Presentation of Johanna Eleonora Petersen, née von und zu Merlau. 1715.

Kurtze Betrachtungen über die Sprüche Von der Im Geist des Glaubens erkannten Hoch-Heiligen Person Jesu Christi/ Davon In den vier Evangelisten Theils nach seiner Hoheit/ Theils nach seiner Niedrigkeit/ Theils nach Beyden zugleich gehandelt/ Und davon gezeuget/ und mitgetheilet wird Von Johanna Eleonora Petersen/ gebohrne von und zu Merlau. 1715.

This work comprises a preface to the reader, three sections with altogether 105 "Observations" based on biblical quotes.

1716

Supplement of Several Edifying Questions and Answers, Designed by Johanna Eleonora Petersen.

Zugab einiger erbaulichen Fragen und Antworten/ entworffen von Johanna Eleonora Pertersenin.

This was published with a separate title page as an appendix to Johann Wilhelm Petersen's 1716 *Proof of Our Lord's Universal Compassion . . .* , a response to the attacks on the dogma of universal salvation by a Reformed theologian in Hesse.

1717

Short Observations on the Usefulness of the Dear Cross, How It Is a Folly and an Obstacle to Worldly People but to the Faithful a Wholesome Way to Salvation. Recited by Johanna Eleonora Petersen, née von und zu Merlau. Berleburg. Printed by Christoph Konert, 1717.

Kurtze Betrachtungen Von der Nutzbarkeit des lieben Creutzes/ Wie solches Denen fleischlichen Menschen eine Thorheit und Aergerniße/ Denen Gläubigen aber Göttliche Weißheit/ und ein heilsames Mittel zur Seeligkeit ist. Vorgetragen von Johanna Eleonora Petersen/ Gebohrnen von und zu Merlau. Berleburg/ Gedruckt bey Christoph Konert/ 1717.

The short treaty of eighty pages may well be based on a sermon by Petersen (it was *vorgetragen*—presented orally) in Berleburg Berleburg (in Hesse) became a center of Pietism under Count Casimir Sayn-Wittgenstein-Berleburg (1687–1741), whose residence was in this small town. Until 1712, his mother (converted to Pietism by the preacher Hochmann von Hochenau) acted as regent for him and prepared the way for Pietism. *Short Observations* was published by the Berleburg printer Konert, who specialized in Pietist and dissident religious literature censored or suppressed elsewhere. There are fifty variations, each based on a biblical quote, on following Christ and justifying theologically men's sufferings. Perhaps this was written much earlier, since there is no trace of chiliasm as yet.

1717 (?)

Observations in Three Epistles: The First on Christ's Words about Faith, the Second about the Eight Benedictions Christ Has Pronounced for the Believers, The Third about the Eight Labors Christ Has Threatened the Infidel. Written in Simplicity by Johanna Eleonora Petersen, née von und zu Merlau. [no place, no date]

Betrachtungen In Drey Send-Schreiben/ Das Ite über die Worte CHRISTI vom Glauben, Das IIte Von den 8 Seeligkeiten so CHristus über die Gläubigen ausgesprochen. Das IIIte Von den 8. Wehen, so CHristus den Ungläubigen gedrohet und kund gemacht in Einfalt auffgesetzet Von Johanna Eleonora Petersen/ Gebohrnen von und zu Merlaw.

This devotional book comprises seventy-one pages. In the preface to the reader Petersen states: "In the beginning I wrote down these simple sighs only for myself and for my edification." The printer's marks point to Konert, Berleburg; the book could have been printed earlier.

1718

The Life of Lady Johanna Eleonora Petersen, née von und zu Merlau, Wife of Dr. Johann Petersen, Written by Herself and Given to the Public Because of Many Edifying Events, As a Sequel to Her Husband's. Payed for by Worthy Friends. 1718.

Leben Frauen Joh. Eleonora Petersen/ Gebohrnen von und zu Merlau, Hrn. D. Jo. Wilh. Petersen Eheliebsten; Von Ihr selbst mit eigener Hand aufgesetzet, und vieler erbaulichen Merckwürdigkeiten wegen zum Druck übergeben, daher es als ein Zweyter Theil zu Ihres Ehe=Herrn Lebens= Beschreibung beygefüget werden kan. Anno MDCCXVIII. Auf Kosten guter Freunde.

This work with a separate title page was appended to Johann Wilhelm Petersen's autobiography *Das Leben Johann Wilhelmi Petersen . . .* 1718, and reprinted in 1719. It contains Petersen's portrait.

OTHER PRIMARY SOURCES

Arndt, Johann. *True Christianity*. Translated and edited by Peter Erb. New York: Paulist Press, 1979.

Arnold, Gottfried. *Das Geheimnis der göttlichen Sophia* [1700]. Reprint. Stuttgart-Bad Cannstadt: Frommann, 1963.

Astell, Mary (1666–1731). *A Serious Proposal to the Ladies, For the Advancement of Their True and Greatest Interest.* Edited with introduction and notes by Patricia Springborg. London: Pickering & Chatto, 1997.

Augustine, Saint. *The Confessions*. Translated and edited by Philip Burton. Introduction by Robin Lane Fox. New York: Knopf, 2001.

Böhme, Jacob. *The Way to Christ* [1624]. Edited and translated by Peter Erb. New York: Paulist Press, 1978.

Bourignon, Antoinette (1616–1680). *An Admirable Treatise of Solid Virtue: Written in 24 Letters to a Young Man, Who Sought After the Perfection of His Soul.* Translated from the French. Amsterdam: Henry Wetstein, 1693.

————. *An Apology for M. Antonia Bourignon*. London: Printed for D. Brown, 1699.

Cavendish, Margaret, Duchess of Newcastle (1623–1673). *A True Relation of My Birth, Breeding and Life*, appended to *The Life of William Cavendish, Duke of Newcastle*. Edited by C. H. Firth. London: Routledge, [no date].

Ferrazzi, Cecilia (1609–1684). *Autobiography of an Aspiring Saint*. Edited and translated by Anne Jacobsen Schutte. The Other Voice in Early Modern Europe. Chicago: University of Chicago Press, 1996.

Feustking, Johann Heinrich. *Gynaeceum Haeretico Fanaticum, Oder Historie und Beschreibung der falschen Prophetinnen, Quäckerinnen, Schwäremerinnen, und andern sectirerischen und begeisterten Weibes-Personen.* Frankfurt and Leipzig, 1704. Reprint edited by Elisabeth Gössmann. Archiv für Philosophie- und Theologiegeschichtliche Frauenforschung, 7. Munich: Iudicium, 1998.

Glückel of Hameln (1646–1724). *The Life of Glückel of Hameln, Written by Herself.* Translated from the original Yiddish and edited by Beth-Zion Abrahams. London: East and West Library, 1962.

Goethe, Johann Wolfgang von. "Confessions of a Beautiful Soul." In *Wilhelm Meister's Apprenticeship*. Translated by Eric A. Blackall in cooperation with Victor Lange. New York: Suhrkamp, 1989.

————. *Truth and Fiction Relating to My Life*. Translated by John Oxenford. Boston: F. A. Niccolls & Co., [no date].

Gottsched, Luise. *Pietism in Petticoats and Other Comedies*. Translated and introduced by Thomas Kerth and John R. Russell, Columbia, SC: Camden House, 1994.

Gyon, Jeannne Marie Bouvier de la Motte (1648–1717). *The Exemplary Life of the Pious*

Lady Gyon. Translated from her own account in the original French by Thomas Digby Brooke. Philadelphia: Printed by Joseph Crukshank, 1804.

The Holy Bible Containing the Old and the New Testaments. Set Forth in 1611 and Commonly Known as the King James Version. New York: American Bible Society [no date].

Hoyers, Anna Owena (1584–1658). *Geistliche und Weltliche Poemata* (1650). Edited by Barbara Becker-Cantarino. Deutsche Neudrucke, Barock, 36. Tübingen: Niemeyer, 1986.

Julian of Norwich (ca. 1342 to after 1416). *Revelation of Love*. Edited and translated by John Skinner. New York: Doubleday, 1997.

Kempe, Margery (ca. 1373—ca. 1439). *The Book of Margery Kempe*. Edited by Barry Windeatt. New York: Longman, 2000.

Lead, Jane. *A Fountain of Gardens Watered by the Rivers of Divine Pleasure and Springing Up in All the Variety of Spiritual Plants*. . . . London, 1697–1701.

Mechthild of Magdeburg (1210–1297). *The Revelations of Mechthild of Magdeburg (1210–1297), or The Flowing Light of the Godhead*. London, 1953.

Petersen, Johann Wilhelm. *Das Leben Johann Wilhelmi Petersen*. . . . N.p., 1717.

Pirckheimer, Caritas (1466–1532). *Die "Denkwürdigkeiten" der Caritas Pirckheimer*. Edited by Josef Pfanner. Landshut: Solanus-Druck, 1962.

Reitz, Johann Henrich. *Historie der Wiedergebohrnen* [1698–1745]. Edited by Hans Jürgen Schrader. Deutsche Neudrucke, Barock 29. Tübingen: Niemeyer, 1982.

Rich, Mary, Countess of Warwick (1625–1678). *Autobiography of Mary Countess of Warwick*. Edited by T. Crofton Crooker. London: Percy Society, 1848.

Schurman, Anna Maria van (1607–1678). *Whether a Christian Woman Should Be Educated and Other Writings from Her Intellectual Circle*, edited and translated by Joyce L. Irwin. The Other Voice in Early Modern Europe. Chicago: University of Chicago Press, 1998.

Schwarz, Sibylle (1621–1638). *Deutsche Poetische Gedichte* (1650). Reprint, Mittlere Deutsche Literatur in Neu- und Nachdrucken, 25. Bern: Lang, 1980.

Spener, Jakob. *Pia Desideria, or Heartfelt Desire for a God-Pleasing Reform of the True Evangelical Church, Together with Several Simple Proposals Looking Toward this End* [1675–76]. Edited and translated by Theodore Trappert. Philadelphia: Fortress Press, 1964.

Teresa de Avila (1515–1582). *The Life of Saint Teresa of Avila by Herself*. Translated by J. M. Cohen. New York: Viking Penguin, 1957.

Wilson, Katharina, and Frank J. Warnke, eds. *Women Writers of the Seventeenth Century*. Athens: University of Georgia Press, 1989.

SECONDARY SOURCES

Becker-Cantarino, Barbara. *Der lange Weg zur Mündigkeit: Frau und Literatur in Deutschland, 1500–1800*. Stuttgart: Metzler, 1987.

———. "Erbauung und Autorschaft bei Johanna Eleonora Petersen (1644–1724)." In *Erbauung in der Frühen Neuzeit*, edited by Andreas Solbach. Tübingen: Niemeyer (forthcoming).

———. "'Erwählung des besseren Theils': Zur Problematik von Selbstbild und Fremdbild in Anna Maria Schurmans *Eukleria* (1673)." In *Autobiographien von Frauen:*

Beiträge zu ihrer Geschichte, edited by Magdalene Heuser, 24–48. Tübingen: Niemeyer, 1996.

————. "Pietismus und Autobiographie. Das 'Leben' der Johanna Eleonora Petersen (1644–1724)." in: *"Der Buchstab tödt — der Geist macht lebendig": Festschrift zum 60. Geburtstag von Hans-Gert Roloff,* edited by James Hardin, 930–36. Bern: Lang, 1992.

————. "Wilhelm und Johanna Eleonora Petersen und England: Die *Philadelphian Society,* Jane Lead und die Böhmisten." In *Das Theologen-Ehepaar Johann Wilhelm und Johanna Eleonora Petersen,* edited by Markus Matthias and Udo Sträter. Tübingen: Niemeyer (forthcoming).

Benstock, Shari, ed. *The Private Self: Theory and Practice of Women's Autobiographical Writings.* Chapel Hill: University of North Carolina Press, 1988.

Brecht, Martin, Klaus Deppermann, Ullrich Gäbler, and Hartmut Lehmann, eds. *Geschichte des Pietismus.* Vol. 1. Göttingen: Vandenhoeck & Ruprecht, 1993.

Bynum, Caroline Walker. "' . . . and Woman His Humanity': Female Imagery in the Religious Writing of the Later Middle Ages." In *Gender and Religion: On the Complexity of Symbols,* edited by Caroline Walker Bynum, Stevan Harrel, and Paula Richman, 257–88. Boston: Beacon Press, 1986.

————. "Women Mystics in the Thirteenth Century: The Case of the Nuns of Helfta." In *Jesus as Mother: Studies in the Spirituality of the High Middle Ages,* 170–246s. Berkeley: University of California Press, 1982.

Daly, Mary. *Beyond God the Father: Toward a Philosophy of Women's Liberation.* Boston: Beacon Press, 1973.

Davis, Natalie Zemon. *Women on the Margins: Three Seventeenth-Century Lives.* Cambridge, MA: Harvard University Press, 1995.

De Baar, Mirjam, Machteld Löwensteyn, Marit Monteiro, and A. Agnes Sneller, eds. *Choosing the Better Part: Anna Maria van Schurman (1607–1678).* Archives Internationales d'Histoire des Idées, 146. Dordrecht: Kluwer Academic Publishers, 1996.

Delaney, Paul. *British Autobiography in the Seventeenth Century.* London: Routledge & Kegan Paul, 1969.

Demers, Patricia, ed. *Women as Interpreters of the Bible.* New York: Paulist Press, 1992.

Durnbaugh, Donald F. "Pietism. A Millennial View from an American Perspective." *Pietismus und Neuzeit* 28 (2002): 11–29.

Ebner, Dean. *Autobiography in Seventeenth-Century England.* The Hague: Mouton, 1970.

Foley-Beining, Kathleen. *The Body and Eucharistic Devotion in Catharina Regina von Greiffenberg's "Meditations."* Columbia, SC: Camden House, 1977.

Fraser, Antonia. *The Weaker Vessel: Woman's Lot in Seventeenth-Century England.* London: Weidenfeld and Nicolson, 1979.

Gawthrop, Richard L. *Pietism and the Making of Eighteenth-Century Prussia.* Cambridge: Cambridge University Press, 1993.

Gibbons, B. J. *Gender in Mystical and Occult Thought: Behmenism and Its Development in England.* Cambridge: Cambridge University Press, 1996.

Gierl, Martin. *Pietismus und Aufklärung: Theologische Polemik und die Kommunikationsreform der Wissenschaft am Ende des 17. Jahrhunderts.* Veröffentlichungen des Max-Plack-Instituts für Geschichte, 129. Göttingen: Vandenhoeck & Ruprecht, 1997.

Gilmore, Leigh. *Autobiographics: A Feminist Theory of Women's Self-Representation.* Ithaca: Cornell University Press, 1993.

Gleixner, Ulrike. "Zwischen göttlicher und weltlicher Ordnung: Die Ehe im lutherischen Pietismus." *Pietismus und Neuzeit* 28 (2003): 147–84.

Goodman, Katherine R. *Amazons and Apprentices: Women and the German Parnassus in the Early Enlightenment*. Rochester, NY: Camden House, 1999.

Harth, Erica. *Cartesian Women: Versions and Subversions of Rational Discourse in the Old Regime*. Ithaca: Cornell University Press.

Hawes, Clement. *Mania and Literary Style: The Rhetoric of Enthusiasm from the Ranters to Christopher Smart*. Cambridge Studies in Eighteenth-Century Literature and Thought, 29. Cambridge: Cambridge University Press, 1996.

Heyd, Michael, ed. *Be Sober and Reasonable: The Critique of Enthusiasm in the Seventeenth and Early Eighteenth Centuries*. Leiden: E. J. Brill, 1995.

Hoffmann, Barbara. "Libertäre Sophienmystik und keusche Ehe. Wandel und Kontinuität weiblicher spiritueller Vorbilder im radikalen Pietismus (17.–18. Jh.)." In *Maria in der Welt, Marienverehrung im Kontext der Sozialgeschichte des 10. bis 18. Jahrhundert*, edited by Claudia Opitz et al., 191–209. Zurich: Chronos, 1993.

————. *Radikalpietismus um 1700: Der Streit um das Recht auf eine neue Gesellschaft*. Geschichte und Geschlechter, 15. Frankfurt: Campus Verlag, 1996.

Irwin, Joyce, "Anna Maria van Schurman and Antoinette Bourignon: Contrasting Examples of Seventeenth-Century Pietism." *Church History* 60 (1991): 301–15.

————. "Anna Maria van Schurman: From Feminism to Pietism." *Church History* (1977): 48–62.

Jacob, James R. *Henry Stubbe, Radical Protestantism, and the Early Enlightenment*. Cambridge: Cambridge University Press, 1983.

Jelinek, Estelle C., ed. *Women's Autobiography: Essays in Criticism*. Bloomington: Indiana University Press, 1980.

Kelso, Ruth. *Doctrine for the Lady of the Renaissance*. Urbana: University of Illinois Press, 1958.

King, Margaret. *Women of the Renaissance*. Chicago: Chicago University Press, 1991.

Kord, Susanne. *Little Detours: The Letters and Plays of Luise Gottsched*. Rochester, NY: Camden House, 2000.

Kormann, Eva. *Ich, Welt und Gott: Autobiographik im 17. Jahrhundert*. Cologne: Böhlau, 2004.

Langen, August. *Der Wortschatz des Pietismus*. 2d revised edition. Tübingen: Niemeyer, 1968.

Luft, Stephan. *Leben und Schreiben für den Pietismus: Der Kampf des pietistischen Ehepaares Johanna und Eleonora und Johann Wilhelm Petersen gegen die lutherische Orthodoxie*. Herzberg: Bautz, 1994

Lüthi, Kurt. "Die Erörterung der Allversöhnungslehre durch das pietistische Ehepaar Johann Wilhelm und Johanna Eleonora Petersen." *Theologische Zeitschrift* 12 (1956): 362–77.

Mack, Phyllis. *Visionary Women. Ecstatic Prophecy in Seventeenth-Century England*. Berkeley: University of California Press, 1992.

Maclean, Ian. *The Renaissance Notion of Woman: A Study in the Fortunes of Scholasticism and Medical Science in European Intellectual Life*. Cambridge: Cambridge University Press, 1980.

Martin, Lucinda. "Female Reformers as Gatekeepers of Pietism: The Example of Johanna Eleonora Merlau and William Penn." *Monatshefte* 95 (2003): 33–58.

Mason, Mary C. "The Other Voice: Autobiographies of Women Writers." In *Autobiography. Essays Theoretical and Critical,* edited by James Olney, 207–35. Princeton: Princeton University Press, 1980.

Matthias, Markus. "Enthusiastische Hermeneutik des Pietismus, dargestellt an Johanna Eleonora Petersens 'Gespräche des Herzens mit Gott' (1689)." *Pietismus und Neuzeit* 17 (1991): 36–61.

———. *Johann Wilhelm Petersen und Johanna Eleonora: Eine Biographie bis zur Amtsenthebung Petersens im Jahre 1692.* Arbeiten zur Geschichte des Pietismus, 30. Göttingen: Vandenhoeck & Ruprecht, 1993.

———. "Mutua Consolatio Sororum: Die Briefe Johanna Eleonora von Merlaus an die Herzogin Sophie Elisabeth von Sachsen-Zeitz." *Pietismus und Neuzeit* 22 (1996): 69–102.

McDowell, Paula. *The Women of Grub Street: Press, Politics, and Gender in the London Literary Marketplace, 1678–1730.* Oxford: Oxford University Press, 1998.

McGinn, Bernard. *Apocalypticism in the Western Tradition.* Variorum Collected Studies Series, CS 430. Brookfield, VT: Ashgate, 1994.

McKee, Elsie Ann. *Katharina Schütz.* 2 vols. Leiden: Brill, 1999.

McKenzie, Edgar C. "British Devotional Literature and the Rise of German Pietism." Ph.D. diss., University of St. Andrews, 1984.

———. *A Catalog of British Devotional and Religious Books in German Translation from the Reformation to 1750.* Berlin: W. de Gruyter, 1997.

Modrow, Irina. "Religiöse Erweckung und Selbstreflexion: Überlegungen zu den Lebensläufen Herrnhuter Schwestern als einem Beispiel pietistischer Selbstdarstellung." In *Ego-Dokumente: Annäherungen an den Menschen in der Geschichte,* edited by Siegfried Schulze, 121–29. Selbstzeugnisse der Neuzeit, 2. Berlin: Akademie Verlag, 1996.

Monson, Craig A. *The Crannied Wall: Women, Religion, and the Arts in Early Modern Europe.* Studies in Medieval and Early Modern Civilizations, 4. Ann Arbor: University of Michigan Press, 1992.

Moore, Cornelia. *The Maiden's Mirror: Reading Material for German Girls in the Sixteenth and Seventeenth Centuries.* Wolfenbütteler Forschungen, 36. Wiesbaden: Harrassowitz, 1987.

Nordmann, Walter. "Im Widerstreit von Mystik und Föderalismus: Geschichtliche Grundlagen der Eschatologie bei dem pietistischen Ehepaar Petersen." *Zeitschrift für Kirchengeschichte* 50 (1931): 145–85.

Olejniczak, Verena. "Heterologie: Konturen frühneuzeitlichen Selbstseins jenseits von Autonomie und Heteronomie." *LiLi* 26 (1996): 6–36.

Perry, Ruth. *The Celebrated Mary Astell: An Early English Feminist.* Chicago: University of Chicago Press, 1986.

Podmore, Colin. *The Moravian Church in England, 1728–1760.* Oxford: Clarendon Press, 1998.

Rippl, Gabriele. *Lebenstexte: Literarische Selbststilisierungen englischer Frauen in der frühen Neuzeit.* Munich: Fink, 1998.

Ritschl, Albrecht. *Geschichte des deutschen Pietismus.* [1880–86]. 3 vols. Reprint, Berlin: de Gruyter, 1966.

Saxby, T. J. *The Quest for the New Jerusalem, Jean de Labadie and the Labadists, 1610–1744.* Archives Internationales d'Histoires des Idées, 115. Dordrecht: Nijhoff, 1987.

Schmidt, Martin. "Biblisch-apokalyptische Frömmigkeit im pietistischen Adel. Johanna Eleonora Petersens Auslegung der Johannesapokalypse." In *Text, Wort, Glaube: Studien zur Überlieferung, Interpretation und Autorisierung biblischer Texte. Kurt Aland gewidmet*, edited by Martin Brecht, 344–58. Arbeiten zur Kirchengeschichte, 50. Berlin: de Gruyter, 1980.

Schneider, Hans. "Der radikale Pietismus in der neueren Forschung." *Pietismus und Neuzeit* 8 (1982): 15–42; 9 (1983): 117–51.

Schrader, Hans-Jürgen. *Literaturproduktion und Büchermarkt des radikalen Pietismus: Johann Henrich Reitz' "Historie der Wiedergebohrnen" und ihr geschichtlicher Kontext.* Palaestra, 283. Göttingen: Vandenhoeck & Ruprecht, 1989.

———. "Philadelphian Hope: The Attitudes of Pietist Immigrants in Pennsylvania towards Jews." *Pietismus und Neuzeit* 28 (2002): 185–212.

Schulze, Winfried. *Ego-Dokumente: Annäherungen an den Menschen in der Geschichte.* Selbstzeugnisse der Neuzeit, 2. Berlin: Akademie Verlag, 1996.

Smith, Catherine F. "Jane Lead: The Feminist Mind and Art of a Seventeenth-Century Protestant Mystic." In *Women of Spirit: Female Leadership in the Jewish and Christian Tradition*, edited by Rosemary Ruether and Eleonor McLaughlin, 184–203. New York: Simon and Schuster, 1979.

———. "Jane Lead's Wisdom: Women and Prophecy in Seventeenth-Century England." In *Poetic Prophecy in Western Literature*, edited by Jan Wojcik and Raymond Frontain, 55–63. London: Associated University Presses, 1983.

———. "Jane Lead: Mysticism and the Woman Clothed in the Sun." In *Shakespeare's Sisters*, edited by Sandra Gilbert and Susan Gubar, 3–18. Bloomington: Indiana University Press, 1979.

Smith, Nigel. *Perfection Proclaimed: Language and Literature in English Radical Religion, 1640–1660.* Oxford: Clarendon Press, 1989.

Sperle, Joanna Magnani. "God's Healing Angel: A Biography of Jane Lead." Ph.D. diss. (microfilm), Kent State University, 1995.

Stecher, Henry Frederic. *Elizabeth Singer Rowe, the Poetess of Frome: A Study in Eighteenth-Century English Pietism.* Europäische Hochschulschriften Reihe, 14, no. 5. Bern: Herbert Lang, 1973.

Stein, K. James. *Philipp Jakob Spener: Pietist Patriarch.* Chicago: University of Chicago Press, 1986.

Stoeffler, F. Ernest. *German Pietism during the Eighteenth Century.* Studies in the History of Religions, 24. Leiden: Brill, 1965.

Sträter, Udo. *Sonthom, Bayly, Dyke und Hall: Studien zur Rezeption der englischen Erbauungsliteratur in Deutschland im 17. Jahrhundert.* Beiträge zur historischen Theologie, 71. Tübingen: Mohr, 1987.

Taylor, Charles. *Sources of the Self: The Making of the Modern Identity.* Cambridge, MA: Harvard University Press, 1989.

Temme, Willi. *Krise der Leiblichkeit: Die Sozietät der Mutter Eva (Buttlarsche Rotte) und der radikale Pietismus um 1700.* Göttingen: Vandenhoeck & Ruprecht, 1998.

Thune, Nils. *The Behmenists and the Philadelphians.* Uppsala: Almquist and Wiksells, 1948.

Van Dülmen, Richard, ed. *Entdeckung des Ich: Die Geschichte der Individualisierung vom Mittelalter bis zur Gegenwart.* Cologne: Bölau, 2001.

Ward, Reginald. *The Protestant Evangelical Awakening.* Cambridge: Cambridge University Press, 1992.

Walker, D. P. *The Decline of Hell: Seventeenth-Century Discussions of Eternal Torment.* Chicago: University of Chicago Press, 1964.

Wallmann, Johannes. *Philipp Jakob Spener und die Anfänge des Pietismus.* Beiträge zur historischen Theologie, 42. 2d revised edition. Tübingen: Mohr, 1986.

Wiesner, Merry. *Gender, Chrurch, and State in Early Modern Germany.* London: Longman, 1998.

Wilson, Renate. "Continental Protestant Refugees and Their Protectors in Germany and London: Commercial and Charitable Networks." *Pietismus und Neuzeit* 20 (1995): 107–24.

Witt, Ulrike. *Bekehrung, Bildung und Biographie: Frauen im Umkreis des Halleschen Pietismus.* Hallesche Forschungen, 2. Tübingen: Niemeyer, 1996

Wodtke, Verena, ed. *Auf den Spuren der Weisheit: Sophia, Wegweiserin für ein neues Gottesbild.* Freiburg im Breisgau: Herder, 1991.

Woods, Jean, and Maria Fürstenwald, eds. *Schriftstellerinnen: Künstlerinnen und gelehrte Frauen des deutschen Barock. Ein Lexikon.* Stuttgart: Metzler, 1984.

Wright, Luella. *The Literary Life of the Early Friends.* New York: Columbia University Press, 1932.

THE LIFE OF LADY JOHANNA ELEONORA PETERSEN, NÉE VON UND ZU MERLAU, WIFE OF DR. JOHANN WILHELM PETERSEN, WRITTEN BY HERSELF AND PUBLISHED BECAUSE OF MANY EDIFYING EVENTS, BEFITTING AS A SEQUEL TO HER HUSBAND'S MEMOIRS. PAID FOR BY WORTHY FRIENDS (1718).[1] A SHORT NARRATION OF HOW GOD'S GUIDING HAND HAS LED ME HITHER AND WHAT HE HAS DONE FOR MY SOUL.

EDITOR'S INTRODUCTION

Johanna Eleonora Petersen first published her autobiography at the age of forty-five, an account from childhood until her early married years, under the title *A Short Narration of How God's Guiding Hand Has Lead Me Until Now and What He Has Done For My Soul*. She appended this "narration" as the final section to her first devotional publication, *The Heart's Conversations with God*, in 1689 (see the annotated bibliography of Petersen's works). This version was expanded (to sixty-seven printed pages) in a publication almost thirty years later (1718) and appeared together with her husband's autobiography, but as a separate part with its own title page: "The Life of Lady Johanna Eleonora Petersen, née von und zu Merlau, Wife of Dr. Johann Petersen. Written by Herself and Given to the Public Because of Many Edifying Events, As a

---

1. "Worthy friends" was a formula for an anonymous donor; neither the publisher nor the place of publication was mentioned on the title page. The publisher was most likely Johann Gottfried Renger, active in Halle from 1698 to 1718, because on the last pages of the autobiography volume Renger advertised books to be found at the Leipzig book fair. Halle was the new center of Pietism; August Hermann Francke had built his schools there after his professorial appointment at the new University of Halle in 1692. The Petersens had visited Halle and corresponded with Francke.

Sequel to Her Husband's. Payed for by Worthy Friends" published in 1718 (see the annotated bibliography). Johann Wilhelm Petersen's autobiography makes up the first part of the volume. The husband's life is fashioned like a professional scholar's vita as the title indicates: *The Life of Jo. Wilhelm Petersen, Doctor of Theology, Formerly Professor at Rostock, then Preacher at St. Egid's in Hannover, After that Superintendent for the Bishop of Lübeck and Court Chaplain, Finally Superintendent in Lüneburg. As Witness to Christ's Truth and His Realm, According to His Great Economy in the Return of All Things. Printed at the End of 1717, at the Expense of Good Friends.* The husband's autobiography is about three times as long, wordy, and defensive of his theological dogmas and professional activities.

My translation of Johanna Eleonora Petersen's autobiography follows the 1718 edition, which comprises the "Narration" of 1689 augmented by the addition of some twenty-two pages. A short transitional section has been inserted between the old and the new part, and the division of the text into thirty-eight long, thematic paragraphs is new here. Some very minor changes in wording are insignificant and probably due to printer's errors or corrections.

My translation into English intentionally stays close to the original for two reasons. Johanna Eleonora Petersen's German is, on the surface, disarmingly plain and accessible even today, because it is based in biblical language, often called "Luther's German," because Luther's translation of the Bible was so successful that it became the common language for Protestants and to a large extent also for Catholics by the late seventeenth century. It superseded the regional dialects as the *written* language in printed books (not as the spoken language). "Luther's German" was the language used in sermons, prayer books, and devotional literature, by far the most popular and most widely read literature until the second half of the eighteenth century in the German-speaking lands.

The notes are intended to aid in an immediate understanding of the text only; further historical, cultural, and theological information and discussion of issues raised in the autobiography can be found in the preceding introduction. Occasionally, the German word for a key term is given in the note. Readers interested in the German text can now consult a modern edition of Petersen's *Leben* by Guglia Guglielmetti, in Kleine Texte des Pietismus 8 (Leipzig: Evangelische Verlagsanstalt, 2003).

TRANSLATION

§ 1. So that you, dear reader, will know how wonderfully the Lord has guided me since my childhood and has drawn me to him on many occasions, I have written down the story of my life[2] in a short version; especially since I, following the example of the Savior, had to endure many and various libels and lies. For many people resented that in my young years I did not run along with the crowd in a wasteful life, and they derided me for this. Some said I must have committed a great sin, because I wanted to atone in such a way; others said I had lost my senses, since the devil was in me and that my behavior was from the devil. I would not do good and would meet a bad end, and more such things. And when I could not be deterred by these and similar accusations, but tried to choose the path of truth and to pursue it, more malicious libel began that I was wrong in my faith. Soon they accused me of this, then of another heretical act of which I had never heard nor seen anything. In the beginning this was very strange to me, because I lived a simple life according to holy scripture and according to the words that the preachers uttered from the pulpit on how one should live. And when I tried to follow them, when I talked about them and went along, I was attacked, though I was considered Christian and virtuous in many places then. However, when I strove to become a doer of such words (according to my lowly status), I was accused from that moment on of many errors, so that I became very upset. And I felt compelled to talk to my God with the following prayer: *Oh my God, you see my heart and that I seek nothing more than to do what I have heard of your word, and in the sermon of the word; you have moved me to this, since you have revealed to me in holy scripture that he who listens to your word without doing it resembles a foolish man and that not those who say Lord, oh Lord, will go to heaven, but those who do your bidding. Now, that I have turned my heart to you, have let your spirit move me to do what pleases you, it seems strange not only to the godless people but also to those who carry such words in their mouth whose doer I would like to be. Oh my God! Reveal to me why I am offensive to my neighbor; you see that I do not seek a new way but am only a follower of your beloved son whom you have given me as a model so that I may follow in his footsteps. Why does it confound those who read your word and who know that I seek nothing but what is said in your word and what has been demanded? It is a sign of our love that we keep your commandments. What is it, my Lord?* Such words I had with my Lord until it was revealed to me from his word that it had to be thus: the beautiful words of grace blind mankind. The word and the power of the deed

---

2. The author uses here the expression *Lebenslauf* (life's course), also used by her spiritual mentor Johann Jakob Spener for his autobiography. See the volume editor's introduction, p. 40.

have been mocked for a long time. Thereupon I was content and learned to be happy that I would be worthy to be derided because of his holy name. Almost daily I received new humiliation but also a new strength and grace in the word and in the recognition of all the good we have in Christ. Indeed, I learned that what Paul says is a holy truth: "Yea, and all that will live godly in Jesus Christ shall suffer persecution."[3]

§ 2. Only when we bend under the Father's hand and accept the punishment do we learn how much such holy guidance by the Lord who tests his children through temptation can benefit us. Then we understand the lesson of the cross, then we see how beneficial this is and how the people's gossip gives us cause for a strict examination of how we stand before God: whether we have something about us that we do not know as yet, whether we earlier believed something evil about others, whether we gave way to the gossip to believe or to repeat what we had heard, and whether we agreed with it and thought that there was something to it. These and similar impurities are being purged out by such sufferings,[4] and we are made observant of all that happens to us.

§ 3. I wanted to place this as an introduction to my life[5] so that the Christian reader will not take it amiss when reading in my little treatise[6] that I speak of much uncleanliness and complain as if the slander of the deceitful world were true, and that such things had driven me to leave this world and its indifference.[7] I am witness before God that it was the Lord's power and his almighty word that led me away from worldly pleasures, that it was God who saved me from the crude sins that this world can punish, and that there will be no one on earth who can truthfully prove only one of all the scandalous things said about me. Everyone will have to confess that what they have heard and credulously believed were other people's hot air and words. On

3. 2 Tim. 3:11. Translations from the Bible are all taken from the King James Version (1611), which corresponds most closely to Petersen's biblical German.

4. The 1689 edition reads "in solcherley Leyden" (in such sufferings); the 1718 edition has "in solcherley Leuten" (in these people). The latter is probably a misprint or copyist's error.

5. The author uses here the word *Leben* (life) to stress the congruence of her "narration" with her actual life.

6. The author calls her autobiography here *mein Tractätlein* (my little tract or treatise), since she expresses firm opinions in it and argues against those who scorned her religious turn.

7. The term *Gleichstellung der Welt* (worldly indifference) refers to the *adiaphora*, practices of secondary importance, worldly things that are morally indifferent—that is, neither bad nor good. In the late seventeenth century, Pietists and orthodox Lutherans disputed whether such activities as dancing, theater, and playing games of cards were "indifferent" or morally reprehensible. The author represents those who rejected these activities for themselves (and for true Christians), because they detracted from the path to God.

the contrary, I can assure you with humility in my heart that there are still many people alive who have witnessed my life from childhood on and who have praised God's grace in me.

What I have written in my little book[8] aims at totally different things. It speaks of the evil in our heart that we have to acknowledge if we want to recognize Jesus Christ, his holy service, and the forgiveness of our sins. For how will he who does not know man's condition after Adam's fall[9] recognize the Savior? Or, how can he who has not felt the misery in which he exists believe in the necessity of precious salvation, each according to his own measure, inasmuch as he partakes in Christ or as he is in need for his self-awareness, and for his heart's true humility that only comes from self-recognition?[10] I thank my Lord that he hid his grace from me for a short moment and that he let me recognize my inability to do good and the wicked nature of the human heart, so that I may understand in truth that all we think, talk, and act is grace; and that there is no sin so great that we might not fall into if we lack grace. Therefore I have not prided myself in God's grace, have not considered myself better than others who fell into evil sin, but I have only God's grace to thank for protecting me. And I have realized that for some of us, who recognize our own wickedness, our fall would turn out for the better, while the hypocrites falsely believe they are just and good. But they have not yet washed off their profanity and they are inflated in vain in their mortal mind. I say this so that you do not think I would pride myself in not falling into such sins because of God's grace. Rather, with all my heart I credit everything to God's grace and understand that likewise within me is the sordid ground from which all kinds of impure desires might arise if we tolerate it. Sin had to be created not that we have a cause for pride, but so that we work for our salvation with fear and trembling, according to the words of Saint Paul.[11]

§ 4. The fear of the Lord has protected me and his grace and faithfulness have guided me; to him alone be praise, honor, and glory. I am writing

---

8. The author uses the diminutive my *Büchlein* (little book), a trope of modesty for her own publication; this section of her autobiography had been appended in 1689 to her first published work *The Heart's Conversations with God*, a devotional book.

9. How to overcome hereditary sin was a much discussed and disputed question; Pietists like the Petersens elaborated the ancient doctrine of universal salvation and the restoration of all things; see also § 31 below.

10. The author uses the term *Selbst-Erkenntnis*, then a modern coinage for the individual's self-reflection to gain self-awareness, here in the theological sense. The mind is illuminated by the knowledge of God, and illumination is a gradual process of increasing self-awareness; this almost approaches the Calvinist theology of knowledge.

11. "Work out your own salvation with fear and trembling," Phil. 2:12.

this so that you, dear reader, may recognize his manifold wisdom, how he attracts people to him in sundry ways, some in their tender youth, others at a more advanced age. As far as I am concerned, I have felt the influence of his kind spirit since early childhood but I have often opposed this same kind spirit out of ignorance. I have hindered him with many a worldly activity[12] because of my mundane nobility, until I came to my senses when the wholesome word affected me with its persuasive power. For when I was about four years old it happened that my parents, who had lived in Frankfurt for a while because of the war,[13] moved back into the country since there was peace everywhere; many things had been taken again into the country. Also my late mother with my two sisters and myself moved to the Philippseck estate near Heddernheim[14] and all went well. One day the servants came and reported that a company of soldiers on horseback was approaching. Everyone quickly tried to save his own possessions and left my mother alone with three small children. The oldest was seven, I was four years old, and the youngest was still a baby. My mother took her youngest in her arm, took us other two children by the hand, and walked without a nursemaid all the way to Frankfurt, a distance of well over five miles.[15] It was summer and the corn was in the fields. We could hear the noise of the soldiers passing by on another road, only a pistol shot away. My mother became very frightened and admonished us to pray. When we had reached the city gates and were safe, my mother sat down with us and made us thank the Lord for protecting us. My oldest sister who was three years older than I said: "Why should we thank the Lord now when they can no longer attack us?" Then I felt a deep concern in my heart about these words: it hurt me that she did not want to thank the Lord and thought it was no longer necessary. I chided her for this out of a fervent love for God, whom I thanked with all my heart. Likewise, when I was told that it is the midwife[16] who brings little children from heaven, I felt the desire to talk to her. I told her to give my greetings to Jesus, and I wanted to know

12. *Gleichstellung*, see note 7.

13. The Thirty Years' War ended with the Peace of Westphalia, or Münster and Osnabrück (two neighboring towns in northern Germany, then Westphalia), in 1648.

14. The knightly manor of Philippseck was situated in the village of Heddernheim, today a suburb of Frankfurt.

15. The author is using a "large" or "land mile" of about fifteen thousand feet (about three modern miles); the actual length of a mile (one thousand Roman steps) varied considerably in each European country and within the various German principalities in the seventeenth century.

16. For "midwife," the author uses the central German term *Bademutter* (bath mother), derived from the ritual bath (water with some salt and holy water) for newborns; in other parts of Germany it is supposed to be the stork who brings the babies.

from her whether Jesus loved me, too, which I felt with all my heart. These were the first thoughts in childhood of which I can recall only very little.

§ 5. When I was six years old and my mother was once again about to give birth, I noticed that my mother was crying a lot. Then I asked my oldest sister what the reason for my mother's crying was. She told me that a well-known noblewoman had turned into a whore. I did not really know what a whore was, but I thought that it had to be something very bad since my mother was crying so hard. I went outside alone, fell on my knees, and prayed to God with tears that he should protect me that I would not become a whore. The Lord has listened to this simple child's prayer, and he not only saved me from any such situation but also gave me a heart that abhors uncouth talk and gestures, so that I stayed only with such people as were honorable and refined. Nevertheless, the malicious gossip-devil has spread his lies against me through his instruments, fabricating the rumor that my sister's daughter who has been living with me was my illegitimate child and that she was born in Praunheim, an hour's way from Frankfurt, and baptized by the minister Johann Harff who is still living. However, at that time I lived more than two hundred miles away at court and I returned home only nine years later. Her father is a von Praunheim and her mother is my middle sister.[17] Thus the devil does not shy away from telling gross, obvious lies that for a child of God are not worth complaining about, since anyone who loves the truth can easily find out that such gossip is nothing but lies, especially since there are people who travel to these places where one can find out the truth..

§ 6. When I was nine years old, we lost our mother and we had a very difficult time. Since our father lived at court[18] quite a distance away from our estate, he hired a teacher's widow for the household, who had her own children in the village and who gave to them what was ours. She let us starve so that we often gladly ate what others did not want. She also had the habit of often leaving us alone in the house when people dressed in white robes, their faces covered with honey and flour, walked around with torches in the house, forced open chests and cupboards and took what they wanted. We were so frightened by this that we hid behind the stove in fear. This happened until the house was almost empty. Since our father was very strict

17. Johanna Eleonora was the godmother of her niece Anna Elisabeth Eleonora Magdalena von Praunheim, one of the daughters of her middle sister, Christina Sibylle Maria Philippina, who was married to Wilhelm von und zu Praunheim, the owner of a neighboring estate.

18. The father Georg Adolph von Merlau (died 1681) served as steward of the household to the Landgrave Wilhelm Christoph of Hessen-Homburg (reigned 1650–1669) in Homburg, a residential city near Frankfurt.

with us, we did not dare tell him, but we were relieved when he had gone again. We suffered through this for a long time until one day von Praunheim (who is now married to my sister and who was then very young) visited us and we told him about our troubles. He decided to stay in the house until evening to see if the ghosts would come again. When the ghosts arrived, went to the cupboard, forced it open and were about to take things from it, Praunheim jumped out of his hiding place and discovered that they were people from the village, sons of a coach builder, who were well acquainted with the widow. But since he was alone, they escaped and denied that they were the thieves. But the ghosts did not reappear and we retrieved also many things that they had hidden in the attic above our kitchen.

§ 7. Our father dismissed the widow and hired a captain's wife who had a good reputation as a housekeeper and in other areas as well. Now our father believed he had provided for us well. But she was an un-Christian woman who had not yet forgotten her soldier's tricks. For when she once saw a group of wild turkeys, she had them driven into the house, grabbed the best one and let the others escape. She wanted to have dry wood with which to cook this stolen roast and sent me to get it from a tower five stories high. The tower was built like a square and where a pigeon house had been in the attic there were a number of dry boards, some loose, some still nailed down. I was to get some of that wood. After I had thrown down several pieces of wood, I pulled so hard at a plank that was still partly nailed down that I bounced back, fell down two flights of stairs and came to rest so close to another set of stairs that I would have tumbled down two more flights, if I had moved. I lay there unconscious for about half an hour and did not know anything about it until I regained my senses. At first I did not know how I had gotten to this place; I got up and realized that I was very weak, climbed down the stairs and lay down in a bed that was in one of the tower's rooms and in which my father used to sleep when he was home. I slept several hours; then I got up and felt refreshed and well. During all this time nobody looked for me, and when I said that I fell down two flights of stairs I was scolded for not having used more caution. I turned away and did not want to eat anything of the stolen roast; it seemed a real disgrace for me, but I did not dare say anything.

§ 8. When I was ten years old going on eleven my older sister, who was three years my senior, was sent to the minister to be taught about the holy communion.[19] Then I felt a strong desire to go along, but my father did not

19. The customary age for the Lutheran confirmation, official introduction into the church with a first communion preceded by catechism classes, was fourteen; it also meant the official

want me to participate because I had recently had only my tenth birthday. I pleaded so long that my father agreed on the condition that the minister find me ready to understand not only the words but also the meaning. God gave me such grace with my answers that I was admitted by the minister with pleasure. But the devil planned again a trick for me: a close relative who also attended the lessons told the other children that I had said I would drink much from the sacred chalice—this was told in a way that made it seem I was crazy for wine. This was neither my thinking nor my words. I was really distraught about such talk, and when the minister learned about it he first thought that my youth had made me say such childish things. But when he learned that I denied it with great sorrow and that I showed the proper devotion for the sacred chalice (which is the communion with Christ), he recognized my innocence and scolded the liar for merely inventing the lie, and she confessed that she had.

§ 9. Some time later my sister was sent to Stuttgart to my father's brother[20] and I had to take over the household and all the accounting. This was very difficult for me, because my father, whenever he returned home, was very strict with me and scolded me for everything that was broken or otherwise not to his liking. Often he punished me without reason. Such a slavish fear beset me that I trembled whenever I heard a voice that was like my father's. I sent many a sigh to God because of this, but when my father had gone I was again happy and content, was singing and skipping up and down, was of high spirits but had at the same time a real distaste for what was lewd or childish. I likewise did not want to have anything to do with wedding games, baptisms and the like, and was embarrassed by them.

§ 10. When I was twelve years old, I was sent to the court of the Countess of Solms-Rödelheim,[21] who was to fall mentally ill six weeks into her pregnancy. But at that time she was still relatively well. When she had given birth to twins, a girl and a boy, she got worse from day to day so that she several times mistook me for her dog, which looked like a baby lion. She

---

end of childhood and for girls the beginning of their marriageable state. The Pietists stressed the educational aspect: the church was to teach piety, repentance, and personal faith. The confirmation became an important public ceremony for the teenager.

20. Johanna Eleonora's uncle, her father's older brother, was Albert Otto von Merlau (1616–1679), privy councillor to the Duke of Württemberg, serving at an important court. The sister was to be introduced there to court society and to find a husband in her social class.

21. Eleonora Barbara Maria von Solms-Rödelheim, née Creutz von Scharffenstein (1629–1680), was mentally unstable. The arrangements for Johanna Eleonora had been made hurriedly in 1657, because the Philippseck estate had been forcefully occupied by another nobleman and the three daughters needed a place to live; the Solms-Rödelheim were neighbors. Rödelheim is in the vicinity of Frankfurt.

called me by the dog's name and beat me. It also happened that we took
a boat several times, since the meadows between Frankfurt and Rödelheim
were flooded and the water reached up to the stagecoaches. Then coaches
went empty and we used boats to the very end of the water and then entered
the coaches. She tried to push me into the water, telling me I was to swim.[22]
But the Lord saved me. One time I happened to notice that she took a knife
from a cupboard and carried it with her in a sheath. I told the chambermaid,
who was already a bit elderly, about it. But she did not want to believe me
and said that the countess did not carry a knife, I had invented a childish
story. The countess's bedroom was connected with ours through a door and
the count had to pass our suite to get to the countess. On the other side of
the countess's room was a door to the count's chamber. When night came
and everyone was to go to bed, I did not want to lie down, because the knife
was on my mind. The chambermaid was angry with me and threatened to
tell the count how childish I was. Thus I lay down on my bed fully dressed.
During the night I heard a clamor, I woke up everybody, and climbed out of
bed. Then we heard the count running from his chamber and after him the
countess with a night light and the bare knife in her hand. When she saw
all of us awake, she got frightened and dropped the knife. Then I stepped
forward as if I were to hand the knife to her but instead I ran down the stairs
with it into the dark. When I was at the stairs I heard the count yell, "Where
is my wife?" I answered that I had the knife, but I was so afraid that I did
not dare to return but entered into a large room, the so-called Great Hall, a
very intimidating place. Here I remained. The chambermaid, who was from
Bohemia, a serf[23] of the countess's mother who lived in Bohemia, left and did
not return. For several weeks I was alone with the countess and had to dress
and undress her by myself. This was a very difficult time for me.

§ 11. Somebody informed my father that I was in such danger
and he took me away from there. Then I came to the Duchess von
Holstein-Sonderburg.[24] Her husband Duke Philipp Ludwig II von Holstein-

22. Not yet a sport in those days, most people did not know how to swim. A trial by water,
pushing a suspected criminal and especially witches into the water often loaded with stones,
was customary. The swimming episode may have been a test of, or allusion to, witchcraft.

23. In most parts of central Europe peasants were still serfs (*Leibeigene*), personal property of the
landed gentry; their labor belonged to their master (or landowner), who had to approve their
residence and marriage, and also owned their children.

24. Anna Margaretha von Holstein-Sonderburg, née von Hessen-Homburg (1629–1686), was
married to Duke Philipp Ludwig von Holstein-Sonderburg and lived in Wiesenburg near the
city of Zwickau in Saxony. She was Johanna Eleonora's godmother. The position of lady-in-
waiting (*Hofjungfer*) entailed helping the women in the ducal family with dressing, all social
events, and often also reading aloud to the duchess.

Sonderburg had a daughter from his first marriage who was to be married to Count Sinzendorff, an Imperial Chamber president. I was about fifteen years old and was employed as lady-in-waiting for this noble bride, who already had one lady-in-waiting, a thirty-year-old Lady von Steinling. Soon after I arrived, we set out for Linz[25] where the wedding was to be celebrated. We traveled on the river Danube. It was a merry time when trumpets and drums resounded on the water and the entire company was received royally everywhere thanks to the efforts of those who were sent to meet the noble bride. This was a very happy time for me compared to my former fears, of which none were left except that I often wondered whether it would harm my soul because I was going to a popish place.[26] Whenever we returned to our quarters, I looked for a quiet place, fell on my knees, and prayed that God might prevent any harm to my salvation. The bride's lady-in-waiting noticed this, followed me one day, and wanted to know what I was doing all by myself, since she considered me to be still rather childish because of my small size. When she found me on my knees praying she quietly left again so that I did not know that she had seen me. When the noble bride later asked if I prayed, the lady-in-waiting answered in my place that this was not a matter of concern. Then I realized that she had seen me praying. When we came to Linz, the wedding was celebrated in the imperial castle and everything was very elaborate. On the second day the noble bride had to enter the chapel to be blessed, and a golden cup with wine was presented to her from which she and the count had to drink. They called it Saint John's blessing.[27] I prayed to God that he save me from the popish. After the wedding when everyone was to return to their own place, a quarrel about me arose between my duke and the Imperial Chamber president. The latter said he could not take more than one lady-in-waiting to his table and that the other one would have to eat with the head housekeeper. The duke did not want to agree to this and said that the housekeeper was only of the bourgeois class. Thus I would likewise be treated like a bourgeois, although I was from an old noble family and no less than the other lady-in-waiting. A

25. Austrian city on the Danube.

26. Linz is Catholic, as is all of Austria and most of southern Germany. In the seventeenth century Protestants commonly used the derogative term popish (*Papistisch*) for Catholics. Fear of Catholics was widespread in Protestant areas of Europe because of the forced conversions to Catholicism under the Hapsburgs. In 1678 the (imaginary) Popish Plot led to antipapal tracts and the ensuing anti-Catholic mass hysteria also in England.

27. The *Johannissegen* is an old Catholic marriage custom in Germany; in a special mass and with wine blessed on the Apostle's Day (December 27), the priest wishes for conjugal love for the newlyweds in the name of John the Evangelist, who was known for his affection and love.

great difference would be made between us and he could not agree to that, since I was his wife's godchild.

§ 12. When this argument did not convince the other side, they decided to take me back with them. When this decision was announced to me with the reasons for it, I could not help but consider it very strange that for such a reason I was to return with them. For I would have preferred to eat with the head housekeeper rather than with my duke and duchess. What I did not know then was that God's mercy had arranged for this and that he had heard my prayers. I learned this later when I was told that all the persons who traveled with us including the princess herself had converted to the popish religion! Then I saw God's ways on my poor soul and praised the Lord. But I had been very sad that I was sent back and thought that people might say I had not been serviceable enough. Also, I was afraid of coming again under the supervision of my strict father.

§ 13. When we returned to Lißborg,[28] which belonged to the Landgrave of Darmstadt and was only on loan to my duke as a security, and when we then moved to Saxony, because he received the castle at Wiesenburg[29]— ten large miles from Leipzig and one large mile from Zwickau—from the Elector of Saxony, the duchess decided to keep me with her. I perfected all kinds of skills and tasks so that I became popular. Even in dancing I was the best, which flattered my vanity. Thus I became interested in luxurious clothing and the like, which looked good on me and was praised by everyone. There was no one who said this was not right, but everyone praised such vanities and considered me blessed and pious, because I read, prayed, and went to church and was often able to recapitulate the sermons in every detail. I remembered what had been said about the biblical passage the year before. This pleased everybody. I was considered a pious lady by all, clerics and laypeople, although I led a life with love and desire for the goods of this world. I had not yet entered the following of Christ.

§ 14. God's grace arranged for the son of a lieutenant by the name of Bretewitz to fall in love with me. When he had his father ask my employer and he himself asked my father for my hand, all agreed. He was to serve one year as a cornet,[30] then he was to receive his father's military command. His father was a lieutenant colonel in the employ of the Elector of Saxony, and

---

28. Lissberg was a castle (now a small town) north of Haunau in Wetteravia, Hesse.

29. Duke Johann Georg II von Holstein-Sonderburg purchased the estate of Wiesenburg, a castle with some surrounding territory—the small city of Kirchberg and twenty-two villages— from the Elector of Saxony in 1664.

30. A cornet was a junior position in the cavalry.

the company was stationed in the country. When he had joined the army, I heard from various sides that his life was not pious but rather worldly. I was secretly very sad about this and lay down on my face before God and prayed that either he change his mind or that our betrothal be dissolved. I did not know that the Lord had let this happen so that I would be saved from other marriages with noblemen. I was then still young and several matches were offered that were prevented by this betrothal, even though he had changed some and he accepted an employment here and there. That lasted for several years, during which time I suffered secretly, and worldly joys became less and less important for me. I had to participate, but my heart was not in it as it had been before when I was pleased to be praised very much. Then the noblewomen who came to court with their daughters admonished them to watch my manners and to imitate them, because my elders liked them. During these years, von Bretewitz changed ten times, his views were different, he was pursuing different things, and when they failed he turned around and wrote about constancy. All this I left to the Highest and I tried to be closer to God.

§ 15. I found solace in scripture, asleep in god-sent dreams when speaking God's words with such force, and then awakening so that my roommate who had a God-fearing heart was very much saddened by it, since she did not receive such messages. I always consoled her saying that she should consider me a child whom the father is enticing with sugar. She, on the other hand, was someone who had proven herself and who did not need such enticements. This was after my heart, for I saw that the world was pulling me toward it because of the cheerful spirit that was in me. But God pulled me over to his side through his joyfulness and love, and he often revealed the word to me so that my heart and my soul rejoiced. I was strengthened in this more and more.

§ 16. Then the person who had changed his mind so many times came and visited our court. He disliked my spiritual nature and mind, because he thought it unfit for a soldier's wife to read so much in the Bible. He would have liked me to renounce him, because his father had found a wealthy bride for him in Dresden, if he could properly dissolve the engagement with me. He did not want to be known as unfaithful, but he would have liked for me to be the one. But I remained quiet[31] and did not take offense, and I trusted the Heavenly Father that he would do it right. When all this dragged on

---

31. The author repeatedly uses the phrase *ich blieb still* (I remained quiet), a reference to Quietism, a mystical brand of Pietism, with its emphasis on humility, Christ-centeredness and trials associated with religious experience. Quietists such as Miguel de Molinos (1640–1697), An-

and on, a person called von Fresen realized that all this was treacherous and wanted to warn me. He thought that I had not noticed that von Bretewitz was dishonest. He sent me a letter, because he had no chance to talk to me, since I was almost always in my lady's chamber. Bretewitz got hold of this letter and believed he had evidence for accusing me of liking other men or having affairs with them. His father who then happened to be present likewise felt that it would be a good thing for them and that they could now arrange politely a wealthy marriage contract; he went to the duke and showed him the letter as proof that others were negotiating a wedding with me and that his son had no chance with me but had to look elsewhere for his happiness. The duke was annoyed to hear this about me, since I had until then to his surprise declined many opportunities and turned down all offers. A good friend reported that this was said about me. But I did not know what was in the letter and had not even given permission for Friesen to talk to me. Then I thought to myself: God almighty, you know that many a treachery has been plotted against me and that for my conscience's sake I have been quiet and have endured all changes and given the matter over to you. How can this unfaithful man now be considered faithful, and I with my loyalty disloyal? I was in great pain and very much embarrassed that my duke and duchess should think of me in such a way. When I went into my chamber in tears, the words came to me: "What I do thou knowest not now; but thou shalt know hereafter."[32] Then I was content and thought the Lord would make things right; innocence lies open before him and what are men other than mortals who perish like this matter will perish. The next day the letter was read more thoroughly and it turned out that the person was asking for an opportunity to talk to me in order to express his appreciation and honest love for me, since he knew how false the other one had acted against me by preventing me from accepting another's offer. Then they realized that I was innocent and that I had not acted unfaithfully. Von Bretewitz could not proceed. The duke and the duchess asked my opinion in order to conclude this matter. Then I asked that von Bretewitz not be compelled to marry me, since I had enough reasons to believe that they would like to find something against me. Von Bretewitz sent two gentlemen to me to find out how I was disposed toward him, whether I would want to wait for some time for his happiness. I gave him back his freedom, to find his happiness wherever he

toinette Bourignon (1616–1680), and Madame de la Mothe Guyon (1648–1717) were Catholic, but many of them renounced the church that persecuted Quietists severely at that time.

32. John 13:7. This quote is Jesus' reply to Peter when he asked why Jesus was washing the disciples' feet at the Last Supper.

wanted, for I felt no longer obliged to turn my mind to such an unfaithful heart who would have accused me of all kinds of disloyalty if that had been possible. Then came a false compliment, as if he were sorry that such misunderstandings had happened, but this now would mean that he had no more obligations toward me. The wealthy marriage did not take place; it was thereafter canceled.

§ 17. I was no longer troubled by anything else, but I recognized that through such an opportunity God had given freedom to my questioning mind,[33] since I was always worried with the thought that I would disappoint him or that this or that might not be true. Thus I was freed from this burden and gained so much strength that I no longer considered marriage at all. Rather, I was constantly thinking about how much abuse of Christianity there was among the nobility: for one, they have more opportunity and occasion for drinking than other persons of quality; secondly, they have to risk body and soul for every injustice and careless word, lest they appear dishonorable.[34] These things made me think about the fact that very evil things happen in Christianity, that people can consider themselves Christians but live totally contrary to Christ's teachings and that they are not even told to drop such customs or to leave the community of Christ. That took away from me all desire to marry. For, though I had known some very fine persons who abhorred such things, I thought that surely the offspring would be placed in danger. Thus I turned away from marriage as if not a single male person was living in this world who could be of interest to me. I would not be allowed to marry a person of another class, I thought, since my father strictly held to his old lineage.

§ 18. When later after some time a cleric in a high office[35] showed interest in me and traveled a long distance in order to persuade me to marry him, I had a tough fight in my mind because I did not want to marry. Then after a long struggle I had to put myself into the Lord's hands. I left it up to my mortal father from whom I wanted to learn the will of the Heavenly Father. But before I did this, I wrote to two pious men who were well known

33. The author recognizes her *streitendes Gemüthe* (questioning mind), an important feature to find the right path; this was characteristic of religious dissenters.

34. The honor code of the nobility required men to duel over verbal or other perceived infractions; in this ritual usually one of the two was killed, a custom that was officially outlawed and only very slowly eliminated in the nineteenth century.

35. The minister was Johann Winckler, a widower and well connected in Pietist circles. The author does not mention that it was her father's older brother Albert Otto von Merlau who objected to this marriage with a commoner. This episode took place in 1674 when Johanna Eleonora was about thirty years old.

to me for their true devotion, and I put some questions to them. The answers were such that I knew of no escape in my mind but that I would let God's will speak. I believed I would learn his will through my father's will. My late father announced his decision to my duke and duchess, and they sent their decision to the cleric. I had insisted on my father's decision, and did not want to say either yes or no. My father's "yes" was to be my "yes," and his "no" was my "no." Then my father made up his mind and said no, and no it was. Until the news had come back from my father, who was then two hundred miles away from us, and until they had reached the cleric, I was considered a bride at court whether I liked it or not. At court nobody thought that my father, after having given me over to the noble family, could still make any decisions on my behalf; and had the cleric insisted on this, it would have become a quarrelsome affair. But this was not the Lord's will; the cleric accepted my father's "no" and was content with it. Then I felt a new disgrace in my heart, because I noticed that there was much talk about this event.

§ 19. But all these tribulations were for the benefit of my soul so that it would enter into God's tranquility. And God showed me more and more of his grace. For I had met two venerable servants of God from Frankfurt before this last marriage proposal took place. Because of the illness of our oldest princess, the entire family traveled to Bad Ems[36] and I became acquainted through God's wondrous ways at first with one pious friend,[37] since he got to sit next to me on the boat with which we traveled to Bad Ems. We entered into a spiritual conversation that lasted several hours, so that the twenty miles from Frankfurt to Mainz, where he disembarked, appeared less than a quarter of an hour to me. We talked together without stopping and it was as if he were looking into my heart and everything that had given me doubts until then came out. Not a word was lost that was not in God's spirit. I remembered all when the time came for actual practice. Yes, I found in this friend what I had doubted would exist in anyone in this world, because I had looked for so long to see whether there were true active Christians,[38] and not finding any I had given up. When I realized that this man had such an insight and that he could see to the bottom of my heart and that he showed such

36. Bad Ems in the Taunus Mountains northwest of Frankfurt is a spa still populartoday; so is visiting one of the many German spas for a stay of several weeks as a "cure" for all kinds of illnesses.

37. This was the eminent theologian Philipp Jakob Spener (1635–1705), the father of German Lutheran Pietism. See the volume editor's introduction, p. 8.

38. The author uses a term here that becomes the guiding light of her own life: to be an active Christian, *Täter des Wortes* ("doer" of God's word).

humility, meekness, clemency, holy love, and seriousness in revealing the path of truth, I was really comforted and fortified. I tried to break away from those whom my ignorance had prevented me turning away from until then. And I parted with those who could have helped me advance but who instead had made me grow doubtful about the things I was laboring under as if they were unworthy to be thought about. But when I realized that my friend's mind and God's word were one, that all doubts about not knowing anyone had disappeared, that he followed the word of the Lord in all simplicity and talked to me as if it were not so simple to understand that one should do it, and that there was enough knowledge though I saw no one using it—then I was strengthened by my new friend in believing that we should not look at men as examples, but that we should look at the example of the Lord, the word of truth. Compared with him, all men are liars.

§ 20. There was a divine persuasion in my heart. I became acquainted with other friends[39] by whom I was strengthened mightily in all good endeavors. More and more I despised the world and its indifference.[40] God made the words come alive in my heart: "Ye might be partakers of the divine nature, having escaped the corruption that is in this world through lust" (Petr. 2:4). Then I said to myself: Should I deprive myself of my godly nature because of this base mortal desire? No, I will persist with God's help, cost what it may. Thereupon I wrote to the first friend who had given me a heavenly gift through God's grace, that I loved him like a father and that I planned to free myself from all the world's indifference. He was worried that I would not be strong enough to endure what was ahead of me and he admonished me to detach only my heart from everything. Then God would send means and occasion to free myself of all the outward things that weighed me down. I should trust in God and remain faithful to him in my love. But God's persuasive spirit in my heart did not leave my mind in peace but convinced me with the strongest sayings, as for example: Love not the world, neither the things that are in the world[41]; let him deny himself[42]; the benevolent grace castigates us, so that we don't love the world. Likewise: work out your own

---

39. Pietists addressed and called each other *Freund* (friend), as did the Quakers in England and America (known as "The Society of Friends") and members of the Philadelphian Society, which the Petersens joined.

40. "Gleichstellung," see note 7, above.

41. 1 John 2:15.

42. Mark 8:34: "Whosoever will come after me, let him deny himself, and take up his cross, and follow me."

salvation with fear and trembling[43]; strive to enter in at the straight gate[44]; he who denies me before men[45]; the devil as a roaring lion walks about![46] The parable of the five foolish virgins[47] and similar instructive passages from the Bible were always in my heart and pushed me to give up the worldly competition. Yet there remained the fear of my duke and duchess that I could not overcome. Then I often danced with tears in my eyes and was helpless. I wished I were a cowherd's daughter, then I would not be hindered from becoming a follower of Christ; no one would take notice. Then I realized that my class standing should not be an excuse for me, because I would have to reject everything if I wanted to follow Christ, and that nothing could hinder putting aside other people's gossip and tolerating this gladly in order to partake in Christ.

§ 21. With the help of God's grace I decided to take this up in earnest and to let neither life nor death hinder me. I went to my duchess since departed and requested my discharge, which was promptly denied. When they asked what had moved me to such a request, I freely told them that the way I had to live my life at court was contrary to my conscience. My esteemed duchess wanted to talk me out of it, considering this to be a fit of melancholy. She said: you are living like a virtuous young lady, you read and pray diligently; look at this one or that one who are Christians, they participate in these activities; they are not forbidden, if you only don't put your heart into them. But I did not want to hear any examples, I merely pointed to the example of Christ and his word that I followed. I would not judge others, but I could not be content with their example and would need a greater assurance of my calling and election in Christ. Since my beloved duchess realized that I would not change my mind for anything, she agreed to release me from any activity that was against my conscience. I should only stay with them and do my duties as before. I told them how many a service they would miss especially when visitors were coming. It might happen that the other lady-in-waiting would be ill and then they would be without any attendant, since I did not want to participate in entertainment and give them cause for mockery. Still they did not let me leave but promised me that I did not

43. Phil 2:12.

44. Luke 13:24. She elaborates on this passage in *The Nature and Necessity of the New Creature in Christ* (see appendix B).

45. Luke 12:9: "But he who denieth me before men shall be denied before the angels of God."

46. 1 Peter 5:8: "Be sober, be vigilant; because your adversary the devil, as a roaring lion, walketh about, seeking whom he may devour."

47. Mat. 25; see also her use and explication of that story in *The Nature and Necessity of the New Creature in Christ* (appendix B).

have to serve at festivities and party games. When told of this, the duke was displeased with me, thinking that I was sick with melancholy.[48] He spoke to me harshly, saying that it was the devil in me, that I was a lady who was liked by high and low and now wanted to make a fool of myself, and what would my family say to all this? I answered confidently that my plans were not of my own doing but according to the words of the Savior, who was the truth. I would accept in good spirits whatever happened to me now that I had heard his voice and would follow it; he would help me tolerate the world's mockery. When none of the conversations could change my mind, several so-called ministers were sent to me. They wanted to convince me that I did not understand scripture the right way, that I had sinister thoughts for which I had no reason, that I was Christian and righteous and should guard myself against sinister thoughts. But I answered according to my Savior's words and asked their conscience which of the two things would be the safest: to follow Christ's footsteps in innocence, or in a worldly life to talk about and to show interest in following Christ without any action? Then they said: the former was, indeed, better, but who could live like that? We all are sinners. Then I said: I was commanded to choose the best,[49] I let my God, who has promised to give me his holy spirit and who is not weak but powerful in our weakness, take care of ability and opportunity. If I were to undertake this out of my own strength, I would be in great fear and pain, because I know my inability well. But since I have undertaken this with the power of Christ according to his command, I know and am confident that I can accomplish this through him and that he, who began this in me, is faithful; he will do it and carry it out until his day. Then they let me go.

§ 22. They also tried another way; they thought they could stop me through contempt, when at the ducal table they exchanged glances and then looked at me, laughed, and often talked about women reading too much in the Bible and becoming too learned. But I let them laugh at me and was strengthened in the love of my God. A year had passed and it seemed that even the lowest person, with the exception of some pious hearts, was ridiculing me at court. But I did not pay much attention and suffered for Christ's sake, and things changed completely. The great wonderful God instilled such reverence in all the hearts of the high and the low that they were afraid

48. Melancholy was considered a widespread emotional and physical illness, an imbalance of the bodily fluids and a sickness of one's imagination. The illness, supposedly affecting women especially, would produce depression, hallucinations, or confusion.

49. This is a reference to Anna Maria van Schurman's autobiography, *Eukleria or Election of the Better Part* (Altona, 1673); see the volume editor's introduction, pp. 37–38.

to say or do something wrong in my presence and became totally silent in my presence, though they did not fear the court chaplain. Even the otherwise wild young people became very quiet and respectable when they saw me coming. Then I often thought with tears in my eyes, my God, wonderful God, who has instilled such fear into their hearts? And how did I bring it about that adults and children are afraid to do wrong in my presence? I have lowered myself below all others, have readily accepted everybody's mockery. Who has brought about this turn? O Lord, it is your almighty power, your presence is causing this; you raise the low and you look at misery, and you lift them up from the dust, yours is the honor and things are happening in your honor. Such developments did not cause an inflation in my heart, but led me to humility and dissipated as it were in front of my God when I felt his greatness and saw that he could guide the hearts of princes like streams of water. In this state I remained three more years at court and can say that I experienced great kindness not only from my duke and duchess but from everybody, who loved me as children love their mother. But with the help of God's grace, I refrained from accepting the favors of the powerful and from using it for something worldly. I saved it for furthering God's honor. I fled everything else that made me high and mighty in the eyes of men; I only used the favor of others so that I would have a place in their hearts.

§ 23. Then it pleased God to draw people of different rank, high and low, to him through my example, so that we felt true change—it had been the very opposite in the beginning. The last trick Satan played on me was that he had me almost confused through well-meaning people who said that I was giving up any opportunity to please other people by turning my back to the world and refusing aristocratic clothes, showing my limbs, and other worldly pleasures. When those who had earlier talked to me in a beautiful religious conversation avoided me, then the devil's trick was almost success-ful with me as I thought: you could have declined everything in your heart, if you had only kept some outward appearance, you could have been use-ful for them. But the spirit of truth soon lifted me up again and gave me other ideas, and I thought: what have you accomplished in all this time with your beautiful words other than that they have learned about piety but done nothing and thus have earned double punishment? Where is the persecu-tion that the Holy Spirit has proclaimed for the followers of Christ, if one outwardly maintains indifference to this world? Where is Christ's confes-sion for his followers in such a performance? Would not obedience to one's faith when in self-denial be more beneficial than obedience in mere words without strength? Since a youth is not better than the master, how could one make others into followers with a weak faith? With such thoughts I overcame everything and realized through God's grace that in one word with a deed there is more bliss and grace than in a thousand words without a deed.

§ 24. Three years passed in which I stayed my course in all simplicity at court. I endeavored to do nothing else but what could be done in God's presence and with calling for his grace. I rejected all worldly pleasures by which only the flesh but not the spirit would be nourished. Then it happened that my late father called for me, because my stepmother had died in childbirth and the baby survived. I was to take care of my father's household and to leave court service. But it was very difficult to get my release, because my duchess since departed loved me very much, as if I were her child. She shed many tears at my departure and sent after me that I should return; she did not give up until I promised to return to them if I went back into service at court. When I reached home, the baby had died and my father had decided to take a position as a steward at the court of the Princess of Philippseck,[50] and I received permission to board with a noble, pious widow Bauer von Eyseneck, née Hynsberg, in Frankfurt. Everybody knew of her impeccable life. She had a blessed death,[51] a proof of her upright life before men and God. I lived with her for six years and we loved each other like heart and soul. The Lord has done much good for me; during this time he gave me so much strength in a dangerous situation on the water, that I rejoiced while others were trembling and afraid. It so happened that I was traveling on the market boat from Frankfurt to Hanau in order to visit my sister Charlotte.[52] There were different people aboard, among them several soldiers who made very crude advances to four lewd women. My soul was troubled that people would forget about their souls. I leaned against the side of the boat and tried to go to sleep so that I would not have to listen to their conversation. In my sleep I dreamed of the line from the first Psalm: "The Lord looked down from heaven upon the children of men,"[53] whereby I awoke. When I was all

---

50. The princess was Anna Elisabeth von Hessen-Homburg, the divorced wife of Wilhelm Christoph von Hessen-Homburg; she resided at the castle Philippseck in Wetteravia, close to the city of Butzbach. This castle was built in 1628 and destroyed in 1773. This was a ducal residence, much larger than the Philippseck manor house in Heddernheim, the Merlau family estate.

51. Juliana Baur von Eyseneck died in 1684; this gives us a date after which von Merlau wrote the (first part) of her autobiography. Heinrich Reitz's *Historie der Wiedergebohrnen* . . . (Offenbach, 1698), the first and friendly contemporary account of Pietists' lives, provides a short biography of Baur (112 ff.).

52. The youngest sister, Charlotte Auguste Philippina, was born about 1650 and was married in 1677 to the widower Johann Reinhard von Dorfelden, who served as court administrator in Hanau, a residential town about twenty miles east of Frankfurt.

53. Psalms 1:4.

awake it was as if a great storm was coming and turned the boat around. I was frightened and thought: you are awake, how do you feel? Not long thereafter a real whirlwind came and touched the boat. We were in great danger so that everybody screamed with fear and called out for help to Jesus whose name they had used superfluously before in their bantering. Then God opened my mouth so that I might show them what horror death will bring and how they had used Christ's name unnecessarily while they were now calling on him for help. I pointed out how important it was to live in fear of the Lord, so that one have a refuge in distress. When by the grace of God the unforeseen and violent storm abetted, one of the women brazenly joked that the little boat had almost been covered by waves, and she laughed about this very loudly. I became very angry about that and said: you insolent woman, don't you know that the Lord's hand could easily find us here in this very place and let the storm and waves grab us? I had hardly closed my mouth when the wind and waves arose again and made a hole into the boat so that everyone feared for his life. But I was filled with an unusual pleasure thinking: shall I now see my Jesus? What now will remain in the water is but my mortal body that has often weighed me down. The life within me will not die. This my inner joy was noticed by Dr. Mige from Hanau who marveled at it, and it lifted up his spirit. We thought the ship would sink, because it already had a lot of water and plugging up the hole and scooping out the water were useless while the storm continued. We could not go on land either to the right nor to the left. Then all of a sudden a quiet set in, the captain reached the shore, and they jumped from the boat. The wild soldiers had taken my words to heart, paid attention to me that I would get ashore safely, and thanked me that I had admonished them. Dr. Mige asserted that he would never again forget my joy in the face of death. He told many people about this, and many a soul has been strengthened in the Lord. But in turn the devil created a lot of blasphemies and lies against me so that I had my share of the Savior's sufferings also in Frankfurt in different ways.

§ 25. After I had been a year with the widow, my dear duke and duchess learned that my father did not need me any more. My dear duchess herself let the privy councillor von der Strassen write to me that I should return and resume my services; they would send a coach and horses and double my salary. Also, I was also to have the title of head stewardess.[54] But I made excuses that I would have to supervise my father's estate, to be present there and have

---

54. In the seventeenth century a stewardess (*Hofmeisterin*) at court, here the castle at Wiesenburg of the Duke of Holstein-Sonderburg, was in charge of the ceremonial, social, and cultural needs of the lady of the house; she would ensure correct etiquette at social gatherings, festivities,

to keep an eye upon everything. Later they sent for me orally through the privy councillor Gerhard. But I remained with my earlier decision because it would have been difficult for me to enter life at court anew now that I had accustomed myself to a simple life.

When I was living with Mrs. Baur and my sister von Praunheim was visiting, she saw what an excellent boarding school for girls Mrs. Baur had established and asked me whether I would take one of her daughters to me so that she would be raised in a Christian manner like myself. She gave me the daughter, named after me, who was eight years old and did very well.

§ 26. When I was living in my sixth year with Mrs. Baur, it was God's will that my dear husband, who had met me in Frankfurt several years earlier and seen my devotion to God, made up his mind to marry me. He asked a certain person[55] in Lübeck that he talk to me, who did so only after some time when the opportunity presented itself. When I learned about it I could not entertain any thoughts of marriage in my mind. I prayed to God, turned down the offer, and suggested another very able person.[56] But my dear husband was not to be deterred; he wrote to a dear friend and eminent minister[57] as well as to my late father. I soon received this letter, and my conscience told me to leave the decision on this marriage to my father, since it was only a matter of honoring God. I wrote this to my father, sent him the letter and was so totally quiet as if this had nothing to do with me. Everything it dealt with was strange to me, and I did not believe that my father would agree. In his answer he said that at his age he had many a reason not to let me go that far away from him and that he had never agreed to a marriage outside of his class for any of his children, but that he could not go against God's will. That went to my heart and I thought that it had to be God's will, since contrary to all expectations my father's heart had been touched. He left the decision up to me, which I did not want to accept but left it totally up to him. My brother-

and family celebrations and assist with readings and the education of the very young children before a tutor was hired for the boys.

55. This "certain person" was the Amsterdam book dealer Heinrich Betke (1625?—1708), a native of Lübeck, who supplied Johann Wilhelm Petersen with scholarly and theological books and who traveled to the important Frankfurt book fair.

56. Johanna Eleonora suggested as a suitable bride Anna Elisabeth Kißner, née Eberhard, the young widow of a physician, a close friend of Spener's, and a member of her Pietist Frankfurt circle.

57. The minister was Johann Jakob Spener, who may have suggested the marriage in the first place. The higher ranking (Protestant) ministers (superintendents, those at a prestigious church in a large city, court chaplains) were very interested in marrying a woman from a patrician, upper bourgeois or noble family. Matchmaking is a common topic in the clerics' correspondence at the time.

in-law von Dorfelden, the steward at the court in Hanau, was much opposed,
but my dear father since departed answered him in a very Christian manner.
He wrote that it was not fair that we Protestants consider our ministers to be
of so low a class, when in the false popish church the clergy is held in high
esteem. Also, his daughter was not fit for a man with a secular profession;
she was not marrying out of her station because of thoughtlessness; everyone knew that she followed God's calling. With this response they had to
be quiet, and my dear father gave his "yes." Thereupon my dear husband
traveled to Frankfurt; Dr. Spener[58] married us on September 7, 1680, in the
presence of the Princess of Philippseck,[59] my late father, and several aristo-
crats, altogether some thirty people. Everything was very Christian and went
well so that everybody was happy. But the scurrilous devil could not forgo
his tricks; he resented that the wedding was not a worldly one with feasting,
drinking, and wild dancing. Carping tongues made up such lies as that the
Holy Ghost had appeared in the chamber in which we were married in the
shape of fire, and that we had then begun to interpret the Apocalypse—at
that time I did not have the insight that I have now in great fullness, nor did I
recognize with great certainty God's judgment and glory for his church here
on earth as a retribution for the pain we suffered for Christ's sake. Such lies
were told to Dr. Heiler[60] by those who did not know that he had attended
our wedding. When he protested against this, saying that he himself was
present at the wedding and that the wedding was Christian and well done,
they had to be ashamed of their lies.

§ 27. When we moved from Frankfurt, we were allowed to take my niece
along because she wanted to stay with me. When we arrived in Amsterdam,
my dear husband became very ill and did not want to lie down because of
his job. We took a boat so that he would soon be with his employers and
his flock. During the entire trip he was very ill and my niece also became ill,
so that I was all alone with two sick people in places where I did not know
anybody. That was very difficult for me and I thought: I did not marry on
account of my own will and pleasure, why am I in such a spot that I have
no help or advice here in these strange places? When we came to the inn
at noon, I could put my dear husband on a bench and I went into the field,
cried, and begged my Lord for help. Then I was comforted in thinking about

58. Spener preached on Eph. 5:32 and published the wedding sermon in Frankfurt the same
year. He was an outstanding preacher and his numerous published sermons were very popular.
59. See above, note 50. Johanna Eleonora's father was the princess's steward at court.
60. Günther Heiler was superintendent in Hanau.

the words in Heb. 2:17.[61] Since Moses trusted the one he did not see as if he were seeing him, I thought: Even if I am in a strange land, God is here and will not give you more than you can bear. When we came to Lübeck[62] a doctor was consulted, who noticed that I was deadly ill and did not know it, although I had often fainted for weakness. But the attendance to my husband had been so important to me that I had forgotten about myself until the physician came and pointed out the danger. I was put to bed and was very ill. But I recovered before my dear husband whom I had to deliver often to God like my dear Isaac[63] between hope and fear for a quarter of a year. Afterward many lies were told about me in this place and many reasons were fabricated why I had married below my class. Some said that I had behaved badly at court, others invented other evil things and passed them off for truth. Such lies were told to our superiors that my dear duchess,[64] who was very Christian, wrote to her sister, the reigning duchess of Gotha,[65] to find out the truth. They knew me well, how I had behaved at court, and gave a good report about me. It was shortly before their death when they attested to my innocence so royally: this will not be forgotten in the presence of the Lord. Our duke told that later to my dear husband when they received the letter about my innocence. Afterward people thought of new lies and said secretly that my niece, of whom I spoke earlier, was my illegitimate child and that she was the reason why I married out of my class. We could not find out where such lies had come from and I praised my Lord, because I knew what he had done for my soul that he had given me a chaste heart since my youth. I can say with humility in my heart that I have lived my life as a single woman in chastity and that I led my married life with God's grace with a chaste heart bearing also this mockery with joy. It is almost unnecessary to explain this, because it can easily be verified: both parents of my

61. "Wherefore in all things it behooved him to be made like unto *his* brethren, that he might be a merciful and faithful high priest in things *pertaining* to God, to make reconciliation for the sins of the people."

62. Lübeck is a port city in northern Germany situated on the Baltic Sea, member of the ancient Hanseatic League and quite wealthy. Johann Wilhelm Petersen grew up and went to school there. From 1678 he held the position of court preacher in the neighboring city of Eutin, the residence of Duke August Friedrich of Holstein-Gottorp, and of superintendent of churches (the highest clerical office) in the princely bishopric of Lübeck.

63. The author refers to God's instructing Abraham to sacrifice his son Isaac to him (Gen. 22).

64. The Duchess Christine von Holstein-Gottorp, née von Sachsen-Weißenfels, had intervened with Johanna Eleonora's father for the marriage with Petersen.

65. The Duchess von Sachsen-Gotha, née von Sachsen-Weißenfels, knew Johanna Eleonora when both lived at neighboring courts in Saxony.

niece are still living in Praunheim, only an hour from Frankfurt. The minister who baptized her is likewise still alive, as is Lady von Solms-Rödelheim,[66] her godmother, only half an hour away from Rödelheim. Any lover of truth could get more accurate information, since the Duchess of Ratzeburg's[67] sister is at Philippseck[68] and knows my sister and brother-in-law, the parents of the young von Praunheim, who was with me. They had the oldest son at their court as a page, the older brother of the young girl. May the Lord forgive also these lies, and may he grant that I delight in all that is happening to me on account of my Savior. For I know that I suffer because I am his follower and because I was praised before when I was a listener and not yet a doer.[69] Now I am being mocked from the very hour onward that I desired with all my heart to do what pleases the Lord. I can be happy with good reason in the Lord. I do not rejoice when others fall into sin or become guilty in the eyes of the Lord because of their fellow men. No, I have often prayed to God that they may be forgiven, since so much good has happened to me since I approached my God. May he likewise have mercy on them. Yes, I have often tasted love for my enemies[70] truly through God's grace, so that I had wanted to take it into my heart and carry it with God. My love was very deep when I realized that I gained more from them than from my best friends. But no hour is like the next, and often it may happen that at first we do not feel with such a love what happens to us unjustly, especially if we have not experienced it for some time and have been quiet. Then we have to learn anew how to love our enemies and to accept everything from the hand of the Lord. This has happened to me so often that I have to turn back again and explore thoroughly the benefit of this or that suffering before I can accept it and bear it with joy.

§ 28. After this first reproach, I experienced much good in my marriage by the grace of God so that I not only have a peaceful and blessed married life and such a beloved husband who is showing me much love and loyalty, but I have also been blessed with children. I have borne my husband two sons of

---

66. See above, note 21.

67. Sibylle Hedwig von Sachsen-Lauenburg (1625–1703); Ratzeburg is a town in Schleswig-Holstein; the author's justification was addressed especially to readers in that area.

68. Philippseck, see above, note 50.

69. Johanna Eleonora uses here a key word to describe her role as active Christian: *Täterin*, (female) doer.

70. Johanna Eleonora's physical expression "ich habe oft die Liebe der Feinde . . . geschmecket" (I have often tasted love for my enemies) is also a reference to an important Pietist tenet: to love one's enemy and to refuse all warlike actions.

whom the firstborn[71] is still alive and will hopefully become a faithful servant of Jesus Christ. He is a son of great promise, since some things occurred before his birth: a year before his birth I opened the Bible at Rom. 9:9 for my husband, when we were at a minister's house in Holstein,[72] and I had my thumb[73] on the words: "For this is the word of promise. At this time I will return and Sarah shall have a son." My husband believed in this saying and wrote on the minister's table: "In a year Johanna will have a son." When half a year had passed, we had forgotten about this and thought that the minister's wife who had been pregnant had fulfilled this prophecy. But when twenty weeks were left in the year, I happened to get up early in the morning and my husband blessed me, there was a movement in my body. It felt as if something were skipping. Then I said, God has blessed me; and we praised God together, remembered the saying, and realized that the birth of our son would occur as promised within the year. We also believed it would be a son as did indeed happen. When he was born at the appointed time he was very small, but he lifted his head already as a one-day-old and looked around. And he has given many a good sign, so that we hope he will be a son of promise. Some people have objected to these words[74] and have thought that I wanted to make something special out of me. But nothing else was in my heart than what one can say of any child of God—that he will be with Isaac a child of promise.[75] The apostle Paul applies this also to himself and to his brothers in the letter to the Galatians (4:28) and says: "Now we, brethren, as Isaac was, are the children of promise," what we also hoped about our son.

§ 30.[76] God then has done so much good for my soul and has opened his cherished word for me, especially the prophets and the blessed Book of Revelation, which is a key for the prophets and is understood well through

71. The surviving son August Friedrich was born on August 2, 1682, and became a Prussian civil servant, not a theologian. He had a large family and died in 1732, outliving his mother by only eight years. The author omits the birth of two daughters, who are mentioned in her husband's autobiography (p. 397), perhaps because they died early or because female children were generally considered less important. She was already in her late thirties when she had her four children.

72. Holstein is the duchy in which the city of Lübeck is situated.

73. *Däumeln* (thumbing), blindly opening the Bible and putting your finger on a passage and predicting the future from these words, was a common practice in some religious groups.

74. This sentence (to the end of paragraph 29) was added in the 1618 edition of the autobiography in response to criticism of the practice of Bible divination.

75. The covenant, God's promise to Abraham that his son Isaac and all his descendants would be the chosen people.

76. Paragraph 29 is missing from the original text, probably due to a printer's oversight.

the prophets. God does good things for my body and my soul daily, so that I can say: the Lord has done great things for me; it is good to rely upon the Lord, for he is true and loyal; he will assist me also in the future and complete the good things he has begun until the day of Jesus Christ. True is he who has promised and who will fulfill the promise.

§ 31. Up to this point I had published my life story as an appendix to my treatise *A Heart's Conversations with God* a few years ago when good friends asked me to relate how God's leading hand had directed me from the beginnings of my youth and how the Lord attracted me to him in many a way during these early years. Now I wanted to add to it how the true Lord has revealed his secrets to me one after another and how he has nourished me with them so that I was drawn away from the love of the world and toward God's love. I will talk about these revelations in this part and of the sufferings that my ungrateful brother-in-law and other detractors made me go through. Their detractions have not done damage to me; they will be my crown on that distant day. My husband is mentioning a few in his autobiography.[77] Since all the suffering that happened to me brought much good for my soul, I will not complain about it but praise the Lord for it. Here I will only record how the Lord has looked upon me with grace.

§ 32. Since my early youth, the faithful Lord has let me get into a great struggle when I could not grasp how God, who is essentially love, would condemn so many to eternal condemnation, as was believed in those days everywhere. That the poor heathens who had never had the opportunity to know God were to remain eternally in such pain, I could not understand. Was this to happen out of essential love? Yet these words were always on my mind: "He that believeth not shall be condemned."[78] And I thought to myself: that is more hate than love. But I fought against it in my heart saying: my God is essential love; and although I cannot understand what seems to me to be contrary to this love, he shall be revered and loved by me as essential love. When I was in such submission, the following was revealed to me: what is said in Peter,[79] "For, for this cause was the gospel preached also to them that are dead, that they might be judged according to men in the flesh, but live according to God in the spirit" (1 Pet. 4:6). Namely, that those

77. See Johann Wilhelm Petersen, *Das Leben Johann Wilhelmi Petersen . . .* (n.p., 1717), who records numerous fights with other theologians including those who attacked Johanna Eleonora. See the volume editor's introduction, p. 18.

78. Macc. 16:16.

79. "For Christ also hath once suffered for sins, the just for the unjust, that he might bring us to God, being put to death in the flesh, but quickened in the spirit. By which also he went and preached unto the spirits in prison" (1 Pet. 3:18–19).

whose bodies were killed at the time of the Great Flood because of their lack of faith and whose spirits were imprisoned, were visited by Christ at the time when his body was killed at the cross and thereafter was resurrected in the spirit. Christ had then preached the gospels to these imprisoned spirits who had been judged according to men in their flesh, but are now living in God's spirit. From this I learned that they had become believers because of Christ's sermon when he had gone to them in the prisons, and they had been redeemed from condemnation through his sacrifice. In addition, the verses Zech. 9:11–12 were revealed to me: "By the blood of thy covenant I have sent forth thy prisoners out of the pit wherein there is no water. Turn you to the stronghold, ye prisoners of hope: even today do I declare *that* I will render double unto thee." I was still puzzled by Matt. 12:31–32 when Christ says: "All manner of sin and blasphemy shall be forgiven unto men; but the blasphemy against the *Holy* Ghost shall not be forgiven unto men . . . neither in this world, neither in the *world* to come." By the previous quotes I was clearly assured that there would be also a redemption from hell and that Christ's blood would also have its validity after death and that everyone will again be redeemed from hell, except for the sinners against the Holy Spirit and the fallen angels. For at that time the return of all things[80] had not been revealed to me, since this phrase was unknown to me in this world and in the other. I stumbled over the word "eternal" and did not yet understand that the ages only have their special durations. Yet I was released from a hard struggle and thought that such sinners would deserve eternal pain. And I praised God that he had given us Jesus Christ as such a great conciliator, until God took away also such doubt in that I found in scriptures that all creatures would praise God and that he, when all is again subject to Christ, would be all in all and that all would be done anew (1 Cor. 15:22, 28; Rev. 5:13; Rev. 21:5).[81] "And he that sat upon the throne said, Behold, I make all things new. And he said unto me, Write: for these words are true and faithful" (Rev. 21:5).

§ 33. The second secret that was revealed to me before I was married is the future conversion of heathens and Jews, which the faithful God revealed

---

80. The return of all things—*apokatastasis panton*—became an important dogma in the (radical) Pietists' credo. See the volume editor's introduction, p. 21.

81. "Wherefore tongues are for a sign, not to them that believe, but to them that believe not: but prophesying serveth not for them that believe not, but for them which believe" (1 Cor. 14:22).

"But if there be no interpreter, let him keep silence in the church; and let him speak to himself and to God" (1 Cor. 14:28).

"And every creature which is in heaven, and on the earth, and under the earth, and such as are in the sea, and all that are in them, heard I saying, Blessing, and honor, and glory, and power, *be* unto him that sitteth upon the throne, and unto the Lamb for ever and ever" (Rev. 5:13).

to me in 1664 in a dream. I was dreaming that I was led into a beautiful rectangular house that was built upon the twelve apostles so that they were the foundation on which the house rested. In the center of the house, in the middle floor, there were once again the twelve apostles in life-size, three on each side. Each one had a special musical instrument. When I entered the house, all these voices came alive so that my heart was filled with joy. Then the roof of the house opened and I came with my body into the clouds where I saw in the sky five suns, of which two did not yet send out rays but appeared in themselves bright and shining. The other three were shining in the following way: one was bright but had no warmth as the moon's rays are without warmth; the second glowed brightly and did have warmth; the third appeared pale like a sun drawing rain. I had my own thoughts about these three suns during my sleep by applying these to the three religions, because at that time I did not know any other sect but Lutheran, Papist, and Reformed. Then I thought that the sun without warmth is the Papist religion, the pale the Reformed, and the one with warmth and glow the Lutheran. When I was mulling this over, I saw to my right a person in a white linen dress, a green wreath on his head, and a golden scepter in his hand with which he pointed to the two suns as yet without rays and said: "Do you want to know the secret of the two suns?" And when I with humility in my heart answered yes, he told me that they indicated two people who did not yet believe in Christ but who would become believers: one was the Jewish people and the other the heathen people, especially those who sprang from Abraham's concubines.[82] He told me about these such deep secrets that I realized in my sleep that it was something very important and that I wanted very much to wake up. But it disappeared as quick as lightning and I remember only as much as I have written down here; he said nothing of the three suns. I again searched in scripture and received an illumination about the conversion of Jews and heathens, of which conversion I had neither heard nor known could be hoped for. This was especially attested to by Rom. 2:25[83] and 4:13: "For the promise, that he should be the heir to the world, *was* not to Abraham, or to his seed, through the law, but through the righteousness of faith" (Rom. 4:13), where it is said that Abraham was to be the heir to the world. When I told my dream to several learned teachers at that time, I was assured that it was a god-sent dream.

82. According to Gen. 16, the descendants of Ishmael, son of Abraham and his concubine Hagar, did not belong to the chosen people.

83. "For circumcision verily profiteth, if thou keep the law; but if thou be a breaker of the law, thy circumcision is made uncircumcision" (Rom. 2:25).

§ 34. When I was as yet unmarried, the article of justification from the writings of Paul was revealed to me as a third tenet through an awakening and on the occasion of the following vision. In a dream I saw the Apostle Paul of small but very pleasant stature with a large light in his hand. When I looked at him intensely, he handed me a light and told me to follow him. We came onto a beautiful green meadow about which I had to follow him, but through which many ropes had been fastened crosswise. This path appeared to me very tedious in the beginning, but became more and more easy while walking until all ropes had been passed. Then I saw a beautiful green tree in the meadow above which there was an angel holding a large golden cup filled with wine. He offered the cup to me. I drank and received such strength from it that in waking up my heart was really refreshed. I learned from this that I should diligently read Paul's writings, which I then endeavored to do and accomplished with God's grace. When I had read and thought about the Epistles to the Romans and to the Galatians I learned that it was God's pure grace through which we can become righteous in our belief in Jesus Christ and can reach eternal salvation, and that with this article of justification one could get lost to the right or the left of it and could miss the divine truth: to the right, if one pursues works and tries to bring a saint to Christ before one has attained one's justification through faith; to the left, if one claims vindication through one's old sinful life, receives grace in vain, and puts one's trust in wantonness. Then I understood that when we seek his grace in Jesus Christ and follow him, God accepts us as godless but does not leave us godless; rather he makes us just and holy so that we turn away from sin and live in righteousness. This holy truth came to me clearly like the sun from the writings of Saint Paul, and with it an affection for Luther's teachings,[84] which agree very much with Paul's on this point. Luther really abhors popish teachings (of which I have been in awe and danger because of my relatives, who belong to that church) that are totally opposed to truth.

§ 35. While I was married, the following secrets were revealed to me. In the year 1685 I received for the first time a revelation concerning the

---

84. Petersen is always very concerned to preserve a pure Lutheran doctrine of justification; she emphasizes God's role in salvation, giving his gift when he chooses. The sinner plays only a passive and negative part in his own salvation. This is squarely directed against the Catholic practice of indulgences, or buying release from purgatory for oneself and even for a deceased person. Luther fought strongly against indulgences, especially those bought during his campaign in the 1520s, when the Catholic church needed and used indulgence money for building St. Peter's Cathedral and for maintaining a Renaissance-style papal court in the Vatican in Rome. Luther totally abandoned the practice of indulgences (by then an elaborate system of what "good deeds" or money could buy what reduced time in purgatory) for economic, national, and theological reasons.

Apocalypse of Jesus Christ.[85] I had never before thought much about this book but had always bypassed it, thinking that I would not understand anything in it. When I once retired to my room and opened the Bible to find a passage, I chanced on the words in Rev. 1:3: "Blessed *is* he who readeth, and they that hear the words of this prophecy, and keep those things which are written therein: for the time is at hand." These words went deep into my heart and I thought: you have put aside the Book of Revelation and passed it by, yet great things are in it. And though I found an excuse for having passed it by because I did not understand its content, I took it to heart and realized that great prophecies were in this book and also great threats. The faithful Lord would grant me the grace to understand what I had to do to become part of such prophecies and to flee what could drag me into such judgments. With such thoughts I fell on my knees before God, praying to him with sighs to open my eyes so that I might understand and recognize his very divine will and live as a true doer[86] after his word. When I arose from my prayer, I intended to read the blessed book. But I did not have any idea that immediately something was to be revealed to me. When I started reading, it appeared to me as if my heart was totally filled with the light of God. And I understood everything, whatever I read. Also, many passages came to my mind that were concordant with Revelation. And when I looked those up, I immediately understood them. I was very much moved by this and humble before God that he had shown me, his lowly maid, such grace. I took a sheet of paper, wrote down the places that harmonized with what I had found in Revelation, took it to my husband and said: look what God has revealed to me in Revelation. He took the sheet to read and was amazed, passed to me his sheet of paper that was still wet,[87] having been written on in the very same hour. In it all fundamentals could be found that were also on my paper. He said to me: the Lord has as truly revealed this to you as he has to me. Go on, we shall show to each other again what the Lord may reveal to us. Thus it happened that, when I showed him something that the Lord had revealed to me, it had already been revealed to him; likewise, when he brought something to me, I had also already received something. Then we remembered the vision in a dream that I had in 1662, in the eighteenth year of my life. In the dream I saw in the sky the number 1685 of which the first two numbers disappeared quickly into the clouds, but the other two

85. Petersen means especially the Book of Revelation, which in German is often referred to as Book of the Apocalypse.

86. "Eine wahre Täterin nach seinem Wort." See above, note 38.

87. The paper was wet from ink; a sharpened goose quill and ink were used for writing.

numbers remained as 85. I saw a man standing to my right who pointed to the number and said: "Behold, at that time great things will begin to happen, and something will be revealed to you."[88] This really happened, for in 1685 the great unrest and persecution in France[89] started and in the very same year the blessed thousand-year-realm of Jesus Christ in the Book of Revelation was opened up to me.

§ 36. The other secret that was revealed to me during my marriage is the return of all things. This happened in the following way: A noble gentleman[90] sent us a manuscript he had received from England titled *The Eight Worlds* and asked us to tell him our thoughts about it, that is to say individually, I alone for myself and my husband likewise for himself alone. In my mind I was quite opposed to the idea contained in the manuscript that the return of the fallen angels can be expected in eight thousand years, because from reading scripture I had learned that in the year eight thousand only the downfall of the fallen angels[91] into a fiery pool would occur and that they would be tortured in it from eternity to eternity. For in seven thousand years, when the marriage of the lamb[92] will take place, the fallen angel will be shut in and sealed in an abyss (Rev. 20:3 etc.)[93] And cast him into the bottomless pit. And shut him up, and set a seal upon him . . ." (Rev. 20:2–3). And after these thousand years they must again be freed for a short while and perform their last evil deed on earth and then be thrown into the fiery pit. Thus this matter (the return of the fallen angels) appeared to me as being totally against scripture; and there were even more passages that would contradict this. Then I went into my chamber for prayer and sighed to my Lord

---

88. Biblical language, but not a direct quote.

89. With the revocation of the Edict of Nantes in 1685, Louis XIV stepped up the prosecutions of Huguenots in France and of Protestants in the Palatinate and Upper Rhine region that he had occupied. Large numbers of refugees from these areas (and from the Hapsburg lands) made their way to Brandenburg-Prussia (where the Petersens then resided), which granted them freedom of religion.

90. The Prussian official and Pietist Baron Dodo von Knyphausen sent a manuscript copy of the English visionary Jane Lead's book, *The Wonders of God's Creation Manifested in the Variety of Eight Worlds* (London 1695), which contained an exposition of the doctrine of universal salvation. See the volume editor's introduction, p. 15.

91. Fallen angels (or demons) and the devil or devils were believed to be creatures who instead of praising God had opposed or fallen away from God from the beginning; they were out to steal human souls away from God.

92. The marriage of the lamb refers to the triumphal return of Christ, Rev. 19:7: "For the marriage of the Lamb is come, and his wife hath made herself ready," the "wife" referring to the believers, the church as community of believers.

93. "And he laid hold on the dragon, that old serpent, which is the Devil, and Satan, and bound him a thousand years."

to lend me grace and strength that I might complete this task. This person[94] was not to think I was setting myself above her talents but would learn that we should give preference to holy scripture over visions and should examine everything according to this divine rule. I do not consider my dream visions as grounds of divine truth but as true instruction with which God the Lord has guided my investigations in holy scripture. Behold, I received courage in my prayer, as if all my senses waned and I was placed with my mind into the fulfillment of all things, hearing with John[95] in my mind that after the end of time all creatures will praise God. Then God will be everything for everybody after he will have renewed and reconciled everything through Jesus Christ. Paul's words became alive in my heart and I repeated these words after him with an ardent spirit: "O the depth of the riches both of the wisdom and knowledge of God . . ."[96] For of him, and through him, and to him *are* all things . . ." (Rom. 11:33, 36). I then understood many deep points: I learned that the Fall means that all of God's qualities are included in revelations. God did not like the fall, nor sin, but he has also given the strength to guard oneself against it. But since he as an all-knowing God has already seen this beforehand, he has also known the end, how he will best finish and reconcile everything through Christ. Because in the very beginning a woman's seed has been promised who will crush the snake's head, and in due time Christ's atonement for the sins of all the world will take place, those who do not accept this sacrifice of reconciliation but reject it will be afflicted with eternal pain. But if they accept what their deeds are worth, they will hear the Gospel of Christ so that they will receive hope for an everlasting reconciliation. If they embrace the belief in Christ with heart-felt humility, then they will achieve salvation, each according to his own place (1 Cor. 25:23), some earlier, others later, according to the example of the jubilee.[97] It was also revealed to me that the seven following years of reconciliation will accomplish this and will reconcile and return everything, except the fallen angel, who will only in his fiftieth year recover his angelic form, if he has been made pliable after a thousand years in the fiery pool and if he comes to Christ with a meek heart and accepts reconciliation, which has been done also for him with a very meek heart, and becomes a eulogizer

94. Jane Lead.

95. Petersen is referring to Rev. 16.

96. " . . . how unsearchable are his judgments."

97. According to the Old Testament, the jubilee was every fiftieth year (seven times seven plus one) and was to be celebrated with festivities, return of the Israelite slaves, reduction of debts, etc.

of God. All this came very much alive to me, and the biblical passages that appeared at first contradictory turned into testimony to this truth like: "A woman's seed shall crush the head of the snake." Then I understood that such a snake's head had to be crushed likewise in the fallen angel. If not, fulfillment would be wanting, and sin that was to be eliminated by Christ the redeemer would remain as long as there is God.

The other passage that was opposing my view was Matt. 25:31 and 46,[98] since I did not understand that it dealt with the realm where the firstborn will reign with Christ in all eternity. Likewise the devil's firstborn will be tormented in the lake of fire in all eternity, and the lake of fire will last as long as Christ's reign, and the last enemy that is the other death like the lake of fire (Rev. 20:14)[99] must be eliminated, before Christ can deliver the kingdom to his father (1 Cor. 15:24).[100] At this delivery there will be no more resistance and God will be all in all.

This was likewise revealed to me: I thought earlier that after the elimination of the first death after one thousand years, Christ would deliver the realm to God; and I did not consider that one death still remained into which the first death would be thrown (Rev. 20:14). But Christ will reign not only a thousand years but from eternity to eternity (Rev. 2:15) until everything will have returned. Then he will deliver the realm to his father, that is to say the entire reborn creation. Then the last enemy, the other death will likewise be eliminated and thus, since a tormenter no longer exists, no creature will be tortured any longer. And it is remarkable that this other death has been called the "last" enemy (1 Cor. 15:26). Since the fallen angel must first be rescued from his hostility and must be restored before this other death is finally eliminated, he has been called "the last enemy" and will be eliminated after all restored beings so that God will be all in all. When I had thoroughly understood this truth, I responded afterward and have proven from scripture what that person[101] had seen and heard in a vision. I have shown them that the time was wrong and that the return of the fallen angel should be expected not in eight thousand but in fifty thousand years. They[102] were much

---

98. "When the Son of men shall come in his glory, and all the holy angels with him, then shall he sit upon the throne of his glory." "And these shall go away into everlasting punishment: but the righteous into life eternal."

99. "And death and hell were cast into the lake of fire. This is the second death."

100. "Then *cometh* the end, when he shall have delivered up the kingdom to God, even to the Father; when he shall have put down all rule, and all authority and power."

101. The person is Jane Lead. Petersen refers to her publication *The Everlasting Gospel of the Return of All Creatures* (1698). See the annotated bibliography of Petersens's works.

102. Members of the Philadelphian Society. See the volume editor's introduction, p. 16.

pleased with my knowledge and often wrote to us from England from where we recognized their affection for us.

§ 37. The third secret revealed to me during my marriage is the notion of the divine God-man, the firstborn of all creatures, revealed to me in the following way. In the year 1708 my dear husband was asked by a noble person of rank in Silesia to attend the Children's Prayer.[103] They organized under the open sky and to give his thoughts about it. When I accompanied him to the neighboring town it happened that I met two learned persons, one a Lutheran and one a Reformed.[104] These two got into an argument: the Lutheran thought that the Reformed could not attain salvation because they did not have the two sacraments[105] in a pure form; the Reformed contested that he found all his comfort in the teaching of predestination.[106] I listened to the argument with dismay and reminded them that we should not condemn one another because of opinions, but that we should strengthen one another in the following of Christ. If we want honestly to grow in it, we will more and more approach each other in our understanding. When I was alone, I remembered that the prophet[107] (Ez. 37:16 ff.) had to take two wooden sticks, had to write on one the tribe of Judah and on the other the tribe of Israel, and had to take both in his hand so that they would become one. This foreshadowed that Judah and Israel, after they separated from each other, would

103. In Silesia in 1708, large groups of Protestant children went out into the fields for prayer sessions and assemblies to call attention to the Protestants' forced conversions to Catholicism. In 1648 Silesia had come under Hapsburg rule, who promised to tolerate Lutherans. But after the deaths of the Protestant princes who owned and governed large parts of Silesia, all Protestants were forced to convert, their churches were closed, and their ministers driven away. The open-air prayers were to call attention also to the lack of churches and ministers for Protestants, especially the Reformed (Calvinists) who were not covered by the 1648 peace. In 1708 the Protestant Swedish King Charles XII was able to exert sufficient military pressure for an agreement (the Altranstädt Convention) to tolerate all Protestants and to reopen some of their churches in Silesia. Johann Wilhelm Petersen considered the children's prayer movement a divine mission from God and published a treatise: *The Power of the Children in the Last Days* (Die Macht der Kinder in der letzten Zeit, 1708).

104. Petersen tells of this meeting also in the preface to her work *The Secret of the First-Born* (1711). See the annotated bibliography of Petersen's works (1711), and the volume editor's introduction, p. 48. The Lutheran and the Reformed Churches were the two officially recognized Protestant churches in seventeenth-century Germany.

105. Baptism and the Eucharist were the two sacraments over whose interpretation Lutherans and the Reformed (Calvinists) disagreed vehemently.

106. In the Reformed Church the doctrine of predestination meant that God had selected an individual for salvation or condemned him or her to eternal torment even before their birth and without correspondence to their individual, personal merit. The subjects of predestination and salvation were hotly debated theological issues in the seventeenth century.

107. The prophet Ezekiel tells this story in the Book of Ezekiel.

once again become one kingdom. Thus I thought in my heart, these two religions have both come from the Reformation of Babel,[108] just like those; they were divided into two sects—just like those into two kingdoms—who judge and condemn each other. I fell on my knees, prayed to God: since such promises were still in store for Israel of the flesh, that he might have mercy on his spiritual Israel, and unite both religions in one understanding, bringing them together in love and harmony. When I had sighed so heartily, the secret of the divine God-humanity of Jesus Christ[109] came very much alive in my heart. I was assured in my mind that such revelation would be an instrument to bring the two religions together when such truth was recognized and understood.

Then I understood many passages that explained the truth (such as Col. 1:18; John 1:1; 1 Cor. 10:14; Heb. 13:8; Gen. 32:28; Prov. 8:22; Mic. 5:1; Eph. 3:9).[110] "And to make all *men* see what is the mystery of the fellowship, which from the beginning of the world hath been his in God, who created all things by Jesus Christ" (Eph. 3:9) and many more places. These assured me that before the creation of this world Jesus Christ had taken his beginnings from the preworldly, mediating Force-Being[111] and had become the original from which and after which we were created, a picture and likeness of God. This could not have been done from a pure divinity. I was assured in my mind that, if this truth was rightly received, not only would the quarrels between us and the Reformed be ended, but also the Socinians[112] would see their errors. They take offense at some passages that have until now been

---

108. Gen. 11:9.

109. The German reads "die himmlische Gott-Menschheit Jesu Christi"; Petersen is coining new word combinations to express her theological notions, a tradition with the mystics and spiritualists who often created their own terminology to express their religious ideas.

110. "And he is the head of the body, the church: who is the beginning, the firstborn from the dead; that in all things he might have the preeminence" (Col. 1:18).

"In the beginning was the Word, and the Word was with God, and the Word was God" (John 1:1).

"Wherefore, my dearly beloved, flee from idolatry" (1 Cor. 10:14).

"Jesus Christ, the same yesterday, and today, and forever" (Heb. 13:8).

"And he said, Thy name shall be called no more Jacob, but Israel; for as a prince hast thou power with God and with men, and hast prevailed" (Gen. 32:28).

"The Lord possessed me in the beginning of his way, before his works of old" (Prov. 8:22).

"Now gather thyself in troops, O daughter of troops: he hath laid siege against us: they shall smite the judge of Israel with a rod upon the cheek" (Mic. 5:1).

111. The German reads "das vorweltliche mittele [mittlere] Krafft-Wesen," a paraphrase for Jesus.

112. Faustus Socinius (1539–1604) denied the divinity of Christ and atonement, rejected the sacraments and the authority of scripture; he held that the soul of man was born pure.

understood as concerning pure divinity. They have taken their consequences from this and denied even the divinity of Jesus. If they would realize that these places refer to the divine God-humanity, they could be convinced of both: that Jesus Christ was the divine God-man[113] before the creation of the world as well as the true God with the Father and the Holy Ghost since eternity. Yes, he has had to have been that, because, according to Mic. 5,[114] he has taken his beginnings and his end from eternity, in which God the Word has become flesh in the fulfillment of time to suffer for us in the guise of a servant and has appeared in order to absolve us.

If the Reformed would recognize this heavenly God-man, it would not appear strange to them to believe that he, according to the community of his divine God-humanity, could also be present among us as a human being, because he has been our head and mediator in this world. They would also not take offense in that we believe in the communion of bread and wine partaking in his flesh and blood, since it is not only the flesh he received from Mary, but he has also been elevated to sit at the right of God. And he is in the communion of flesh and blood from heaven: "He that eateth my flesh, and drinketh my blood, dwelleth in me, and I am in him" (John 6:51, 53, 56).[115] Without this we have no life within us. But by partaking in it, we stay in Christ and Christ stays in us.

Let us now look at the teachings of predestination. The Reformed can likewise recognize this truth that nothing that was created according to Col. 1:16[116] by Christ and for Christ was created for damnation. The truth about the return of all things is likewise a great instrument to recognize that everything has been created for salvation by Christ and for Christ. When this truth was revealed to me, I remembered what happened to me in my early youth. At that time I once pondered how time could have emerged from eternity, since eternity has neither beginning, middle, nor end. When I was thinking about this, I remembered a sermon about how Saint Augustine had

113. The German reads "Jesus Christus der Gottes-Mensch."

114. Mic. 5 is interpreted as the coming of Christ, especially verses 4–5: "And he shall stand and feed in the strength of the Lord, in the majesty of the name of the Lord his God; and they shall abide: for now shall he be great unto the ends of the earth. And this *man* shall be the peace . . ."

115. "I am the living bread which came down from heaven: if any man eat of this bread, he shall live for ever: and the bread that I will give is my flesh, which I will give for the life of the world."

"Then Jesus said unto them: Verily, verily, I say unto you, Except ye eat the flesh of the Son of man, and drink his blood, ye have no life in you."

116. "For by him were all things created, that are in heaven, and that are in earth, visible and invisible, whether *they be* thrones, or dominions, or principalities, or power: all things ere created by him and for him."

once wandered in deep thoughts wanting to know the secret of the Holy Trinity.[117] Then he saw a young boy who was digging a hole in the ground. When Augustine asked the boy what he was doing, the boy answered that he wanted to capture the sea in his hole. Augustine then said: you will not be able to do this; the boy answered: you too will in your thoughts not be able to understand the secret of the Holy Trinity. This caused me to likewise stop my investigation and to surrender to God, that he has done well with everything, although I cannot reach it with my thoughts.

When after some time I no longer remembered this, the place in Mic. 5:3 became so very much alive in my heart that I did not understand why and thought: since his, Christ's origin, has been from the beginning and will be in all eternity, then he who was born and had already existed where he was born had to be a new revelation, and so forth.

There were many deep thoughts in my heart that I cannot express. Likewise I thought that God would not have started to reveal himself at the creation of the world, but since eternity had revealed much through Jesus Christ. Later in the blessed state, one great depth after another would be unveiled and all would be an inexpressible glory. I had great feelings about these thoughts, but I sacrificed them again to my Lord and was recently delighted when in 1708 the secret of the firstborn, the divine God-man, was revealed to me by the Lord. Then this passage in Mic. 5[118] became alive again within me and I remembered the secrets that had been disclosed to me in my youth.

In conclusion I want to add something here that I have later interpreted as pertaining to this secret.

§ 38. Last year I had a dream about the year 1685: I was with other people in a big house, as if imprisoned. In the house there were twenty-four pictures of great importance in that they portrayed how one could free oneself from such captivity. These pictures were disclosed to me and I understood that in the first twelve pictures one had to learn to descend into the deep and in the remaining twelve pictures to ascend again from the deep to the height. Also, every picture had special markers from which one could learn if descending and ascending was correct, that is to say, if all that was shown in the pictures would occur in reality.

When I decided to make my way, I selected a few people to come along. I did not reveal my intentions to them because I thought it would appear too

---

117. This is a popular story attributed to Saint Augustine since the Middle Ages.

118. "Now gather thyself in troops, O daughter of troops: he hath laid siege against us: they shall smite the judge of Israel with a rod upon the cheek" (Mic. 5:1).

difficult to them. When descending I encountered in reality everything I had learned from the pictures. When I had completed the twelve pictures of descent, I realized that the ascension would be even more difficult than the descent. But it also went well, because everything I had seen in the pictures came alive in reality. In awakening I forgot everything except the last, the nightingale, whose voice I had to reach. Since everything had been completed well and only the one exercise shown in the last picture remained, I came before a door leading into a chamber with a great secret. But when I stood in front of this door, I had forgotten what to do so that the door would open, and I could see the secret in the room (in which there was a father, a mother, and a son). Since I could not remember at all what I had seen in the picture, I became very sad and thought that all troubles had been in vain. When I prayed with sighs to God, I remembered that I had seen a nightingale in the picture and that I had learned from the picture to raise my voice like a nightingale. When I began to raise my voice louder and louder, the door opened and I felt very well, whereupon I woke up from the sleep.

I have understood to a certain extent what the pictures meant and interpreted them: that in the very same year the secret of the kingdom was revealed to my dear husband and to me, about which we had to suffer much and had to descend deep into humility. With our confidence we had to ascend high to our Lord, who has stood by us benevolently in all distress.

After the divine God-humanity[119] and the heavenly Jerusalem[120] had been revealed to me, I interpreted the room's last picture with the secret of the father, the mother, and the son as the dove-spirit out of which we are born as spirit from spirit. With this picture the secret of the Holy Trinity, of Father, Son, and the Holy Ghost, who in the Hebrew language appears in the feminine gender like a fruit-bearing mother and a hatching dove, has come into Revelation. With this the transformation into the intermediate power-being and the invisibility of God has become visible. Therefore, if we understand rightly and well such a divine God-humanity, the entire scripture will become more and more clear and understandable to us. May the Lord himself reveal his truths clearer and clearer to us, for his sake, Amen.

---

119. The German reads "die himmlische Gott-Menschheit." See also above, note 109.

120. See Petersen's *Instructions for a Thorough Understanding of Christ's Holy Revelations* (1696) and the volume editor's introduction, pp. 34–35.

APPENDIX A

EDITOR'S INTRODUCTION

During her stay in Frankfurt from 1675 until her marriage in 1680, Johanna Eleonora von und zu Merlau was active in charitable and religious work. She taught girls in the Saalhof mansion she shared with the widowed Juliana Baur von Eyseneck, and she invited friends for religious meetings, similar to the conventicles Philipp Jakob Spener had instituted in his parish. Such activities by a layperson and single woman aroused envy, gossip, and the suspicion of the authorities. Archival sources and letters indicate that it was indeed the gatherings by the two women that caused the gossip; in particular Balthasaar Mentzer, the court chaplain to the Landgrave in Darmstadt, agitated against Merlau. Spener wrote a lengthy account and defense of Merlau and Eyseneck and sent copies to several friends in Germany to defend and restore the good reputation of the two women as well as his own. He summarized the gossip in a letter of June 16, 1677: "Miss von Merlau and Mrs. Baur are supposedly entertaining two *collegia* in the *Saalhof*: an open one to which everybody is admitted and where there is much confusion; and a private one in which four or five persons meet and one does not know what is going on there, but one can readily guess that it is nothing good."[1] Besides these insinuations, people complained that men and women sat in a mixed group (not separated by gender), that they were keeping others from going to church, that they talked too much with great enthusiasm, that they taught Greek and even Hebrew to girls and instigated them to unruliness against their parents and elders, that a woman had preached, and that they gave too much money to the poor. Supposedly it was Spener who was the instigator of these religious enthusiasts, and the

---

1. Philipp Jakob Spener, *Briefe aus der Frankfurter Zeit 1666–1686*, ed. Johannes Wallmann with Udo Sträter and Markus Matthias (Tübingen: Mohr Siebeck, 1992), vol. 3, 191.

entire city of Frankfurt was said to be full of such fools, many of whom were pale and sickly in appearance and dressed in a strange way.

The Frankfurt city council reacted to such gossip and Mentzer's accusations by trying to get rid of Johanna Eleonora von und zu Merlau, requesting that she move on. Apparently they did not have any clear or convincing proof of any infractions. In response to the council's request (delivered only orally by a messenger), she wrote the following supplication, which her acquaintance and lawyer Johann Jakob Schütz presented to the council, since a woman could not represent herself. In her supplication she points to her noble station and her impeccable conduct in order to defend herself; she does not mention the gatherings nor her teaching. The supplication impressed the city council, but the rumors persisted. She decided in 1680 to accept Johann Wilhelm Petersen's marriage proposal and left Frankfurt after their wedding in September of that year. The ongoing rumors and distrust of Pietists was one of the reasons why she published her autobiography in 1689 (and enlarged it in 1718).

My translation is based on the original supplication preserved in the Frankfurt city archives.

A SUPPLICATION TO THE MAGISTRATE OF FRANKFURT

Your Worship, Most Honorable, Gracious and Highly Learned, Most Provident and Most Prudent Lords, Lord Mayor and Council, Peerless and Highly Esteemed Gentlemen![2]

Yesterday, on the 21st of February of this year [1678], a man came to me saying that he was a messenger of the city council of this city and was to report to me the order of the esteemed city council: that, although I have never been under the protection of this city, they nevertheless rescind such protection, that is to say, I should proceed on my journey.[3]

When I asked who had brought a complaint against me or what the reason was, he humbly answered that he did not know and excused himself

---

2. Such a formulaic address was required; each person of rank and every official body had to be addressed with their specific titles. "Gracious" (*gestreng*) was the proper address and title of the lower nobility.

3. The legal expression used here (*den Stab weitersetzen*) was usually employed with journeymen, traveling scholars, and vagrants. Johanna Eleonora von und zu Merlau considers this inappropriately below her rank as a woman of nobility or patrician member of the Council. Frankfurt was a Free Imperial City (subject directly to the emperor, not to a prince) and the city council was, of course, not elected by popular vote but composed of representatives from the upper class, only a handful of old patrician families.

with all courtesy, saying that he simply had to follow the council's bidding. Thereupon I thanked him for his civility in the same way.

Now, I am entitled to learn what has been said: that I proceed on my journey, and whether I have earned such a dishonor as some kind of punishment or reprimand.

It may be customary that for good reasons roaming vagrants are requested to proceed on their journey. I, however, did not, as is well known, enter this city as a vagrant, but I was born in wedlock[4] into a family of ancient, free nobility, immediate to the emperor,[5] and I was raised accordingly with great decency. I served from my early youth at first as chambermaid, then as stewardess to the women at the court of the Duke of Holstein. I led such an exemplary life that my honorable conduct there is known to many other princes and princesses, also to other canonical and worldly persons of high and low rank. Not one honest person in this entire world will appear who can accuse me of having committed even the least of crimes. Rather, I can surely cite a continuing good relationship with many persons of high rank and with theological gentlemen until this day.

I ask Your Worship to be so kind as to investigate the evil reports, the libel, all the secret lies, which have been spread willfully by the enemies of the pious against many a Christian soul in this very city and by malevolent people throughout Germany. Then it will surely come to light that everything that appears evil will turn out to be falsely fabricated and obvious, notorious lies by which the patience of pious persons is being tested and through which the others, indeed, reveal their malice or at least their thoughtlessness in repeating the lies. Yes, I can surely say to the eternal praise of God's grace: if you can find that I as one of the most honorable matrons and virgins of this entire city have done something criminal, then I will have forfeited without excuse not only all of men's protection but even my very life.

Truly, I have conducted myself all the time in such a way that only by resorting to obvious lies can any actions liable to be punished in this world be attributed to me; moreover, I have done countless charitable deeds[6] with honesty and have gone my way in fear of the Lord, as is well known within and outside this city. None of my accusers dares to step publicly into the

4. "Born into wedlock" is mentioned here because illegitimate children were treated like outcasts or vagrants and as a rule expelled from the city in which they were born, if not already in infancy with their mother, then later at the age of fourteen.

5. The Merlau family belonged to the Knights of the Rhine, subject not to a ruling prince but immediate to the emperor; they were relatively independent.

6. Charity was important; Johanna Eleonora refers here to her teaching of girls and donations for the poor.

light of truth but defames me only secretly. Therefore, Most Esteemed Gentlemen, you cannot say before God, the Judge over the living and the dead, and before all the world, that somebody has accused me of evildoing to your face and presence; much less can you prove it.

Therefore, I am keeping my unchanged good trust to you, My Esteemed Gentlemen, that you are not inclined to expel me, a noble lady who cannot live on her family's nearby estate because of the present warfare,[7] from this city (where moreover I was born and baptized and where I spent a good deal of my childhood); nor are you willing to ban me from the country because of my enthusiasm,[8] as some citizens are saying. In case something specious has been brought against me, I should not be denied an appropriate defense (which is granted to the worst offender). I am agreeable to paying or doing what is customarily requested of noble ladies who live some time in this city. Yours very truly, with submission to God's protection.

My Esteemed Gentlemen,

Your Servant,

Johanna Eleonora von und zu Merlau.

---

7. Although the Thirty Years' War had ended in 1648, wars or warlike actions were going on in several locations in 1678: Louis XIV was occupying Elsass-Lorraine and the Palatinate and fighting the Netherlands, which was also fighting England at sea; the Great Elector of Brandenburg-Prussia was at war with Sweden; and the Turks were marching towards Vienna. As a Free Imperial City, Frankfurt sided with the emperor in Vienna but kept out of all regional wars.

8. The term *Gottseligkeit* or piety had already begun to assume the negative meaning of hypocritical, uncontrolled religiosity or enthusiasm.

APPENDIX B

EDITOR'S INTRODUCTION

"The Nature and Necessity of the New Creature in Christ" is a 1772 translation of Johanna Eleonora Petersen's *Die Nothwendigkeit der Neuen Creatur in CHRISTO* (1699). She may have written this religious epistle addressed to her two sisters much earlier than the actual publication date of the German original 1699 indicates, since the English translator still used the author's maiden name "von Merlau." Perhaps it was written as a farewell letter in 1680 when she married the Pietist minister Johann Wilhelm Petersen and the couple set out for the city of Lübeck (on the Baltic Sea) by way of the Netherlands and northern Germany. A move to such a relatively distant place from the Frankfurt area would have meant that the sisters would most likely not see each other again. Also, with her marriage to a commoner, though a prominent theologian and court chaplain, Johanna Eleonora officially severed ties with her status as a noblewoman and her family. More important, she began to live a life for her faith and wanted to relate what her English translator called "her heart's experience and true practice."

The English translator Francis Okely (1719–94) was a theologian who studied and taught for a while at Oxford University, where he had become acquainted with religious circles interested in the spiritual writings of Jacob Böhme (1575–1624), the so-called English Behmenists and in the revival movement in the 1740s. Together with John Wesley, among others, he became a member of the Fetter Lane Society in 1739, the main seedbed from which the English evangelical revival would spring. In 1742 Okely joined the Unitas Fratrum, a religious group organized by Count Zinzendorf's Herrnhut Brethren as the Moravian Church in England (to be recognized as an "Ancient Protestant Episcopal Church" by Parliament in 1749). Okely worked as a "resident laborer," organizing a community in Bristol for the Moravian Church. Later he became devoted to the then prominent

English mystic William Law's (1686–1761) *A Serious Call to a Devout and Holy Life* (1728). In the early 1750s anti-Moravian tracts claimed that the Moravian Church posed a danger to the state and was also an ecclesiastical menace. Okely left the Moravian Church in 1757 when Lord Dartmouth offered him the curacy of Olney. As it turned out, Okely's ordination in the Moravian Church was not recognized for this office, and he was refused ordination as a priest by the Bishop of Lincoln. Okely lived as a translator and author of religious books and was a vocal mediator of theological and ecclesiastical movements from Protestant Germany until his death in 1794.

Francis Okely published about a dozen religious books, most of them translations or adaptations from the German, such as the mystic Johannes Tauler's *Conversions*, sermons by Count Zinzendorf, the *Memoirs of J. G. Gichtel*, two books on a seventeenth-century German visionary John Engelbrecht (*The Divine Visions of John Engelbrecht* and *A Display of God's Wonders . . . upon John Engelbrecht* [both published in 1781]). Especially important was Okely's translation of *Memoirs of the Life, Death, Burial and Wonderful Writings of Jacob Behmen; now done at large into English . . . from the original German* (Northampton, 1780), the first biography of Böhme by Abraham von Franckenberg (1593–1652).

How did he come across Johanna Eleonora Petersen's writings? Okely states in his introduction that he found the German manuscript among a pile of old and soiled papers; and he translated it because he felt that the epistle's message was of "beautiful simplicity," truthful in the "inward parts" and showing "pure zeal for genuine Christianity" without being of a particular "party." In short, it contained no dogma offensive to the warring factions within English Protestantism—it was ecumenical. Okely's translation followed the printed version that survived closely and is complete.

The epistle is remarkable for containing the Pietist credo as Johanna Eleonora would see it in a very personal way. Christ is the central figure, the one great example to follow to "produce a new creature." Seeking (*suchen*) is not enough, she contends, but striving (*streben*), an active conscious effort on the part of the individual, is necessary. This means leaving the old Adam, "putting off the old man and putting on the new," a complete renewal that cannot be accomplished by merely following religious rituals and practices. The new man is able "to judge and discern things." The parable of the five wise and the five foolish brides illustrates the necessity to be prepared in time; only an active faith has the strength to change and renew. Growing and advancing comes "in the inward man" (*inwendigen Menschen*). Johanna Eleonora's message to her sisters is a "message of life." Spiritual renewal, a recasting and re-creation of the old self, is the goal. It is an almost utopian vision and path, not for the sake of innovation but rather a rebirth of the old in the image of the divine. Johanna Eleonora Petersen's model of a "new creature" is a sign for modernity, not for an empty meaningless modernism at all cost but for a spiritual renewal affirming life. The epistle and Petersen's visionary tracts may explain why, after the devastating religious feuds and wars, people were attracted to the Pietists' call for renewal and the promise of a new life.

The following text has been taken from the second (unchanged) edition of a copy at the Humanities Research Center Library at the University of Texas, Austin. All parentheses and capitalizations for emphasis are in the original; the orthography has been slightly modernized according to American spelling rules, but not the wording or the punctuation.

A LETTER TO HER SISTERS: THE NATURE AND NECESSITY OF THE NEW CREATURE IN CHRIST STATED AND DESCRIBED ACCORDING TO HEART'S EXPERIENCE AND TRUE PRACTICE (1699). TRANSLATED BY FRANCIS OKELY (1772)

To my two dear and worthy Sisters, Christina Sibylla Maria Philippina,[1] and Carolina Augustina Philippina,[2] the grace of God, which is in Christ Jesus, and the power of his death and of his resurrection for the production of a New Creature; together with all the unsearchable riches, lying hid in him for time and eternity; are, with this letter, wished, by

Their faithful Sister,
Joanna Eleonora de Merlau.

I am not unapprized that you both heartily desire to be real partakers of your Savior Jesus Christ; and through him to obtain an access unto the Father. But I have through experience learned that we are not apt to take at once the shortest way to this; but often endeavor, by various exercises, and under divers forms, to get into this way of life. This the precious words of the dearest Savior plainly evince; when he says, "Strive to enter in at the straight gate, for many, I say unto you, shall seek to enter in, and shall not be able"

1. Christina Sibylle Maria Philippina von Merlau (born ca. 1648) was four years younger than Johanna Eleonora; she married in 1665 Johann Heinrich (Wilhelm) von und zu Praunheim and lived on an estate very close to Frankfurt. Johanna Eleonora was the godmother of one of her sister's several daughters; this girl lived with Johanna Eleonora for a number of years.
2. Charlotte Auguste Philippina (born ca. 1650) married the widower Johann Reinhard von Dorfelden, steward at the court in Hanau (near Frankfurt), who objected to Johanna Eleonora's marriage "out of station." Johanna Eleonora's oldest sister is not mentioned; most likely she was no longer alive.

(Luke 13:24). And again, "Straight is the gate, and narrow the way, which leadeth unto life, and *few* there be that find it" (Matt. 7:14).

Which words it very highly concerns us to lay to heart, and diligently to enquire, what may be the proper reason, "why so *few* find this narrow way"; and what that implies, "many shall seek to enter in, and shall not be able." Notwithstanding that it is so clearly pointed out in the holy scriptures, and is in plain words as well as by parabolical[3] expressions, testified of and set forth. Now, if we duly ponder Christ's words, and consider the difference there is between *striving* and *seeking* (to the former of which an entry into life is granted and of the latter a total incapacity of attaining it is affirmed) then let us employ our utmost diligence, not only to investigate the real meaning of this truth, but also to reduce it to practice.

I must ingenuously own to my dear sisters that this meaning of Christ, by his declaration here, remained a secret to me for a long time; and that as often as it recurred to memory, it was with great anguish of spirit; considering that *many* shall seek to enter in at the straight gate, which leadeth to life, and shall not be *able*: Yea, that there are but few who find the narrow way to this gate. So that I have had many a conflict, and employed myself in much seeking and striving to find out this narrow way; till at length the goodness of the most High preventing me, did open my understanding to discern, wherein the proper difference between the *seeking* and *striving* state lies. And I was hereby made acquainted that all the exercises of godliness engaged in without putting off the old man and putting on the new are to no purpose: For instance, the going to public worship, praying, reading, and taking the sacrament, the giving of alms; the drawing up articles of faith according to the words of scripture; and the appropriating to ourselves all the benefits of Christ's propitiatory[4] sacrifice; or, as the scripture in brief expresseth it, " The having a form of knowledge and of the truth in the law," or in our Bible (Rom. 2:20). All this, my dear sisters, have I found in the seeking state; yea, more still, even divine contemplations, and a knowledge of the truth; all which Christ reckons as a part of seeking: The same which Paul also, through the Spirit of Christ, asserts, "If I had all knowledge, and understood all mysteries, it might yet profit me nothing" (1 Cor. 13:1, 13:3). For in the midst of all these things, in themselves good, one may still abide in his old nature and submit to the ascendancy of its lusts, as every day's experience sufficiently

---

3. Allegorical, having a hidden spiritual meaning that transcends the literal sense of the sacred text.

4. Expiatory, serving to atone for, to appease or put an end to.

evinces.[5] Whereas, "If any man be in Christ, he is a new creature" (2 Cor. 5:17). Nor is any other thing but such a new creature of avail in Christ. Whereby I have been taught by the Holy Ghost that by the *striving* to enter in at the straight gate (of which strivers alone our Savior asserts that they enter into life) we are to understand precisely the mortification of the old man by the power of the death of Christ, in order to the resurrection of the new man, by the power of his resurrection.

And although this truth stands in the catechism,[6] we are taught as children, and we learn the words thereof from our infancy, viz. "That our old man must be drowned by daily remorse and repentance; and the new Man come forth, which after God is created in true righteousness and holiness." Yet what Christ tells us remains nevertheless true, when he affirms that *few* there be that find it, that is, the narrow way to life. It also verifies the testimony of the Holy Ghost by Paul; who in his epistles, speaking of the last times, declares, "that they shall retain the form of godliness, or truth; but deny the power of it" (2 Tim. 3:5). Forasmuch as in the practice and course of our day, nothing less than this truth is found, viz. the man in Christ, or, the new creature; whereby, "with open face, beholding as in a glass the glory of the Lord, we are changed into the same image from glory to glory, even as by the Spirit of the Lord" (2 Cor. 3:18). Insomuch, that a man lives no more, but "Jesus Christ lives in him" (Gal. 2:20), as having died for him, and risen again to this very end (Rom. 14:9). Nay, in our day the way of life comes under an evil suspicion; so that every one who only makes the first essay towards a godly life of this sort is immediately exposed to persecution. And although he injures no man in any respect, nay rather is disposed to do good to all men, to the utmost of his power; yet is he nevertheless more maligned and persecuted than any the vilest miscreant (whom they notwithstanding indulge with civil liberties; yea, admit to baptism and the supper of the Lord), which yet they debar[7] him from, who is in good earnest

5. *Note by translator Francis Okely*—Were the Holy Ghost to shew the extent of the flesh's confidence, expressed by St. Paul, Phil. 3:1 f., many a supposed Christian society, and many a professor of Christianity of the first rate, would have occasion to tremble. God grant then, that we may neither deceive our own selves (1 Cor. 3:18; 6:9), nor be deceived by others (Matt. 24:4; Rev. 12:9). "Let us come to the light, that our deeds may be made manifest, that they are wrought in God" (John 3:20–21).

6. The catechism is the summary of religious dogma, usually in the form of questions and answers. The Pietists revived and extended the religious instruction with the catechism.

7. *Note by translator Francis Okely*—The clergy abroad seem to have more authority than ours in England.

about his salvation; rejecting him as a fanatic and enthusiast,[8] who wants to introduce a new religion.[9] All which is an infallible proof, that the old man is not put off, nor the new Man, which is able to judge and discern all things, put on. And yet from this old man it is that all ignorance in spirituals arises; because "the natural man receiveth not the things of the Spirit of God; for they are foolishness unto him, neither can he know them" (1 Cor. 2:14). For were the *one* put off, and the *other* put on, another sort of Christianity would arise, no longer divided and subdivided into so many sects, as is now the case; but like the primitive Christians, as one heart and one soul, it would again make its appearance in the world.

Is it not true, dear sisters, that this has given rise to the present divided state of Christendom? People have endeavored to secure their own salvation by *Articles* and *Forms*, drawn out of the scripture; when one party has framed the scripture-words into this, and the other into another sense and form; wrangling and damning one another without entering any of them into a close examination of themselves, how far they all live in the new creature. Had this been the main point of enquiry, in process of time there would have been no want of real and useful knowledge: For wheresoever Christ dwelleth, and in whomsoever he liveth, no unfruitfulness in all knowledge and purity will remain; because, that "in Him are hid all the treasures of wisdom and knowledge" (Col. 2:3), and he discloseth them to such as are his friends, and do as he hath commanded them; which is to put into practice the genuine self-denial; which also consisteth in this very thing, viz., the putting off the old man with this deeds, and following the Savior; a thing quite impracticable without putting on the new man. But now notwithstanding all this, they will needs extort from merely natural men, that they shall comprehend articles of faith; nay even compile and instruct others in them; although the Holy Ghost has clearly told us that it is a thing impracticable: For the natural man cannot so much as perceive the things of the Spirit of God, being

8. "Enthusiast" (*Schwärmer*) was the derogatory term among the Protestants for religious dissidents with mystical and spiritual interests. The translator seems to sympathize with Johanna Eleonora's lament that such people—and she means the Pietists—are barred from church service and accused of starting their own sect, an idea the Petersens fought vehemently against.

9. *Note by translator Francis Okely*—I heartily wish, that those persons, who are so glib at dubbing other people Enthusiasts etc., might well consider what ground it springs from. There is undoubtedly such a thing as enthusiasm, or a false pretense to inspiration. But must the abuse of any thing, destroy the reality of it? If so, farewell every thing that is sacred. I am bold to assert, that notwithstanding all abuses, if we are not found amongst some of the miscalled Enthusiasts of our day, we shall run a great hazard of not being owned by Christ, when he comes in his own glory and his Father's. Human reason is now strongly at war against superstition. May I be found at all events in the supposed enthusiastical mean between both these extremes.

foolishness unto him, nor can he comprehend them. Consequently a new spiritual man is to this end indispensably requisite; one who can preach the doctrines of faith in *power*; who, as a man of God, and a person regenerated, must endeavor first of all, by the power of God, to make of natural, spiritual men. In a word, he must go through Christ the door into the sheepfold; that the Holy Ghost, the porter, may open to himself, before he can find an open door into the hearts of other men; and before he can challenge from them a right faith concerning Christ. Forasmuch as the acquiring knowledge and certain phraseologies, and the appropriating to ourselves the things, which are written concerning Christ, is not faith; but to possess substantially what the holy scripture testifies concerning Christ, is faith. Do I now find it testifying, that Christ is the Propitiation for our sins, and that he hath redeemed us from them? I must then in my own heart possess such a propitiation, and the efficacy of this redemption to such a degree, that what I am redeemed from must no longer be able to domineer over me; but I to rule and reign over it. Doth the scripture testify, that Christ hath died unto sin once? Then must I also be dead with him unto it; not in the imagination, but in reality. Is he risen again? Then must I be also risen with him, and seek those things only, which are above. Is he ascended up into heaven? I must also ascend with him, and have my conversation, or citizenship, in heaven. Is he, the Lord Christ, righteous? Then must I, by virtue of his righteousness wrought out in his own person, also work righteousness. And more especially do I yield myself up to an egregious delusion, should I presume,[10] that because he is righteous, I may set it down to my own account that I am righteous too. No, no; through him, who hath been made unto me righteousness, I must also become righteous, and lay aside all unrighteousness, the offspring not of the new but of the old man. And where this hath not yet taken place, the man is not yet a partaker of, has no interest in Christ. In this case, he is Christ *for us* and exterior to us; but not yet Christ *in us*; whereas without mincing the matter, *in him* we must be found. And although he did die for all the world ("for he is the propitiation not for our sins only, but also for the sins of the whole world" [1 John 2:2]), yet we believe nevertheless, according to the scriptures, that all men are not now *actually* saved; which would be a consequence inevitable, were it sufficient to have Christ only *for us*.

10. *Note by translator Francis Oakley*—This point has long been a point of contention between Christians. But may we not say, that God's imputation is always a real and immediate communication of righteousness? As surely, and in the same heart wherein one man's disobedience has made us sinners, does the obedience of one make us righteous? Rom. 5:19. It certainly is so; and then what our author alleges is only leveled at one of the most subtle and abominable abuses of God's grace, that Satan ever instigated human nature to.

The having here a strong sensation, impression, or imagination, will in truth be of no avail to us; for it must be real: Otherwise such a sensation, impression, or imagination, will prove too ineffectual to overcome the world; according to the character given of faith in the scripture, "that it is our victory, that it overcometh the world" (1 John 5:4–5). And can any faith subsist but in the new creature? Because in "Christ nothing availeth, but a new creature" (Gal. 6:15), which is, with Paul, of the same import with "the faith that worketh by love" (Gal. 5:6).

Wherefore when the holy scripture treats of faith, it means *the* faith, which is possessed by the new creature; it being impossible for the old man to believe, as unbelief is his essential characteristic. *This* the sacraments also refer to and suppose, viz., baptism and the supper of the Lord; for are we not baptized into the death of Christ, in order that the old man may abide in death, and a new Man come forth? That, "like as CHRIST was raised from the dead, so WE also should walk in newness of life" (Rom. 6:4). Now, if baptism be the laver[11] of regeneration, ought it not to be our grand pursuit to attain the end of it? That we put on the new creature whereunto we are baptized; and lay aside the old man, whom through baptism we have delivered up unto death? Without this effect, it will be said of our baptism what Paul says (Rom. 2:25–26) of circumcision, "That to such as do not attain the end and design of that ordinance, their circumcision is made uncircumcision": So will our baptism, if we do not attain the end and design of baptism, by putting off the old man and putting on the new, whereunto we are baptized; be also not esteemed as Christianity, but mere heathenism. The very same is the case with the Lord's supper too; which has been instituted and given us for a memorial, that we may "shew forth the death of Christ," not only with *words*, but also in *reality* and *power*. Now, this ordinance being instituted for the growth of the inward man, that "Christ may dwell in us and we in him"; and being an immediate consequent upon baptism, wherein we are to put on the new Man; should we use it in the old man, in which we are alive and do his deeds; we then "eat and drink damnation, or a judgment to ourselves" (1 Cor. 11:29), or Christ came into the world for judgment to the old man; that, as the seat of the devil's works, it might be destroyed (1 John 3:8). For as Christ operateth in the new creature to produce the fruits of righteousness to the glory of God; so on the other hand doth the devil actuate the old man to produce his works therein. And the works of the flesh are manifest; for as the tree is known by its fruit, so are the old and the new man distinguishable

---

11. Laver was a large basin used for ceremonial ablutions in the ancient Jewish Tabernacle and Temple worship; here: instrument.

by their several deeds. See, my beloved sisters! I have here, according to the measure of grace in utterance, given unto me, wished to shew you the difference between the *seeking* and the *striving* for an entrance into life; and have evinced the truth of Christ's words, that such as seek after it only in this way, will not be able to compass it. Because all outward exercises, such as the attending on public worship, taking the sacrament, fasting, praying, &c. are things which may be done without putting off the old man; which ought however to be performed and effected by *striving* alone; through which, by the death of the old man, we press through all obstacles into the life of the New. For then all such exercises as reading, praying, giving alms, &c. and all other good works, are profitable and acceptable to Almighty God.

Herein has also the parable of the wise and foolish virgins its ground and reality (Matt. 25).[12] For whereas it is said, that the foolish virgins took pains to go out to meet the Bridegroom, and to trim their lamps; this implies in the first point of comparison and resemblance, the very same as *seeking*. We may take the lamps for the external worship of God; but the vessels filled with oil, which the wise take with them, intimates the *striving* of the new Creature, which has no lack at all. And although a drowsiness may steal upon the truly godly, yet are they possessed of a constant and habitual readiness; so as immediately on the Bridegroom's voice to be in a capacity of obtaining an admission. Whereas the rest, who had always carelessly an entire dependence on others, without the substance of the holy unction in themselves, come too late for admission, and cannot procure it; being repulsed, as these that had neglected to become new creatures; without which in Christ nothing is of any avail. They hoped indeed to have gained admission, because they knocked and said, "Lord, Lord, open unto us"; but they obtained it not. The same is intended by the similitude proposed (Matt. 6:24 seq.), concerning the foolish man, who built his house upon the sand; and the wise man who built his on a rock. For the Fabric on the sand exhibits just the thing in the first point of resemblance, spoken concerning the *seeking* state, viz., that by all the exercises above mentioned, we get the credit and appearance of godliness, in the same manner as the house built on the sand has the form of a proper house, being for all that a groundless fabric, a house without a foundation; which by descending rains, rising floods, and boisterous winds, may be thrown down and demolished. For instance, suppose we have acquired

12. The parable tells of the five wise and five foolish virgins, who did not take enough oil for their lamps when meeting the groom and were at the market buying oil when he arrived. The groom only took the five clever and ready virgins with him "to the marriage and the door was shut. Afterward came also the other virgins saying, Lord, Lord, open to us. But he answered and said: Verily, I say unto you, I know you not" (Matt. 24:10-12).

a habit of meekness and affability, and yet are not dead to the old man; let but a small blast of human words of an irritating nature come suddenly upon us, and it is capable of demolishing this whole fabric and bringing us into such a chase and perturbation, as if we had neither heard of, nor acquired any meekness and affability. But this is not the case with the fabric built on the rock, which has a stable foundation and bears an analogy to *striving*: where the sandy bottom of the old nature, being dug and cleared away, the building rests upon Christ the rock of life, through whom we are become new creatures; so that HE is our inward life, and WE in him are transformed into his own Image, as in the second Adam. Now the fabric, supported by this foundation, is impregnable and immovable; and the virtues built on such a bottom are divine virtues, which we are to shew forth, being merely the instruments of what the Spirit worketh in us; which is the very nature of a fabric, that neither fire consumes, nor winds and inundations sap and throw down; nay, it is rendered more firm and stable. For should any incident surprise a person who is a new creature in Christ, he maintains his ground and manifests his meekness in power: And the more the assaults of the enemy, represented by floods and winds, advance against him; so much the stronger he becomes through the conflict in suppressing the old man, rising like a whirlwind; who will not fail to exert his utmost power on those escaped from him into Christ; though all to no purpose, because not knowledge only, but deed also is ready to receive him. And therefore all virtues are stable in him, which in others not truly found in Christ, having all their ground in notional faith, are so far from being ready at any exigency of action and trial, that then we live and act diametrically opposite to the very things we however profess in words. And were we to expostulate with such as thus think one way and live another, they would immediately rejoin and tell you, "O we are weak human creatures! we are incapable of doing it. And such as conceit themselves to do it, are only inflated faints, etc." Nay, they go so far as to bless themselves, because they ascribe honor to Christ, and confess themselves in fact to be so very weak: And they censure others who labor after a good conversation in truth, as proud Pharisees,[13] going about to establish their own righteousness, and wanting to be saved by their own works.

To such a pitch, dearest sisters! has the devil brought matters, that God's truth is misunderstood and very grossly misapplied. For, whereas man, under the knowledge of his being a weak and worthless creature, without the ability so much as to think a good thought, much less to speak, and least of all to do a good act; is forced to resign all claim to the promised salvation

13. Strict observers of rites, ceremonies, and words; following the letter of the law; hypocrites.

(forasmuch as without doing the will of God none can be saved [Matt. 7:21]). And whereas man for this very reason, because he is by nature in a plight so wretched, ought to fly to Jesus Christ, that in HIM he might become a new creature (whereby he might afterwards be a match for every thing, and be released by Jesus Christ from the old nature, which in divine matters is so incompetent) yet man for all this remains out of Christ, retaining and hugging his sinful weakness, and never attaining to a victory in and through Christ. Think only, how detestable a thing it is, that the old man would fain do honor to Christ, by retaining as it were his old slough, and continuing in sins with the praises of the atonement in his mouth! Whereas the Lord Jesus Christ is hereby dishonored to the highest degree, because his precious atonement is invalidated and rendered so ineffectual as not ACTUALLY to redeem us from sin, but only to bear the *name of doing it.* But a man, renewed in Jesus Christ, knows and feels that he is actually redeemed; and yet does not glory in himself, but his glory is in the Lord Christ. And when he proves by his own example that there is a *reality* in such redemption, he does not do his good works by way of ostentation, like those who still live in the old man; but doth such works as Jesus worketh in him to the glory of the heavenly Father. Wherefore neither doth he attribute them to himself, as seeking honor from men; but he seeks it from God only, merely wishing that the name of God may through him be glorified. And should he remonstrate against his neighbor's perversion of divine things, his aim thereby is not to exalt and make himself respectable; but being cordially affected towards the other's salvation, would fain have him also come to the real knowledge of the truth. But *this* the natural man comprehendeth not, all the saving doctrines of Christ being folly to him. He cannot comprehend them, because they are diametrically opposite to his depraved reason, and appear to him in a light so nonsensical, that he even makes them matter of his banter and ridicule. And yet at the same time he adopts the words thereof, as articles of his faith; and with his mouth professes them to be the words of God, whilst he is vilifying them in fact: A procedure this that would be incredible, had not the Holy Ghost forewarned us, that the things of the Spirit of God would in their practice and substance be mere nonsense and folly to the natural man; the words of which natural men pronounce and confess, but deny their meaning and power.

Our conviction of this ought to stimulate us to *strive,* that we may obtain. And therefore, according to my small ability, I will suggest to you what has been of use to me in this respect. Not, my dear sisters! "as though I count I had already attained, either were already perfect": But all I say is, that with Paul, "I forget those things that are behind, and reach forth unto those things that are before, that I may apprehend that for which also I am apprehended of Christ Jesus" (Phil. 3:12–13). I have in fact and by experience found, that I must devote my entire will to God. For, whereas through the fall of man I departed with my will from God; so must I return again by the conversion of my entire will to God. For so long as we keep any view whatsoever in reserve to ourselves, it is impossible fully to arrive at this. Every one that makes the experiment will find, that no quality of birth, nor any situation in life can obstruct our becoming true disciples and followers of Christ, and consequently new creatures in Christ; provided we do but abandon every view to men, and the reflection upon other creatures. But so long as we retain and foster any such view, we shall not become pure and entire; but, like a blind man groping in the dark, shall abide under perpetual scruples, and arrive at no divine assurance and satisfaction; "we shall be ever learning, and never coming to the knowledge of the truth" (2 Tim. 3:7). Like a man trying to climb a high hill of sand, having almost gained the summit with extreme difficulty; the ground sinks under him, and he slides down again from top to bottom. For though something may with extreme difficulty be surmounted; yet, if our own views be not dead, we may by one or another occasion be drawn away and hurried back again; insomuch that all the pains we have put ourselves to, without a true purity of intention, may prove abortive. This has been my own sad experience. Before I was got above human views and considerations, how many tears have I shed; sometimes imagining the fault lay on my being born of quality,[14] which would not admit of my becoming a simple and thorough follower of Christ; and at other times it seemed to me as though it were owing to the place I had lived in. However the Lord commiserating my unhappy condition, opened my understanding, so that I could discern and acknowledge, that nothing but *human views* were my hindrance, and that I was loth to bear the reproach of Christ (John 5:44 and 7:6–7, 7:48). But no sooner, under this fight and with God's grace, did I fix the resolution of walking in all simplicity, according to the word and pattern of my Lord Jesus Christ; but it happily ended in my salvation: So that now "I know in whom I believe"; and can say, according to my measure with Paul, "I believe, and therefore speak" (2 Cor. 4:13). And although since the time of my having formed such a resolution in the Lord, and put it, by his power, into practice; I have been obliged to undergo many a trial, and have by manifold "experience got my senses exercised to discern both good and evil" (Heb. 5:14). Yet I can affirm, that from that very hour the Lord has been with me, shewing the utmost patience towards me; bearing with

14. Of nobility; Petersen considered the lifestyle of the nobility inimical to Christian ways.

my ignorance and untowardness in divine things; enlightening me more and more with the light of life; working in me genuine heart's humility, through his holy forgiveness; and afterwards opening to me, from time to time, many mysteries and promises concerning events to come: thereby strengthening me for my spiritual warfare, and instigating me unto *true* godliness. Amidst all which I never forgot, that "whosoever would have such a hope in him, ought to purify himself, even as he is pure" (1 John 3:3). And because I met with frequent occasion of being made sensible of my own impotency by his forgiveness, and in the experience, that "without him I could absolutely do nothing" (John 15:5). So he thereby preserved me from being puffed up in reference to my neighbor, whom I pitied; owning that I had nothing of myself, but was solely "by the grace of God what I was" (1 Cor. 15:10). And at length I came so far as to relinquish all self-assuming in divine things; only wishing incessantly that I might be a serviceable instrument to my faithful Creator; an instrument, that takes as little to itself of what HE effects by it; as any earthen vessel in the potter's hand, who forms it to his own ends, assumes any thing to itself. Under such subjection hath my God exercised me a while, till at length I came into the possession of his peace, and descried many depths in his incomprehensible ways and unsearchable judgments; and thus "have known him that is from the beginning" (1 John 2:14). Insomuch that *no occasion of stumbling* is any longer in my way; but every thing tends to forward me to his glory.

Yet must I notwithstanding never be at a stand, but grow and advance in the inward man, and keep upon my guard, that the old man may never cajole and draw me into any defilement; consequently "am to keep myself in the power of God, that that wicked one may not touch me" (1 John 5:18). Which then, dearest sisters! is another thing I would recommend to you. I mean, that having sincerely devoted your whole wills to God, and got all bye-views under your feet; you then take Christ's exhortation to yourselves, when he says, "Watch and pray." One does not at first discern the importance of this: for it being directly perceptible that no outward watching can be hereby understood; and every man from his infancy growing up in inattention to, and an almost total ignorance of his heart, so as to pay no regard to its stirrings and movings, or operations; hence it comes to pass, that a man is plunged into one or another vice, before he is aware. This we see in David, who ascribes it to grace that he had found his heart. "Lord, says he, thy servant has found his heart"[15] (2 Sam. 7:27). For, till we have found our heart, no watching

15. *Note by translator Francis Okely*—This is Luther's version; in ours it runs thus: "found in his heart." In the Hebrew it is "found with his heart, etc."

can properly take place; because that "which defileth a man, cometh forth from the heart" (Matt. 15:18). But so long as a man is unacquainted with his own heart (which, on account of dissipation and distraction, he hath not yet truly found) neither can he discern and distinguish its stirrings and movings. Wherefore we must by the grace of God take good heed to habituate ourselves to abide at home within our own hearts, and take due cognizance of what passeth there; which is precisely what our Savior means by *watching*. Now when we perceive by various incidental occasions, that wrath, hatred, self-complacence, self-love, and the like, will be springing up out of the heart (which indeed the enemy stirs up, but is permitted by God for our good; that we may be able to discern the old man, and learn to mortify him in his power) we must then be roused up to prayer in order to supplicate strength from on high to get this old man out of the heart, and that Christ may be truly formed in us. For although we never, through the whole course of our lives, can sit down in security, and therefore must never dismiss and remit our *watching* and *praying*; yet may we nevertheless by degrees, and through various exercises and experience, arrive through God's grace to such a state, that the old man is no longer able to domineer over us; rather that we enjoy the Presence of Christ to such a degree, that we have a great confidence in our heart towards God, and are filled with all kinds of divine knowledge, unto all the fullness of God; and can grow up "to the measure of the stature of the fullness of Christ" (Eph. 4:13). We may become temples of God and Christ, wherein the Father, Son, and Holy Ghost resideth, walketh, teacheth, testifieth, and discloseth one depth after the other, according to the good pleasure of his own will. Thus one goes on from glory to glory, and our *watch* on the whole grows easier and easier; because we are standing in the power of God, and have the stirrings and movings of the heart under control and command, being habituated with Jacob to the staying at home, to the being turned inward, and not roving abroad like Esau (Gen. 25:27).[16] And thus it must also be amidst a multiplicity of external employments, against the accumulation and oppression of which we must however be on our guard, lest they dissipate, distract, and decoy us out of our fortress (1 Tim. 6:9–10). We have in the state above described all proper liberty, because we use everything with a pure heart. But since all things are not expedient, and may even frequently prove a stumbling block to the weak; therefore we disclaim every privilege, which is not for edification. And here we begin to discern how great and extensive our privileges are, and how true that scripture is, that "godliness

---

16. "And Esau was a cunning hunter, a man of the fields and Jacob was a plain man, dwelling in tents" (Gen. 25–26).

has the promise of the life that now is and of that which is to come" (1 Tim. 4:8), for as soon as a person can in truth make use of all things, as if he used them not, not suffering his heart to cleave to any of them; then the heavenly Father loves to give him joy, and with pleasure to satisfy him, even in temporals; so that he obtains these things into the bargain: And when others, incapable of standing the test, often eat the bread of carefulness and sorrow, these get theirs as it were in sleep, and taste a blessing in all things; which they however possess, as if they possessed them not. Because they do not regard them as their own property; but only as a trust reposed in them, to be employed in the way the Giver of all good things shall best approve and point out. And even though they know that "all things are theirs, whether things present or things to come" (1 Cor. 3: 21 ad fin.), yet do "they not abuse them" (7:31), "by loving the world or the things in the world" (1 John 2:15), but loving the creature in God, as God's creation and handiwork, praising and adoring him for it. Then in the place of former repinings,[17] nothing but thanksgivings succeed: In the place of disquietude, quietness, and assurance; and instead of the horrible apprehensions of things that are to come, which might well make men's hearts to fail in them for fear and dread, comfort and confidence in God, because their redemption draweth nigh. We are satisfied, that the Lord will then shelter and protect his own; nay, that "he will spare them, as a man spareth his own son that serveth him" (Malach. 3:17). "And before the earth be destroyed, and the hour of temptation comes upon the face of the whole earth" (2 Pet. 3:10–11; Rev. 3:10). "They shall be sealed with the seal of the living God" (Rev. 7), "they shall eat when others hunger, drink, when others thirst; sing for joy of heart, when others cry and howl for sorrow of heart; and shall also in the days of famine be satisfied." And after being perfected in this tabernacle of the body, shall either by martyrdom (for which God has imparted sufficient strength unto them) or in some other way, bid adieu to this world, and receive a "glorious kingdom and a diadem of beauty from the hand of the Lord"; and shall commence a never-ending felicity, "the second death having no power over them; being partakers of the first resurrection, and as priests of God and Christ, sitting on the throne, and reigning with Christ a thousand years" (Rev. 20), yea, from eternity to eternity. This is in very deed "the promise of the life which now is, and of that which is to come." And although it be not immediately bestowed, do not on that account despond; seeing victory must precede the enjoyment of the promises. "The striving against sin" (Heb. 12:4), and "the good fight of faith" (2 Tim. 4:7), are first in order; for as we are to strive

17. To feel or express dejection or discontent.

against sin to subjugate or bring under the old man; so must we also "contend earnestly for the faith which was once given to the saints" (Jude 3), that in this faith we may go on "conquering and to conquer." But first of all it must suffice us to do good, because it is the will of God, and we afterwards discern how good that will is; yea, that all God's commandments are lovely, and not grievous: Insomuch that the performing God's commandments is a real self-gratification, being thereby exempted from every thing that can annoy and hurt us. Consequently by being DOERs we learn by the clearest and most natural evidence of our own experience, that the love of God has issued out no other commandments than such as constitute the happiness of mankind; nor any other prohibitions than from such things as are detrimental and af-flictive both to their souls and bodies. Thus in such a "deed we are blessed" (James 1:25), and can have a right knowledge by our own experience that the God, who seeks our salvation and well-being in every thing to such a degree, must needs be *love* itself (1 John 4:8, 4:16). But where *deed* is wanting, and we are unconcerned to advance any further than to notional knowledge; buoying ourselves up with a false imagination, and taking it for granted we are Christians, and so ought to appropriate Christ and his righteousness (as we commonly speak) to ourselves; we shall for all that discover that we were nothing more than heathens. For what though we did not worship stocks and stones; yet we loved and were more addicted to sensual pleasures than to God; and were in various ways wholly attached and devoted to the things of the world. And at the last day, if we continue in the old nature, we shall have far more to answer for (as having professed ourselves Christians, and been really heathens; as having confessed the scriptures, and yet lived counter to them) than they who were outwardly heathens, and had no means of know-ing the will of God, as we had. Neither will it be of the least avail here to any person, that he was received into this or the other church; which presumed they had the genuine faith, because their doctrines of faith were taken in the purest and most sincere manner from the scripture: No, no; this will be the question, How such a one converted it into life? whether such boasted purity of doctrine led him to purity of life, and made him a new creature in Christ Jesus? so that he can say with Paul, "I live not, but Christ liveth in me" (Gal. 2:20). Such a one does indeed not come into judgment, neither does he die; but passeth out of this mortality into life; and upon the demo-lition of this earthly tabernacle obtains a building from heaven, a glorified body according to the likeness of Christ's glorious body. Lo! such is our hope towards him; and moreover, as long as we are here on our pilgrimage to the Lord, "are persuaded that neither things present, nor things to come shall ever separate us from the love of God" (Rom. 8:38–39). Hallelujah!

This, my dearest sisters! is what I had in my heart to propose to you, when I parted and took leave of you as to bodily presence. But may the God of all fidelity, who is able to preserve you from this wicked world, and to impart all the riches of his divine knowledge unto you; so as to outstrip me far, and get an image of Christ formed in your own hearts far more complete than any representation, I (according to my measure) may be able to make of it: May this faithful God be gracious unto you; that in these last days, when both the hour of temptation and the sealing of his faithful ones is approaching,[18] you may stand your ground, and obtain his divine seal. For this I bow my knees in his presence, promising myself a favorable answer; and that in his own good time we may meet and embrace each other before the throne of God and the Lamb: Not only as having been begotten by one and the same earthly father, and born of one and the same earthly mother; but also as having been begotten and born of God and of the heavenly Jerusalem. So run then, dearest sisters! that ye may obtain. And be you hereby, from the very bottom of my heart, commended to the Love Eternal,

By your faithful sister,
Joanna Eleonora de Merlau.

P.S. I heartily salute my dear brother,[19] begotten of the same bodily father, but not born of the same mother with myself. I wish him the birth from above, and that therein we may become near to each other, and be found under one heart. May the Lord teach him to know that not many noble are called; to the end he may be found amongst the few, which are; and who have devoted themselves to God in Christ Jesus, and kept themselves unspotted from the world! Amen.

18. *Note by the translator Francis Okely*—What we love we wish for, and are but too apt to be unduly precipitant in our expectations of. This has been truly the case with respect to our dear LORD'S coming, from the apostles down to the present day. The uncertainty of the time has infinite wisdom in it, to keep us always on the watch. See the following passages: 1 Cor. 1:7; Phil. 3:20, 4:5; 1 Thess. 1:10; 2 Thess. 2:1–2; 2 Tim. 4:8; James 5:7–9; 1 John 2:28; Rev. 22:26. But the Lord will surely come in the fullness of time. Luke 21:7, Acts 1:6–7.
19. The young brother was Christian Philipp von Merlau (born ca. 1670); Johanna Eleonora had been called home from court service in 1670, when her stepmother died while giving birth, in order to care for the infant. This brother became a colonel and died childless in 1709.

SERIES EDITORS'
BIBLIOGRAPHY

PRIMARY SOURCES

Alberti, Leon Battista (1404–72). *The Family in Renaissance Florence*. Translated by Renée Neu Watkins. Columbia: University of South Carolina Press, 1969.

Arenal, Electa and Stacey Schlau, eds. *Untold Sisters: Hispanic Nuns in Their Own Works*. Translated by Amanda Powell. Albuquerque: University of New Mexico Press, 1989.

Astell, Mary (1666–1731). *The First English Feminist: Reflections on Marriage and Other Writings*. Edited and introduction by Bridget Hill. New York: St. Martin's Press, 1986.

Atherton, Margaret, ed. *Women Philosophers of the Early Modern Period*. Indianapolis, IN: Hackett, 1994.

Aughterson, Kate, ed. *Renaissance Woman: Constructions of Femininity in England: A Source Book*. London: Routledge, 1995.

Barbaro, Francesco (1390–1454). *On Wifely Duties* (preface and book 2). Translated by Benjamin Kohl in Kohl and R. G. Witt, eds., *The Earthly Republic*. Philadelphia: University of Pennsylvania Press, 1978, 179–228.

Behn, Aphra. *The Works of Aphra Behn*. 7 vols. Edited by Janet Todd. Columbus: Ohio State University Press, 1992–96.

Boccaccio, Giovanni (1313–75). *Famous Women*. Edited and translated by Virginia Brown. The I Tatti Renaissance Library. Cambridge, MA: Harvard University Press, 2001.

———. *Corbaccio or the Labyrinth of Love*. Translated by Anthony K. Cassell. 2nd rev. ed. Binghamton, NY: Medieval and Renaissance Texts and Studies, 1993.

Brown, Sylvia. *Women's Writing in Stuart England: The Mother's Legacies of Dorothy Leigh, Elizabeth Joscelin and Elizabeth Richardson*. Thrupp, Stroud, Gloucestershire: Sutton, 1999.

Bruni, Leonardo (1370–1444). "On the Study of Literature (1405) to Lady Battista Malatesta of Moltefeltro." In *The Humanism of Leonardo Bruni: Selected Texts*. Translated and introduction by Gordon Griffiths, James Hankins, and David Thompson. Binghamton, NY: Medieval and Renaissance Studies and Texts, 1987, 240–51.

Castiglione, Baldassare (1478–1529). *The Book of the Courtier*. Translated by George Bull. New York: Penguin, 1967. *The Book of the Courtier*. Edited by Daniel Javitch. New York: W. W. Norton, 2002.

Christine de Pizan (1365–1431). *The Book of the City of Ladies.* Translated by Earl Jeffrey Richards. Foreword by Marina Warner. New York: Persea, 1982.

————. *The Treasure of the City of Ladies.* Translated by Sarah Lawson. New York: Viking Penguin, 1985. Also translated and introduction by Charity Cannon Willard. Edited and introduction by Madeleine P. Cosman. New York: Persea, 1989.

Clarke, Danielle, ed. *Isabella Whitney, Mary Sidney and Aemilia Lanyer: Renaissance Women Poets.* New York: Penguin, 2000.

Crawford, Patricia, and Laura Gowing, eds. *Women's Worlds in Seventeenth-Century England: A Source Book.* London: Routledge, 2000.

Daybell, James, ed. *Early Modern Women's Letter Writing, 1450–1700.* Houndmills, England:: Palgrave, 2001.

Elizabeth I: Collected Works. Edited by Leah S. Marcus, Janel Mueller, and Mary Beth Rose. Chicago: University of Chicago Press, 2000.

Elyot, Thomas (1490–1546). *Defence of Good Women: The Feminist Controversy of the Renaissance.* Facsimile Reproductions. Edited by Diane Bornstein. New York: Delmar, 1980.

Erasmus, Desiderius (1467–1536). *Erasmus on Women.* Edited by Erika Rummel. Toronto: University of Toronto Press, 1996.

Female and Male Voices in Early Modern England: An Anthology of Renaissance Writing. Edited by Betty S. Travitsky and Anne Lake Prescott. New York: Columbia University Press, 2000.

Ferguson, Moira, ed. *First Feminists: British Women Writers 1578–1799.* Bloomington: Indiana University Press, 1985.

Galilei, Maria Celeste. *Sister Maria Celeste's Letters to Her Father, Galileo.* Edited by and Translated by Rinaldina Russell. Lincoln, NE: Writers Club Press of Universe.com, 2000. Also published as *To Father: The Letters of Sister Maria Celeste to Galileo, 1623–1633.* Translated by Dava Sobel. London: Fourth Estate, 2001.

Gethner, Perry, ed. *The Lunatic Lover and Other Plays by French Women of the 17th and 18th Centuries.* Portsmouth, NH: Heinemann, 1994.

Glückel of Hameln (1646–1724). *The Memoirs of Glückel of Hameln.* Translated by Marvin Lowenthal. New introduction by Robert Rosen. New York: Schocken Books, 1977.

Henderson, Katherine Usher, and Barbara F. McManus, eds. *Half Humankind: Contexts and Texts of the Controversy about Women in England, 1540–1640.* Urbana: Illinois University Press, 1985.

Hoby, Margaret. *The Private Life of an Elizabethan Lady: The Diary of Lady Margaret Hoby 1599–1605.* Thrupp, Stroud, Gloucestershire: Sutton, 1998.

Humanist Educational Treatises. Edited and translated by Craig W. Kallendorf. The I Tatti Renaissance Library. Cambridge, MA: Harvard University Press, 2002.

Joscelin, Elizabeth. *The Mothers Legacy to Her Unborn Childe.* Edited by Jean leDrew Metcalfe. Toronto: University of Toronto Press, 2000.

Kaminsky, Amy Katz, ed. *Water Lilies, Flores del agua: An Anthology of Spanish Women Writers from the Fifteenth Through the Nineteenth Century.* Minneapolis: University of Minnesota Press, 1996.

Kempe, Margery (1373–1439). *The Book of Margery Kempe.* Translated by and edited by Lynn Staley. A Norton Critical Edition. New York: W. W. Norton, 2001.

King, Margaret L., and Albert Rabil, Jr., eds. *Her Immaculate Hand: Selected Works by and about the Women Humanists of Quattrocento Italy.* Binghamton, NY: Medieval and Renaissance Texts and Studies, 1983; second revised paperback edition, 1991.

Klein, Joan Larsen, ed. *Daughters, Wives, and Widows: Writings by Men about Women and Marriage in England, 1500–1640.* Urbana: University of Illinois Press, 1992.

Knox, John (1505–72). *The Political Writings of John Knox: The First Blast of the Trumpet against the Monstrous Regiment of Women and Other Selected Works.* Edited by Marvin A. Breslow. Washington, DC: Folger Shakespeare Library, 1985.

Kors, Alan C., and Edward Peters, eds. *Witchcraft in Europe, 400–1700: A Documentary History.* Philadelphia: University of Pennsylvania Press, 2000.

Krämer, Heinrich, and Jacob Sprenger. *Malleus Maleficarum* (ca. 1487). Translated by Montague Summers. London: Pushkin Press, 1928. Reprint, New York: Dover, 1971.

Larsen, Anne R., and Colette H. Winn, eds. *Writings by Pre-Revolutionary French Women: From Marie de France to Elizabeth Vigée-Le Brun.* New York: Garland, 2000.

de Lorris, William, and Jean de Meun. *The Romance of the Rose.* Translated by Charles Dahlbert. Princeton, NJ: Princeton University Press, 1971. Reprint, University Press of New England, 1983.

Marguerite d'Angoulême, Queen of Navarre (1492–1549). *The Heptameron.* Translated by P. A. Chilton. New York: Viking Penguin, 1984.

Mary of Agreda. *The Divine Life of the Most Holy Virgin.* Abridgment of *The Mystical City of God.* Abridged by Fr. Bonaventure Amedeo de Caesarea, M.C. Translated from the French by Abbé Joseph A. Boullan. Rockford, IL: Tan Books, 1997.

Myers, Kathleen A., and Amanda Powell, eds. *A Wild Country Out in the Garden: The Spiritual Journals of a Colonial Mexican Nun.* Bloomington: Indiana University Press, 1999.

Russell, Rinaldina, ed. *Sister Maria Celeste's Letters to Her Father, Galileo.* San Jose: Writers Club Press, 2000.

Teresa of Avila, Saint (1515–82). *The Life of Saint Teresa of Avila by Herself.* Translated by J. M. Cohen. New York: Viking Penguin, 1957.

Weyer, Johann (1515–88). *Witches, Devils, and Doctors in the Renaissance: Johann Weyer, De praestigiis daemonum.* Edited by George Mora with Benjamin G. Kohl, Erik Midelfort, and Helen Bacon. Translated by John Shea. Binghamton, NY: Medieval and Renaissance Texts and Studies, 1991.

Wilson, Katharina M., ed. *Medieval Women Writers.* Athens: University of Georgia Press, 1984.

———, ed. *Women Writers of the Renaissance and Reformation.* Athens: University of Georgia Press, 1987.

Wilson, Katharina M., and Frank J. Warnke, eds. *Women Writers of the Seventeenth Century.* Athens: University of Georgia Press, 1989.

Wollstonecraft, Mary. *A Vindication of the Rights of Men and a Vindication of the Rights of Women.* Edited by Sylvana Tomaselli. Cambridge: Cambridge University Press, 1995. Also *The Vindications of the Rights of Men, The Rights of Women.* Edited by D. L. Macdonald and Kathleen Scherf. Peterborough, Ontario, Canada: Broadview Press, 1997.

Women Critics 1660–1820: An Anthology. Edited by the Folger Collective on Early Women Critics. Bloomington: Indiana University Press, 1995.

Women Writers in English, 1350–1850. 15 vols. published through 1999 (projected 30-volume series suspended). Oxford University Press.

Wroth, Lady Mary. *The Countess of Montgomery's Urania*. 2 parts. Edited by Josephine A. Roberts. Tempe, AZ: MRTS, 1995, 1999.

——. *Lady Mary Wroth's "Love's Victory": The Penshurst Manuscript*. Edited by Michael G. Brennan. London: The Roxburghe Club, 1988.

——. *The Poems of Lady Mary Wroth*. Edited by Josephine A. Roberts. Baton Rouge: Louisiana State University Press, 1983.

de Zayas, Maria. *The Disenchantments of Love*. Translated by H. Patsy Boyer. Albany: State University of New York Press, 1997.

——. *The Enchantments of Love: Amorous and Exemplary Novels*. Translated by H. Patsy Boyer. Berkeley and Los Angeles: University of California Press, 1990.

SECONDARY SOURCES

Ahlgren, Gillian. *Teresa of Avila and the Politics of Sanctity*. Ithaca, NY: Cornell University Press, 1996.

Akkerman, Tjitske, and Siep Sturman, eds. *Feminist Thought in European History, 1400–2000*. London: Routledge, 1997.

Allen, Sister Prudence, R.S.M. *The Concept of Woman: The Aristotelian Revolution, 750 B.C.–A.D. 1250*. Grand Rapids, MI: William B. Eerdmans, 1997.

——. *The Concept of Woman*. Vol. 2, *The Early Humanist Reformation, 1250–1500*. Grand Rapids, MI: William B. Eerdmans, 2002.

Andreadis, Harriette. *Sappho in Early Modern England: Female Same-Sex Literary Erotics 1550–1714*. Chicago: University of Chicago Press, 2001.

Armon, Shifra. *Picking Wedlock: Women and the Courtship Novel in Spain*. New York: Rowman & Littlefield Publishers, Inc., 2002.

Backer, Anne Liot Backer. *Precious Women*. New York: Basic Books, 1974.

Ballaster, Ros. *Seductive Forms*. New York: Oxford University Press, 1992.

Barash, Carol. *English Women's Poetry, 1649–1714: Politics, Community, and Linguistic Authority*. New York: Oxford University Press, 1996.

Battigelli, Anna. *Margaret Cavendish and the Exiles of the Mind*. Lexington, KY: University of Kentucky Press, 1998.

Beasley, Faith. *Revising Memory: Women's Fiction and Memoirs in Seventeenth-Century France*. New Brunswick: Rutgers University Press, 1990.

Beilin, Elaine V. *Redeeming Eve: Women Writers of the English Renaissance*. Princeton, NJ: Princeton University Press, 1987.

Benson, Pamela Joseph. *The Invention of Renaissance Woman: The Challenge of Female Independence in the Literature and Thought of Italy and England*. University Park, PA: Pennsylvania State University Press, 1992.

Benson, Pamela Joseph, and Victoria Kirkham, eds. *Strong Voices, Weak History? Medieval and Renaissance Women in their Literary Canons: England, France, Italy*. Ann Arbor: University of Michigan Press, 2003.

Bilinkoff, Jodi. *The Avila of Saint Teresa: Religious Reform in a Sixteenth-Century City*. Ithaca: Cornell University Press, 1989.

Bissell, R. Ward. *Artemisia Gentileschi and the Authority of Art*. University Park: Pennsylvania State University Press, 2000.

Blain, Virginia, Isobel Grundy, AND Patricia Clements, eds. *The Feminist Companion to Literature in English: Women Writers from the Middle Ages to the Present.* New Haven, CT: Yale University Press, 1990.

Bloch, R. Howard. *Medieval Misogyny and the Invention of Western Romantic Love.* Chicago: University of Chicago Press, 1991.

Bornstein, Daniel and Roberto Rusconi, eds. *Women and Religion in Medieval and Renaissance Italy.* Translated by Margery J. Schneider. Chicago: University of Chicago Press, 1996.

Brant, Clare, and Diane Purkiss, eds. *Women, Texts and Histories, 1575–1760.* London: Routledge, 1992.

Briggs, Robin. *Witches and Neighbours: The Social and Cultural Context of European Witchcraft.* New York: HarperCollins, 1995; Viking Penguin, 1996.

Brink, Jean R., ed. *Female Scholars: A Tradition of Learned Women before 1800.* Montréal: Eden Press Women's Publications, 1980.

Broude, Norma, and Mary D. Garrard, eds. *The Expanding Discourse: Feminism and Art History.* New York: HarperCollins, 1992.

Brown, Judith C. *Immodest Acts: The Life of a Lesbian Nun in Renaissance Italy.* New York: Oxford University Press, 1986.

Brown, Judith C. , and Robert C. Davis, eds. *Gender and Society in Renaissance Italy.* London: Addison Wesley Longman, 1998.

Bynum, Carolyn Walker. *Fragmentation and Redemption: Essays on Gender and the Human Body in Medieval Religion.* New York: Zone Books, 1992.

———. *Holy Feast and Holy Fast: The Religious Significance of Food to Medieval Women.* Berkeley: University of California Press, 1987.

Cambridge Guide to Women's Writing in English. Edited by Lorna Sage. Cambridge: University Press, 1999.

Cavanagh, Sheila T. *Cherished Torment: The Emotional Geography of Lady Mary Wroth's Urania* . Pittsburgh: Duquesne University Press, 2001.

Cerasano, S. P. and Marion Wynne-Davies, eds. *Readings in Renaissance Women's Drama: Criticism, History, and Performance 1594–1998.* London: Routledge, 1998.

Cervigni, Dino S., ed. *Women Mystic Writers.* Annali d'Italianistica 13 (1995) (entire issue).

Cervigni, Dino S., and Rebecca West, eds. *Women's Voices in Italian Literature.* Annali d'Italianistica 7 (1989) (entire issue).

Charlton, Kenneth. *Women, Religion and Education in Early Modern England.* London: Routledge, 1999.

Chojnacka, Monica. *Working Women in Early Modern Venice.* Baltimore: Johns Hopkins University Press, 2001.

Chojnacki, Stanley. *Women and Men in Renaissance Venice: Twelve Essays on Patrician Society.* Baltimore: Johns Hopkins University Press, 2000.

Cholakian, Patricia Francis. *Rape and Writing in the "Heptameron" of Marguerite de Navarre.* Carbondale: Southern Illinois University Press, 1991.

———. *Women and the Politics of Self-Representation in Seventeenth-Century France.* Newark: University of Delaware Press, 2000.

Christine de Pizan: A Casebook. Edited by Barbara K. Altmann and Deborah L. McGrady. New York: Routledge, 2003.

Clogan, Paul Maruice, ed. *Medievali et Humanistica: Literacy and the Lay Reader.* Lanham, MD: Rowman & Littlefield, 2000.

Clubb, Louise George (1989). *Italian Drama in Shakespeare's Time.* New Haven, CT: Yale University Press.

Conley, John J., S.J. *The Suspicion of Virtue: Women Philosophers in Neoclassical France.* Ithaca, NY: Cornell University Press, 2002.

Crabb, Ann. *The Strozzi of Florence: Widowhood and Family Solidarity in the Renaissance.* Ann Arbor: University of Michigan Press, 2000.

Cruz, Anne J., and Mary Elizabeth Perry, eds. *Culture and Control in Counter-Reformation Spain.* Minneapolis: University of Minnesota Press, 1992.

Davis, Natalie Zemon. *Society and Culture in Early Modern France.* Stanford: Stanford University Press, 1975. Especially chapters 3 and 5.

————. *Women on the Margins: Three Seventeenth-Century Lives.* Cambridge, MA: Harvard University Press, 1995.

DeJean, Joan. *Ancients Against Moderns: Culture Wars and the Making of a Fin de Siècle.* Chicago: University of Chicago Press, 1997.

————. *Fictions of Sappho, 1546–1937.* Chicago: University of Chicago Press, 1989.

————. *The Reinvention of Obscenity: Sex, Lies, and Tabloids in Early Modern France.* Chicago: University of Chicago Press, 2002.

————. *Tender Geographies: Women and the Origins of the Novel in France.* New York: Columbia University Press, 1991.

Dictionary of Russian Women Writers. Edited by Marina Ledkovsky, Charlotte Rosenthal, and Mary Zirin. Westport, CT: Greenwood Press, 1994.

Dixon, Laurinda S. *Perilous Chastity: Women and Illness in Pre-Enlightenment Art and Medicine.* Ithaca: Cornell Universitiy Press, 1995.

Dolan, Frances, E. *Whores of Babylon: Catholicism, Gender and Seventeenth-Century Print Culture.* Ithaca: Cornell University Press, 1999.

Donovan, Josephine. *Women and the Rise of the Novel, 1405–1726.* New York: St. Martin's Press, 1999.

De Erauso, Catalina. *Lieutenant Nun: Memoir of a Basque Transvestite in the New World.* Translated by Michele Ttepto and Gabriel Stepto; foreword by Marjorie Garber. Boston: Beacon Press, 1995.

Encyclopedia of Continental Women Writers. 2 vols. Edited by Katharina Wilson. New York: Garland, 1991.

Erdmann, Axel. *My Gracious Silence: Women in the Mirror of Sixteenth-Century Printing in Western Europe.* Luzern: Gilhofer and Rauschberg, 1999.

Erickson, Amy Louise. *Women and Property in Early Modern England.* London: Routledge, 1993.

Ezell, Margaret J. M. *The Patriarch's Wife: Literary Evidence and the History of the Family.* Chapel Hill: University of North Carolina Press, 1987.

————. *Social Authorship and the Advent of Print.* Baltimore: Johns Hopkins University Press, 1999.

————. *Writing Women's Literary History.* Baltimore: Johns Hopkins University Press, 1993.

Farrell, Michèle Longino. *Performing Motherhood: The Sévigné Correspondence.* Hanover, NH: University Press of New England, 1991.

The Feminist Companion to Literature in English: Women Writers from the Middle Ages to the Present. Edited by Virginia Blain, Isobel Grundy, and Patricia Clements. New Haven, CT: Yale University Press, 1990.

The Feminist Encyclopedia of German Literature. Edited by Friederike Eigler and Susanne
    Kord. Westport, CT: Greenwood Press, 1997.
Feminist Encyclopedia of Italian Literature. Edited by Rinaldina Russell. Westport, CT:
    Greenwood Press, 1997.
Ferguson, Margaret W. *Dido's Daughters: Literacy, Gender, and Empire in Early Modern England
    and France.* Chicago: University of Chicago Press, 2003.
Ferguson, Margaret W., Maureen Quilligan, and Nancy J. Vickers, eds. *Rewriting the
    Renaissance: The Discourses of Sexual Difference in Early Modern Europe.* Chicago: Univer-
    sity of Chicago Press, 1987.
Ferraro, Joanne M. *Marriage Wars in Late Renaissance Venice.* Oxford: Oxford University
    Press, 2001.
Fletcher, Anthony. *Gender, Sex and Subordination in England 1500–1800.* New Haven, CT:
    Yale University Press, 1995.
French Women Writers: A Bio-Bibliographical Source Book. Edited by Eva Martin Sartori and
    Dorothy Wynne Zimmerman. Westport, CT: Greenwood Press, 1991.
Frye, Susan and Karen Robertson, eds. *Maids and Mistresses, Cousins and Queens: Women's
    Alliances in Early Modern England.* Oxford: Oxford University Press, 1999.
Gallagher, Catherine. *Nobody's Story: The Vanishing Acts of Women Writers in the Market-
    place, 1670–1820.* Berkeley: University of California Press, 1994.
Garrard, Mary D. *Artemisia Gentileschi: The Image of the Female Hero in Italian Baroque Art.*
    Princeton, NJ: Princeton University Press, 1989.
Gelbart, Nina Rattner. *The King's Midwife: A History and Mystery of Madame du Coudray.*
    Berkeley: University of California Press, 1998.
Glenn, Cheryl. *Rhetoric Retold: Regendering the Tradition from Antiquity through the Renais-
    sance.* Carbondale: Southern Illinois University Press, 1997.
Goffen, Rona. *Titian's Women.* New Haven, CT: Yale University Press, 1997.
Goldberg, Jonathan. *Desiring Women Writing: English Renaissance Examples.* Stanford:
    Stanford University Press, 1997.
Goldsmith, Elizabeth C. *Exclusive Conversations: The Art of Interaction in Seventeenth-Century
    France.* Philadelphia: University of Pennsylvania Press, 1988.
———, ed. *Writing the Female Voice.* Boston: Northeastern University Press, 1989.
Goldsmith, Elizabeth C., and Dena Goodman, eds. *Going Public: Women and Publishing
    in Early Modern France.* Ithaca: Cornell University Press, 1995.
Grafton, Anthony, and Lisa Jardine. *From Humanism to the Humanities: Education and the
    Liberal Arts in Fifteenth-and Sixteenth-Century Europe.* London: Duckworth, 1986.
Greer, Margaret Rich. *Maria de Zayas Tells Baroque Tales of Love and the Cruelty of Men.*
    University Park: Pennsylvania State University Press, 2000.
Hackett, Helen. *Women and Romance Fiction in the English Renaissance.* Cambridge: Cam-
    bridge University Press, 2000.
Hall, Kim F. *Things of Darkness: Economies of Race and Gender in Early Modern England.* Ithaca,
    NY: Cornell University Press, 1995.
Hampton, Timothy. *Literature and the Nation in the Sixteenth Century: Inventing Renaissance
    France.* Ithaca, NY: Cornell University Press, 2001.
Hannay, Margaret, ed. *Silent But for the Word.* Kent, OH: Kent State University Press,
    1985.
Hardwick, Julie. *The Practice of Patriarchy: Gender and the Politics of Household Authority in
    Early Modern France.* University Park: Pennsylvania State University Press, 1998.

Harris, Barbara J. *English Aristocratic Women, 1450–1550: Marriage and Family, Property and Careers.* New York: Oxford University Press, 2002.

Harth, Erica. *Ideology and Culture in Seventeenth-Century France.* Ithaca: Cornell University Press, 1983.

———. *Cartesian Women: Versions and Subversions of Rational Discourse in the Old Regime.* Ithaca: Cornell University Press, 1992.

Harvey, Elizabeth D. *Ventriloquized Voices: Feminist Theory and English Renaissance Texts.* London: Routledge, 1992.

Haselkorn, Anne M., and Betty Travitsky, eds. *The Renaissance Englishwoman in Print: Counterbalancing the Canon.* Amherst: University of Massachusetts Press, 1990.

Herlihy, David. "Did Women Have a Renaissance? A Reconsideration." *Medievalia et Humanistica,* NS 13 (1985): 1–22.

Hill, Bridget. *The Republican Virago: The Life and Times of Catharine Macaulay, Historian.* New York: Oxford University Press, 1992.

A History of Central European Women's Writing. Edited by Celia Hawkesworth. New York: Palgrave Press, 2001.

A History of Women in the West.
> Volume 1: *From Ancient Goddesses to Christian Saints.* Edited by Pauline Schmitt Pantel. Cambridge, MA: Harvard University Press, 1992.
> Volume 2: *Silences of the Middle Ages.* Edited by Christiane Klapisch-Zuber. Cambridge, MA: Harvard University Press, 1992.
> Volume 3: *Renaissance and Enlightenment Paradoxes.* Edited by Natalie Zemon Davis and Arlette Farge. Cambridge, MA: Harvard University Press, 1993.

A History of Women Philosophers. Edited by Mary Ellen Waithe. 3 vols. Dordrecht: Martinus Nijhoff, 1987.

A History of Women's Writing in France. Edited by Sonya Stephens. Cambridge: Cambridge University Press, 2000.

A History of Women's Writing in Germany, Austria and Switzerland. Edited by Jo Catling. Cambridge: Cambridge University Press, 2000.

A History of Women's Writing in Italy. Edited by Letizia Panizza and Sharon Wood. Cambridge: University Press, 2000.

A History of Women's Writing in Russia. Edited by Alele Marie Barker and Jehanne M. Gheith. Cambridge: Cambridge University Press, 2002.

Hobby, Elaine. *Virtue of Necessity: English Women's Writing 1646–1688.* London: Virago Press, 1988.

Horowitz, Maryanne Cline. "Aristotle and Women." *Journal of the History of Biology* 9 (1976): 183–213.

Howell, Martha. *The Marriage Exchange: Property, Social Place, and Gender in Cities of the Low Countries, 1300–1550.* Chicago: University of Chicago Press, 1998.

Hufton, Olwen H. *The Prospect Before Her: A History of Women in Western Europe, 1: 1500–1800.* New York: HarperCollins, 1996.

Hull, Suzanne W. *Chaste, Silent, and Obedient: English Books for Women, 1475–1640.* San Marino, CA: The Huntington Library, 1982.

Hunt, Lynn, ed. *The Invention of Pornography: Obscenity and the Origins of Modernity, 1500–1800.* New York: Zone Books, 1996.

Hutner, Heidi, ed. *Rereading Aphra Behn: History, Theory, and Criticism.* Charlottesville: University Press of Virginia, 1993.

Hutson, Lorna, ed. *Feminism and Renaissance Studies*. New York: Oxford University Press, 1999.

Italian Women Writers: A Bio-Bibliographical Sourcebook. Edited by Rinaldina Russell. Westport, CT: Greenwood Press, 1994.

Jaffe, Irma B., with Gernando Colombardo. *Shining Eyes, Cruel Fortune: The Lives and Loves of Italian Renaissance Women Poets*. New York: Fordham University Press, 2002.

James, Susan E. *Kateryn Parr: The Making of a Queen*. Aldershot: Ashgate, 1999.

Jankowski, Theodora A. *Women in Power in the Early Modern Drama*. Urbana: University of Illinois Press, 1992.

Jansen, Katherine Ludwig. *The Making of the Magdalen: Preaching and Popular Devotion in the Later Middle Ages*. Princeton, NJ: Princeton University Press, 2000.

Jed, Stephanie H. *Chaste Thinking: The Rape of Lucretia and the Birth of Humanism*. Bloomington: Indiana University Press, 1989.

Jordan, Constance. *Renaissance Feminism: Literary Texts and Political Models*. Ithaca: Cornell University Press, 1990.

Kagan, Richard L. *Lucrecia's Dreams: Politics and Prophecy in Sixteenth-Century Spain*. Berkeley: University of California Press, 1990.

Kehler, Dorothea and Laurel Amtower, eds. *The Single Woman in Medieval and Early Modern England: Her Life and Representation*. Tempe, AZ: MRTS, 2002.

Kelly, Joan. "Did Women Have a Renaissance?" In her *Women, History, and Theory*. Chicago: University of Chicago Press, 1984. Also in Renate Bridenthal, Claudia Koonz, and Susan M. Stuard, eds., *Becoming Visible: Women in European History*. 3rd ed. Boston: Houghton Mifflin, 1998.

———. "Early Feminist Theory and the *Querelle des Femmes*." In *Women, History, and Theory*.

Kelso, Ruth. *Doctrine for the Lady of the Renaissance*. Foreword by Katharine M. Rogers. Urbana: University of Illinois Press, 1956, 1978.

King, Catherine E. *Renaissance Women Patrons: Wives and Widows in Italy, c. 1300–1550*. Manchester: Manchester University Press (distributed in the U.S. by St. Martin's Press), 1998.

King, Margaret L. *Women of the Renaissance*. Foreword by Catharine R. Stimpson. Chicago: University of Chicago Press, 1991.

Krontiris, Tina. *Oppositional Voices: Women as Writers and Translators of Literature in the English Renaissance*. London: Routledge, 1992.

Kuehn, Thomas. *Law, Family, and Women: Toward a Legal Anthropology of Renaissance Italy*. Chicago: University of Chicago Press, 1991.

Kunze, Bonnelyn Young. *Margaret Fell and the Rise of Quakerism*. Stanford: Stanford University Press, 1994.

Labalme, Patricia A., ed. *Beyond Their Sex: Learned Women of the European Past*. New York: New York University Press, 1980.

Laqueur, Thomas. *Making Sex: Body and Gender from the Greeks to Freud*. Cambridge, MA: Harvard University Press, 1990.

Larsen, Anne R. and Colette H. Winn, eds. *Renaissance Women Writers: French Texts/ American Contexts*. Detroit, MI: Wayne State University Press, 1994.

Lerner, Gerda. *The Creation of Patriarchy* and *Creation of Feminist Consciousness, 1000–1870*. 2 vols. New York: Oxford University Press, 1986, 1994.

Levin, Carole, and Jeanie Watson, eds. *Ambiguous Realities: Women in the Middle Ages and Renaissance*. Detroit: Wayne State University Press, 1987.

Levin, Carole, et al. *Extraordinary Women of the Medieval and Renaissance World: A Biographical Dictionary*. Westport, CT: Greenwood Press, 2000.

Lewalsky, Barbara Kiefer. *Writing Women in Jacobean England*. Cambridge, MA: Harvard University Press, 1993.

Lewis, Jayne Elizabeth. *Mary Queen of Scots: Romance and Nation*. London: Routledge, 1998.

Lindsey, Karen. *Divorced Beheaded Survived: A Feminist Reinterpretation of the Wives of Henry VIII*. Reading, MA: Addison-Wesley, 1995.

Lochrie, Karma. *Margery Kempe and Translations of the Flesh*. Philadelphia: University of Pennsylvania Press, 1992.

Lougee, Carolyn C. *Le Paradis des Femmes: Women, Salons, and Social Stratification in Seventeenth-Century France*. Princeton, NJ: Princeton University Press, 1976.

Love, Harold. *The Culture and Commerce of Texts: Scribal Publication in Seventeenth-Century England*. Amherst: University of Massachusetts Press, 1993.

MacCarthy, Bridget G. *The Female Pen: Women Writers and Novelists, 1621–1818*. Preface by Janet Todd. New York: New York University Press, 1994. Originally published 1946–47 by Cork University Press.

Maclean, Ian. *Woman Triumphant: Feminism in French Literature, 1610–1652*. Oxford: Clarendon Press, 1977.

————. *The Renaissance Notion of Woman: A Study of the Fortunes of Scholasticism and Medical Science in European Intellectual Life*. Cambridge: Cambridge University Press, 1980.

MacNeil, Anne. *Music and Women of the Commedia dell'Arte in the Late Sixteenth Century*. New York: Oxford University Press, 2003.

Maggi, Armando. *Uttering the Word: The Mystical Performances of Maria Maddalena de' Pazzi, a Renaissance Visionary*. Albany: State University of New York Press, 1998.

Marshall, Sherrin. *Women in Reformation and Counter-Reformation Europe: Public and Private Worlds*. Bloomington: Indiana University Press, 1989.

Masten, Jeffrey. *Textual Intercourse: Collaboration, Authorship, and Sexualities in Renaissance Drama*. Cambridge: Cambridge University Press, 1997.

Matter, E. Ann, and John Coakley, eds. *Creative Women in Medieval and Early Modern Italy*. Philadelphia: University of Pennsylvania Press, 1994. (Sequel to the Monson collection, below.)

McLeod, Glenda. *Virtue and Venom: Catalogs of Women from Antiquity to the Renaissance*. Ann Arbor: University of Michigan Press, 1991.

Medwick, Cathleen. *Teresa of Avila: The Progress of a Soul*. New York: Knopf, 2000.

Meek, Christine, ed. *Women in Renaissance and Early Modern Europe*. Dublin-Portland: Four Courts Press, 2000.

Mendelson, Sara and Patricia Crawford. *Women in Early Modern England, 1550–1720*. Oxford: Clarendon Press, 1998.

Merchant, Carolyn. *The Death of Nature: Women, Ecology, and the Scientific Revolution*. New York: HarperCollins, 1980.

Merrim, Stephanie. *Early Modern Women's Writing and Sor Juana Inés de la Cruz*. Nashville, TN: Vanderbilt University Press, 1999.

Messbarger, Rebecca. *The Century of Women: The Representations of Women in Eighteenth-Century Italian Public Discourse*. Toronto: University of Toronto Press, 2002.

Miller, Nancy K. *The Heroine's Text: Readings in the French and English Novel, 1722–1782.* New York: Columbia University Press, 1980.

Miller, Naomi J. *Changing the Subject: Mary Wroth and Figurations of Gender in Early Modern England.* Lexington: University Press of Kentucky, 1996.

Miller, Naomi J., and Gary Waller, eds. *Reading Mary Wroth: Representing Alternatives in Early Modern England.* Knoxville: University of Tennessee Press, 1991.

Monson, Craig A., ed. *The Crannied Wall: Women, Religion, and the Arts in Early Modern Europe.* Ann Arbor: University of Michigan Press, 1992.

Musacchio, Jacqueline Marie. *The Art and Ritual of Childbirth in Renaissance Italy.* New Haven, CT: Yale University Press, 1999.

Newman, Barbara. *God and the Goddesses: Vision, Poetry, and Belief in the Middle Ages.* Philadelphia: University of Pennsylvania Press, 2003.

Newman, Karen. *Fashioning Femininity and English Renaissance Drama.* Chicago: University of Chicago Press, 1991.

Okin, Susan Moller. *Women in Western Political Thought.* Princeton, NJ: Princeton University Press, 1979.

Ozment, Steven. *The Bürgermeister's Daughter: Scandal in a Sixteenth-Century German Town.* New York: St. Martin's Press, 1995.

Pacheco, Anita, ed. *Early [English] Women Writers: 1600–1720.* New York: Longman, 1998.

Pagels, Elaine. *Adam, Eve, and the Serpent.* New York: HarperCollins, 1988.

Panizza, Letizia, ed. *Women in Italian Renaissance Culture and Society.* Oxford: European Humanities Research Centre, 2000.

Parker, Patricia. *Literary Fat Ladies: Rhetoric, Gender, and Property.* London: Methuen, 1987.

Pernoud, Regine, and Marie-Veronique Clin. *Joan of Arc: Her Story.* Revised and translated by Jeremy DuQuesnay Adams. New York: St. Martin's Press, 1998 (French original, 1986).

Perry, Mary Elizabeth. *Crime and Society in Early Modern Seville.* Hanover, NH: University Press of New England, 1980.

———. *Gender and Disorder in Early Modern Seville.* Princeton, NJ: Princeton University Press, 1990.

Perry, Ruth. *The Celebrated Mary Astell: An Early English Feminist.* Chicago: University of Chicago Press, 1986.

Petroff, Elizabeth Alvilda, ed. *Medieval Women's Visionary Literature.* New York: Oxford University Press, 1986.

Rabil, Albert. *Laura Cereta: Quattrocento Humanist.* Binghamton, NY: MRTS, 1981.

Ranft, Patricia. *Women in Western Intellectual Culture, 600–1500.* New York: Palgrave, 2002.

Rapley, Elizabeth. *A Social History of the Cloister: Daily Life in the Teaching Monasteries of the Old Regime.* Montreal: McGill-Queen's University Press, 2001.

Raven, James, Helen Small, and Naomi Tadmor, eds. *The Practice and Representation of Reading in England.* Cambridge: University Press, 1996.

Reardon, Colleen. *Holy Concord within Sacred Walls: Nuns and Music in Siena, 1575–1700.* Oxford: Oxford University Press, 2001.

Reiss, Sheryl E., and David G. Wilkins, ed. *Beyond Isabella: Secular Women Patrons of Art in Renaissance Italy.* Kirksville, MO: Truman State University Press, 2001.

Rheubottom, David. *Age, Marriage, and Politics in Fifteenth-Century Ragusa*. Oxford: Oxford University Press, 2000.

Richardson, Brian. *Printing, Writers and Readers in Renaissance Italy*. Cambridge: University Press, 1999.

Riddle, John M. *Contraception and Abortion from the Ancient World to the Renaissance*. Cambridge, MA: Harvard University Press, 1992.

———. *Eve's Herbs: A History of Contraception and Abortion in the West*. Cambridge, MA: Harvard University Press, 1997.

Rose, Mary Beth. *The Expense of Spirit: Love and Sexuality in English Renaissance Drama*. Ithaca, NY: Cornell University Press, 1988.

———. *Gender and Heroism in Early Modern English Literature*. Chicago: University of Chicago Press, 2002.

———, ed. *Women in the Middle Ages and the Renaissance: Literary and Historical Perspectives*. Syracuse: Syracuse University Press, 1986.

Rosenthal, Margaret F. *The Honest Courtesan: Veronica Franco, Citizen and Writer in Sixteenth-Century Venice*. Foreword by Catharine R. Stimpson. Chicago: University of Chicago Press, 1992.

Sackville-West, Vita. *Daughter of France: The Life of La Grande Mademoiselle*. Garden City, NY: Doubleday, 1959.

Sánchez, Magdalena S. *The Empress, the Queen, and the Nun: Women and Power at the Court of Philip III of Spain*. Baltimore: Johns Hopkins University Press, 1998.

Schiebinger, Londa. *The Mind Has No Sex? Women in the Origins of Modern Science*. Cambridge, MA: Harvard University Press, 1991.

———. *Nature's Body: Gender in the Making of Modern Science*. Boston: Beacon Press, 1993.

Schutte, Anne Jacobson, Thomas Kuehn, and Silvana Seidel Menchi, eds. *Time, Space, and Women's Lives in Early Modern Europe*. Kirksville, MO: Truman State University Press, 2001.

Schofield, Mary Anne, and Cecilia Macheski, eds. *Fetter'd or Free? British Women Novelists, 1670–1815*. Athens: Ohio University Press, 1986.

Shannon, Laurie. *Sovereign Amity: Figures of Friendship in Shakespearean Contexts*. Chicago: University of Chicago Press, 2002.

Shemek, Deanna. *Ladies Errant: Wayward Women and Social Order in Early Modern Italy*. Durham, NC: Duke University Press, 1998.

Smith, Hilda L. *Reason's Disciples: Seventeenth-Century English Feminists*. Urbana: University of Illinois Press, 1982.

———. *Women Writers and the Early Modern British Political Tradition*. Cambridge: Cambridge University Press, 1998.

Sobel, Dava. *Galileo's Daughter: A Historical Memoir of Science, Faith, and Love*. New York: Penguin, 2000.

Sommerville, Margaret R. *Sex and Subjection: Attitudes to Women in Early-Modern Society*. London: Arnold, 1995.

Soufas, Teresa Scott. *Dramas of Distinction: A Study of Plays by Golden Age Women*. Lexington: The University Press of Kentucky, 1997.

Spencer, Jane. *The Rise of the Woman Novelist: From Aphra Behn to Jane Austen*. Oxford: Basil Blackwell, 1986.

Spender, Dale. *Mothers of the Novel: 100 Good Women Writers Before Jane Austen*. London: Routledge, 1986.

Sperling, Jutta Gisela. *Convents and the Body Politic in Late Renaissance Venice*. Foreword by Catharine R. Stimpson. Chicago: University of Chicago Press, 1999.

Steinbrügge, Lieselotte. *The Moral Sex: Woman's Nature in the French Enlightenment*. Translated by Pamela E. Selwyn. New York: Oxford University Press, 1995.

Stocker, Margarita. *Judith, Sexual Warrior: Women and Power in Western Culture*. New Haven, CT: Yale University Press, 1998.

Stretton, Timothy. *Women Waging Law in Elizabethan England*. Cambridge: Cambridge University Press, 1998.

Stuard, Susan M. "The Dominion of Gender: Women's Fortunes in the High Middle Ages." In *Becoming Visible: Women in European History*, edited by Renate Bridenthal, Claudia Koonz, and Susan M. Stuard. 3rd ed. Boston: Houghton Mifflin, 1998.

Summit, Jennifer. *Lost Property: The Woman Writer and English Literary History, 1380–1589*. Chicago: University of Chicago Press, 2000.

Surtz, Ronald E. *The Guitar of God: Gender, Power, and Authority in the Visionary World of Mother Juana de la Cruz (1481–1534)*. Philadelphia: University of Pennsylvania Press, 1991.

———. *Writing Women in Late Medieval and Early Modern Spain: The Mothers of Saint Teresa of Avila*. Philadelphia: University of Pennsylvania Press, 1995.

Teague, Frances. *Bathsua Makin, Woman of Learning*. Lewisburg, PA: Bucknell University Press, 1999.

Tinagli, Paola. *Women in Italian Renaissance Art: Gender, Representation, Identity*. Manchester: Manchester University Press, 1997.

Todd, Janet. *The Secret Life of Aphra Behn*. London: Pandora, 2000.

———. *The Sign of Angelica: Women, Writing and Fiction, 1660–1800*. New York: Columbia University Press, 1989.

Valenze, Deborah. *The First Industrial Woman*. New York: Oxford University Press, 1995.

Van Dijk, Susan, Lia van Gemert, and Sheila Ottway, eds. *Writing the History of Women's Writing: Toward an International Approach*. Proceedings of the Colloquium, Amsterdam, 9–11 September. Amsterdam: Royal Netherlands Academy of Arts and Sciences, 2001.

Vickery, Amanda. *The Gentleman's Daughter: Women's Lives in Georgian England*. New Haven, CT: Yale University Press, 1998.

Vollendorf, Lisa, ed. *Recovering Spain's Feminist Tradition*. New York: MLA, 2001.

Walker, Claire. *Gender and Politics in Early Modern Europe: English Convents in France and the Low Countries*. New York: Palgrave, 2003.

Wall, Wendy. *The Imprint of Gender: Authorship and Publication in the English Renaissance*. Ithaca, NY: Cornell University Press, 1993.

Walsh, William T. *St. Teresa of Avila: A Biography*. Rockford, IL: TAN, 1987.

Warner, Marina. *Alone of All Her Sex: The Myth and Cult of the Virgin Mary*. New York: Knopf, 1976.

Warnicke, Retha M. *The Marrying of Anne of Cleves: Royal Protocol in Tudor England*. Cambridge: Cambridge University Press, 2000.

Watt, Diane. *Secretaries of God: Women Prophets in Late Medieval and Early Modern England*. Cambridge: D. S. Brewer, 1997.

Weber, Alison. *Teresa of Avila and the Rhetoric of Femininity*. Princeton, NJ: Princeton University Press, 1990.

Welles, Marcia L. *Persephone's Girdle: Narratives of Rape in Seventeenth-Century Spanish Literature.* Nashville: Vanderbilt University Press, 2000.

Whitehead, Barbara J., ed. *Women's Education in Early Modern Europe: A History, 1500–1800.* New York: Garland, 1999.

Wiesner, Merry E. *Women and Gender in Early Modern Europe.* Cambridge: Cambridge University Press, 1993.

————. *Working Women in Renaissance Germany.* New Brunswick, NJ: Rutgers University Press, 1986.

Willard, Charity Cannon. *Christine de Pizan: Her Life and Works.* New York: Persea Books, 1984.

Winn, Colette and Donna Kuizenga, eds. *Women Writers in Pre-Revolutionary France.* New York: Garland, 1997.

Woodbridge, Linda. *Women and the English Renaissance: Literature and the Nature of Womankind, 1540–1620.* Urbana: University of Illinois Press, 1984.

Woods, Susanne. *Lanyer: A Renaissance Woman Poet.* New York: Oxford University Press, 1999.

Woods, Susanne, and Margaret P. Hannay, eds. *Teaching Tudor and Stuart Women Writers.* New York: MLA, 2000.

INDEX

17; *The Nature and Necessity of a New Creature in Christ*, 28–29, 48, 103–19; *Supplication* (to the Frankfurt City Council), 11, 100–102

Petersen, Johann Wilhelm (husband of Johanna Eleonora P.), 2, 11, 12, 13, 14, 15, 18, 27, 45, 46, 47, 48, 49, 81, 82, 83, 86, 94, 100; autobiography, 24n.60, 41, 60; *The Power of the Children in the Last Days*, 84n.103; *Proof of our Lord's Universal Compassion*, 50

Philadelphia, 10n.21; the new, 32–33; woman's role in the new, 33

Philadelphianism, 2

Philadelphian Society, 16, 17

Philippseck Castle, 79, 84

Philippseck (Merlau) estate, 4, 64

Pietism, 6, 47, 59

Pietists, 2, 9–10, 11, 14, 17, 32, 39; radical Pietists, 19; theology, 29, 104; women, 12, 43

Pirckheimer, Caritas, 42

Pizan, Christine de, xx; *Book of the City of Ladies*, xv, xviii–xix, xxii; *querelle de femme*, xx

Plato, and women in the *Republic*, xi

Pordage, John, *Theologia Mystica*, 16, 16n.39

power, women and, xv–xvi

Praunheim (estate), 65

Praunheim, Anna Elisabeth Eleonora Magdalena (Johanna Eleonora Petersen's niece and godchild), 65, 65n.17, 81, 83

Praunheim, Christina Sibylle Maria Philippina, née von Merlau (Johanna Eleonora Petersen's sister), 65, 81, 105

Praunheim, Wilhelm von und zu (Johanna Eleonora Petersen's brother-in-law), 45, 46

predestination, 96

Protestant church, 8; theology, 33

Psalms, 29, 45

Puritans, 39

Quakers, 9, 16; women, 18, 39

querelle des femmes (the woman question), xx

Quietism, 71n.31

Reformation, 23, 42

Reformed Church, 38, 47, 88, 93, 95, 96

religion, contributions of women to, 25

Renger, Johann Gottfried, 59

return of all things, doctrine of the, 33–34, 47, 91

Revelation, Book of (Apocalypse), 16, 18, 21, 22, 33, 82, 90, 91

Rhineland, 10

Ribero, Pietro Paolo de, *Immortal Triumphs*, xix

Rich, Mary Countess of Warwick, 39

Roach, Richard, 17

Rodríguez de la Camara, Juan, *Triumph of Women*, xx

Roman Law, and the female condition, xii–xiii

Rostock, 11

Rotterdam, 13

Saalhof, 7

Saalhof Pietists, 1, 9–10

Sachsen-Zeitz, Sophie Elisabeth, 12

Saint John's blessing, 69

salvation, 21, 63, 76; (universal) salvation of all (*Aapokatastasis panton*), 33–34, 33n.80, 50

Sandhagen, 14

Sarah, 65

Saxony, 5, 43, 68; Elector of, 70

Sayn-Wittgenstein-Berleburg, Count Casimir, 50

Schleswig-Holstein, Christine von, duchess, 45

Schongauer, Martin, *Mary in the Rosegrove*, 20

Schütz, Johann Jakob, 9, 11, 38, 100

Schütz, Katharina, 42

Schurman, Anna Maria van, xxvi, 9n.17, 11, 36; autobiography,